LACAN AND THE LIMITS
OF LANGUAGE

CHARLES SHEPHERDSON

AND

THE LIMITS OF

LANGUAGE

FORDHAM UNIVERSITY PRESS

New York

Library of Congress Cataloging-in-Publication Data

Shepherdson, Charles.
Lacan and the limits of language / Charles Shepherdson.—1st ed.
    p.   cm.
  Includes bibliographical references and index.
  ISBN-13: 978-0-8232-2766-2 (cloth : alk. paper)
  ISBN-13: 978-0-8232-2767-9 (pbk. : alk. paper)
  1. Lacan, Jacques, 1901–1981.   I. Title.
BF109.L23S54   2008
150.19′5092—dc22   2008008923

Printed in the United States of America
10 09 08   5 4 3 2
First edition

CONTENTS

E Jacques Lacan. *Écrits* (Paris: Seuil, 1966). A portion of this volume has been translated as *Écrits: A Selection*, trans. Alan Sheridan (New York: Norton, 1977). References will be to the English edition.

FS *Feminine Sexuality: Jacques Lacan and the École Freudienne*. Ed. Juliet Mitchell and Jacqueline Rose. Trans. Jacqueline Rose. New York: Norton, 1985.

SI Jacques Lacan.*The Seminar of Jacques Lacan, Book I: Freud's Papers on Technique, 1953–54*. Ed. Jacques-Alain Miller. Trans. John Forrester. New York: Norton, 1988.

SII Jacques Lacan. *The Seminar of Jacques Lacan, Book II: The Ego in Freud's Theory and in the Technique of Psychoanalysis, 1954–55*. Ed. Jacques-Alain Miller. Trans. Sylvana Tomaselli. New York: Norton, 1988.

SVII Jacques Lacan. *The Seminar of Jacques Lacan, Book VII: The Ethics of Psychoanalysis 1959–60*. Ed. Jacques-Alain Miller. Trans. Dennis Porter. New York: Norton, 1992.

SVIII Jacques Lacan. *Le Seminaire, livre VIII: Le transfert*. Ed. Jacques-Alain Miller. Paris: Seuil, 1991.

SXI Jacques Lacan. *The Four Fundamental Concepts of Psychoanalysis*. Trans. Alan Sheridan. New York: Norton, 1978.

SE Sigmund Freud. *The Standard Edition of the Complete Psychological Works*. Trans. and ed. James Strachey et. al. London: The Hogarth Press, 1953. 24 volumes.

T Jacques Lacan. "Television," trans. Denis Hollier, Rosalind Krauss, and Annette Michelson. In *Television: A Challenge to the Psychoanalytic Establishment*, ed. Joan Copjec (New York: Norton, 1990).

TL Julia Kristeva. *Tales of Love*. Trans. Leon Roudiez. New York: Columbia University Press, 1987.

These chapters were written as occasional essays, each at the invitation of a different host, who invited me to think about a topic of his or her own choosing. The solicitation of thought that is thereby implied, the way in which my own thought, grounded in philosophy and psychoanalysis, was shaped and altered by these invitations, is of intrinsic interest to me, insofar as it suggests how thought, and indeed life itself, unfolds beyond the individual, and beyond one's own preoccupations. At the same time, my own concerns invariably mark each essay. And above all I am struck, looking back at these essays, at how preoccupied I have been with trying to support a conversation across boundaries that have become overly territorialized, overly defended, and exclusive. These boundaries are multiple, and I attempt here to cross them in several ways simultaneously. Several chapters are concerned with the question of the body, which Lacan is often wrongly said to neglect (Chapters 1, 2, 3, and 6). Several are concerned with the complex relationships among Lacan, Heidegger, and Derrida, relationships that I approach, not through explicit references or texts or themes (notoriously, the phallus as a supposed "master signifier," the text of Poe's "Purloined Letter," etc.), but through some fundamental conceptual problems they share in common, in particular, the excruciatingly complex relationship between "structure" and "history" (Chapters 1, 4, and 5); the question of Lacan's relation to topics that he is generally considered to have neglected, such as race (in Chapter 6), affect (in Chapters 2 and 3), and the body—a topic Lacan is thought to discuss endlessly, but only in order to reduce it to the order of the signifier, or to the conservative law of phallic division into two "sexes," both claims being, in my view, greatly mistaken (Chapters 1, 2, 3, and 6).

In general, these crossings between Lacan and other thinkers (feminist theory, Foucault, Derrida, and Heidegger, especially) are subterranean here, in the sense that these relationships are not the "topic" of the essays. But readers will see very clearly, I think, where I am inviting these relationships, and indeed am compelled to initiate them, for what I hope are more authentic reasons—not, in other words, because I sought to produce an academic essay on "Lacan's relation to Derrida" (useful as this could be), but rather because a particular conceptual issue, set before me by others, led me to realize that the issue itself—*die Sache selbst*—called me to encounter the question of these relations. Thus, even while the relationships named above (to a thinker like Derrida, or a concept like affect) remain subterranean, I think they will be the recognizable substructure of this book, and that readers will see how the *issues themselves* should oblige us—and I do see this as an ethical issue, especially today, when so many territorialized camps have been set up in the academy, such that Foucauldians do not read Lacan, philosophers do not touch psychoanalysis (and I use "touch" with all its phobic resonance), with the forceful and important exception of feminist theory, and Lacanians, unfortunately, do not read anyone else, except to demonstrate that so-and-so "only repeats what Lacan already said more profoundly," or "fails to recognize the most crucial point, which only Lacan was able to see for us"—to move across these territorial boundaries, which are only the trivial boundaries of academic turf, and not appropriate to the conceptual work that calls for our attention. Derrida and Lacan, Foucault and Lacan, have much closer and more intimate relations than their reception has allowed, and academic pieties and allegiances, indeed, kinship wars (inheritances of the father), have largely prevented us from engaging these relationships in a serious way. This is not to say that there are no serious differences between these thinkers—on the contrary. But we will never grasp them with any clarity if we begin, and teach our students to begin, with denunciations, excommunications, and imaginary rivalry. Too often, especially in our academic culture, and in the training of our doctoral students, these allegiances have taken the place of thinking, and I hope these essays will encourage some more generous and hospitable encounters.

Let me be somewhat more concrete. Chapter 1 emerged from some questions posed to me by a Mexican student of psychoanalysis, who was trying to understand the concept of the "real" and who asked me to clarify its relation to the symbolic order. I therefore wrote this piece in a very schematic way, somewhat like an encyclopedia article, hoping at least to sketch out some of the major issues that the concept of the real might engage, and also to suggest some general points of intersection between the real in Lacan and other contemporary issues or thinkers—the "trace" in Derrida, the "incest prohibition" in Lévi-Strauss, the critique of Lacan's covert essentialism that one finds in some of Judith Butler's work.

Chapter 2 was written at the invitation of Joan Copjec, for a splendid conference on *Antigone* at the University at Buffalo, and since this community included some people in comparative literature whom I greatly admire (Rodolphe Gasché, Carol Jacobs, Henry Sussman, and others), I tried to emphasize not only the argument of Lacan's *Ethics of Psychoanalysis* but also (1) the literary text itself, (2) Hegel's famous interpretation of Sophocles, and (3) some classical issues stemming from Aristotle's *Poetics*, particularly insofar as they bear on "catharsis," and the problem of *jouissance*.

Chapter 3 was written on the very sad occasion of the death of Teresa Brennan, who died unexpectedly and much too young, and I was honored to be invited by Kelly Oliver and Elizabeth Grosz to a conference in honor of her work and her life, at the University at Stony Brook. In these circumstances, I could not write about anything other than "Mourning and Melancholia," and the concept of affect, which had so occupied Teresa. Here again, as in Chapter 2, I had begun to think that affect, far from being neglected by Lacan, bore very directly on his concept of *jouissance*. The problem is enormously complex, of course, because Lacan appears at some points to say that anxiety is the only affect and that, indeed, anxiety is not an "emotion," which would seem to have a clearer symbolic orientation. The distinction between affect and emotion would thus be one approach to the border between the symbolic and the real, but this is only a first approximation. Any reader of Heidegger will immediately realize that questions of *stimmung* ("mood"), *Befindlichkeit* ("disposition" or "attunement"), and indeed anxiety itself would call for a far more extensive treatment. Nevertheless, the question of affect in Chapter 2, and of the aesthetic effect of tragedy on our emotions (especially "pity" and "fear"), is in some sense continued in Chapter 3, where I also turn briefly from *Antigone* to *Hamlet* for guidance.

Chapter 4 was written at the request of David Goecocheia of Brock University, who organized a conference on Kristeva's *Tales of Love* and invited me to comment specifically on Kristeva's chapter on Plotinus and Ovid. I was thus brought to *The Metamorphoses*, yet another literary text, which complicated greatly what I might otherwise have written, either about Lacan or about Kristeva herself. This chapter is perhaps the best example of what I mean by stressing the gift of these "occasional" origins: having been invited to write on this topic, I could not leave in place what I thought I knew about narcissism, in Freud or Lacan or Kristeva; on the contrary, having been asked to comment on Plotinus, and thus on the philosophical tradition, which is not at all psychoanalytic, and then (even worse) on Ovid, I was pulled irrevocably back to my own origins in literary study, and I found that the text of Ovid, understood not as an "example" or "instance" of psychoanalysis but as a dense literary object, inserted into its own complex literary tradition, compelled me to read *that text* for what it contained. My argument thus became a kind of encounter between literature (Ovid), philosophy (Plotinus), and psychoanalysis (Kristeva and Freud), and the question of love is not unrelated to these crossings. In fact, Lacan says that "love is the sign of a change in discourse," and this may be part of the movement set forth in all the chapters that follow.

Chapter 5 emerged from an invitation to write about "memory," for a special issue of *Research in Phenomenology*, a journal which I had greatly admired as a graduate student, and in which I saw the most rigorous and exciting phenomenological community I knew. I thus took what I understood of Lacan's ideas about memory—a topic so crucial to Freud—and tried to show not simply what Lacan said about the subject, but how his ideas might intersect with some issues in the phenomenological tradition.

Chapter 6, finally, was written at the request of Christopher Lane, who was collecting a set of essays on the topic of psychoanalysis and race for Columbia University Press. I understood, implicitly, (or thought I understood) that this was an invitation to write about psychoanalysis and *racism*, and thus about the various forms of imaginary and symbolic identification that structure our *experience* of race, what we call "racial identity" or "racial practice." But the invitation itself spoke of *race* and not *racism*, and because I have long been interested in biology, and the history of biological thought (indeed Canguilhem was important to me, and Foucault's *The Birth of the Clinic* was a favorite book, no doubt because I had trained as a Romanticist, and was steeped in the early nineteenth century, which saw the rise of biological sciences and the very concept of "life" in its modern form), I decided to try to address the relationship between psychoanalysis and "race" as a concept that claims to have some biological or genetic content. Cultural studies, of course, had long argued—persuasively, in my view—that science always operates within a discursive horizon, and is decisively shaped by concepts and categories that do not have a purely empirical basis, but belong to larger conceptual, discursive, and institutional regimes. And yet, when I think about the attacks on Darwin that are launched by religious fundamentalists in the United States, and I consider the importance of current genetic research, and medical advances, I find it impossible to say with the haughty confidence of some cultural theorists that "race," or "the body," or "sex," or indeed "perception," can be entirely detached from all consideration of biological knowledge, even if that knowledge is, as I believe, a product of culture that will inevitably be shaped in many ways by forces that are not strictly "scientific" (in the sense that scientists would understand that term). In fact, it seemed to me that cultural critics themselves had become all too comfortable with their own appeal to "discursive construction," as if *that* regime of truth, *that* pious certainty, could serve as a magic wand, capable of banishing all the stupidities and blindnesses of *other* thinkers, while leaving cultural theorists blind to the mechanical operation of their own dogma, in which there could be no reference to "sex," no reference to "the body," no reference to "race" as a reality that might escape the reach of language.

Of course, as Judith Butler has relentlessly reminded us, any *talk about* race, or the body, will always involve some kind of discursive organization, which itself requires vigilant attention. But one should not forget that this assertion, that "all knowledge is discursive," is itself prey to the same observation, and we should therefore ask what may be occluded or banished from thought by this insistent reminder, this universal truth of discursive construction, which covers all knowledge and all thinking, no matter what the field of investigation may be. In response to this invitation to write on "race," then, I decided not to speak about racism, which I suspected many other contributors would address, and chose instead to think—almost in the manner of a thought experiment—what psychoanalysis might have to say about the idea of "race" as a biological fact. In other words, setting aside for a moment the obvious and compelling critiques that had been launched against the use of "race" as a biological category—critiques that I thought had been well-circulated and successful—and knowing that one could always rightly develop a critique of any scientific discourse, as Foucault himself did on several occasions, I decided to ask what psychoanalysis might have to say about "race," assuming that something like race is indeed a "reality" of a biological kind, namely, a form of human diversity that has affected our evolutionary history, just as it did the history of other animals. A critique of the anthropological *use* of race, or of the conceptual categories that were generated as an *answer* to the reality of racial difference, would always be possible and necessary, but assuming for a moment that there is some truth to the theory of evolution, and that human beings are not exempt from evolution, what would psychoanalysis have to say about this "reality" of the body? My answer was that human physiological diversity could not be understood in quite the same way that animal diversity is imagined, because humans organize themselves, group together, migrate and exchange, intermarry and reproduce, according to mechanisms and structures that are partly cultural. This is quite obvious, but it seemed to me that evolutionary theory, insofar as I understood it, had not really addressed this fact. Thus, from the standpoint of cultural studies, theory seemed to have avoided the "reality" of race, while from the standpoint of biological knowledge, science had neglected to consider the impact of culture on the body. Psychoanalysis, strangely enough, seemed to me to be the obvious arena for a philosophical reflection on the history of the human body, in which the shortcomings of both biological and cultural theories would become more evident.

A similar argument could be made about "sexual difference," and I had in fact attempted such an argument in a previous book, *Vital Signs*, whose title was explicitly intended to mark this conjunction of the "vital" order and the "signifier"—two realms that were too often separated from one another. "Race," however, as readers will see, does not have the same status as "sexual difference," and the evolutionary perspective that I tried to maintain in this chapter, this thought experiment, remains fairly strong and radically distinguishes "race" from what Lacanians mean by "sexual difference." But the larger point, from the perspective of this book as a whole, is that this chapter tries to dislodge some of the pieties of contemporary academic discourse and seeks to bring into contact areas of thought that are too often separated from one another—literature and philosophy, structuralism and history, Derrida and Lacan, and so on. These "prohibited" relations, these "unthinkable" neighbors, are brought into proximity here, not to dissolve all differences but, on the contrary, to initiate a clearer understanding of the distinct contribution of each tradition, each "method" or "discourse" or form of knowledge.

Each chapter can, in some sense, be read as an investigation of the "limits of language," in that I wanted to show how the dominant reading of Lacan, as a thinker of the symbolic order, mistakenly reduces his work to a thought of *nothing but* the symbolic order, which is obviously a very different thing. As a thinker of the symbolic order, Lacan brought to light many aspects of human existence that are irreducible to language. In Chapter 5, this appears as the *limit to remembering*, which is one of the first formations in Lacan of the concept of the real. In Chapter 1, it appears as the limit of the real itself, understood not as a prelinguistic reality but as an effect of the signifier itself. In Chapter 2, the "limit of language" appears in the figure of Antigone, in a least two respects: first, because she is presented by Lacan in terms of her *appearance*, her *manifestation*, the so-called "beauty" of Antigone (*l'eclat d'Antigone*), a sort of "shining" that not only recalls Heidegger but introduces a profound meditation on the analytic of the beautiful in Kant's *Third Critique* and gives rise to one of the first incarnations of the concept of the "gaze," which reorganizes the familiar account of the "imaginary" in Lacan; and second, because Antigone's ethical position, according to Lacan, can only be understood in connection with a refinement of our familiar understanding of the "law" in Lacan, since, as Lacan himself says, she confronts us with "something that is, in effect, of the order of law, but which does not get inscribed in any signifying chain." This is where Lacan breaks with the Hegelian interpretation. And here too, we are dealing with the limit of language, and its consequences for ethics. In Chapter 3, this limit takes off from the remarks on *jouissance* offered in the discussion of *Antigone* and develops the question of affect more directly, together with a distinction between "affect" and "emotion," which Lacan's work might help us to pursue in a more precise and useful way. Chapter 4 approaches the limit of language in narcissism itself, insofar as the "time" of narcissism, and the very structure of the temporality of the subject, necessarily refers us to something that is not inscribed in history, an absolute past that organizes narrative but cannot be reduced to the narratives that seek to describe it. The tension between "genesis" and "structure" that runs throughout the book is at is highest point here, but despite the philosophical character of this question, it was expressed more precisely though Ovid than through Derrida, who taught me to be aware of the issue. And finally, in Chapter 6, the limit of language is encountered, in a very different way, through the problem of the body.

From my earliest days as a student, I have been impressed and fascinated by the excruciating complexity of literary texts. And when I eventually began to read philosophy in a serious way—partly because poetry was simply too difficult, impossible to speak about, really—I found myself struck by the strange relation between philosophy and poetry. On the one hand, philosophers are notoriously clumsy and incompetent when they read poems, so much so that one should advise philosophers to keep altogether silent on such matters. Recent accounts of *Antigone*, grounded in the interpretations of Hegel and Lacan, have been stunningly ignorant about the literary dimension of Sophocles' text, so much so that can one hardly imagine one is dealing with a tragedy. As with early "deconstructive" readings of literary texts, one can only be shocked at how quickly the literary work disappears—a matter to which Derrida himself was profoundly sensitive. Readings that make literary work into evidence of the "Foucauldian construction of early modern subjectivity," while often extremely illuminating as intellectual history, can only make a literary scholar cringe. Yet I would not have learned to read literary texts without philosophy. I would not have learned to pause and unfold the philosophical consequences of literary works without the guidance of Heidegger, Derrida, and other philosophers. The same is true of Lacan: he is not a philosopher, and I have written many times about the erasure of psychoanalysis that takes place whenever Lacan's work is translated into the linguistic theory of Saussure or the philosophical account of intersubjectivity that one finds in Kojève. Psychoanalysis is not philosophy, and yet its significance, as Lacan always insisted, cannot be grasped from within psychoanalysis alone but requires philosophical elaboration, so that, eventually, the critique of philosophy that one finds in psychoanalysis can eventually emerge with greater force. These neighbors stand in need of one another, precisely in order that their differences can emerge. I have tried to initiate this process in the chapters that follow.

I would like to thank The Pembroke Center for Teaching and Research on Women at Brown University, which provided fellowship support during the time when Chapters 2 and 6 were drafted. I am grateful to Elizabeth Weed for her support, for cultivating an exceptional intellectual space at the Pembroke Center, and for encouraging me to speak in my own voice. I would also like to thank the Institute for Advanced Study for support during the time when Chapters 3 and 5 were completed. Joan Scott not only gave me exceptional guidance and support during my time in Princeton, but provided an unmatched example of the strength and spiritedness that are necessary for intellectual survival, and she has generously continued to support my work. I am also grateful to Bobby Paul of Emory University, who in the face of many demands has generously supported my work and helped me to give my interest in psychoanalysis a broader footing. I am deeply indebted to Charles Scott of Vanderbilt University for his exceptional teaching, for introducing me to Continental philosophy and making its questions real, and for taking me to the Collegium Phaenomenologicum in Perugia, Italy, where my educational path was irrevocably altered. One could not hope for a better and more generous teacher.

Earlier versions of some of this work appeared in the following places. I wish to thank the following publishers for granting permission to reprint.

Humanities Press International and *Research in Phenomenology* for "Vital Signs: The Place of Memory in Psychoanalysis," *Research in Phenomenology* 23 (1993): 22–72.

Oxford University Press, for permission to reprint "The Intimate Alterity of the Real," *Postmodern Culture*, vol. 6, no. 3 (May 1996).

Joan Copjec and the State University of New York at Buffalo, "Of Love and Beauty in Lacan's *Antigone*," *Umbr(a)*, no. 1 (Fall 1999): 63–80.

The State University of New York Press, for "Affect, Emotion, and the Work of Mourning," from *Affect in the Work of Teresa Brennan*, ed. Kelly Oliver and Shannon Lundeen (Albany: State University of New York Press, 2007), 57–77.

The Johns Hopkins University Press, for "Telling Tales of Love: Philosophy, Literature, Psychoanalysis," *Diacritics* (Spring 2000): 89–105.

Columbia University Press, for "Human Diversity and the Sexual Relation," *The Psychoanalysis of Race*, ed. Christopher Lane (New York: Columbia University Press, 1997), 41–64.

LACAN AND THE LIMITS
OF LANGUAGE

CHAPTER I

The Intimate Alterity of the Real

Many readers of Lacan have asked the question: "Is everything really a 'discursive construction,' a product of the symbolic order, and if not, how can we speak of an 'outside' without returning to a naive realism?" This question is especially important for the concept of the "real," and more broadly speaking, it is one of the most important issues in contemporary intellectual life. It might even be said that one's response to this single issue is enough to define one's theoretical orientation today.

A map of postmodernism could in fact be drawn on the basis of the answers that are given to this question. It would have three major areas: in the first, we find an emphasis on the "symbolic order" and certain theories of "social construction"; in the second, we find a reaction against "postmodernism" and a return to "positive" and "empirical" investigation, together with a return to biological, genetic, and endocrinological accounts of consciousness, behavior, and sexuality; in the third, we find an effort to think *through* the "linguistic turn"—not to react against the formative power of representation, but rather to think its *limit*. This is where I believe the most interesting contemporary work is being done, and this is a problem held in common by Foucault, Lacan, and Derrida, though they do not elaborate the issue in the same way. There are many ways to approach the question, as it concerns Lacan, and I will therefore try to touch very briefly on a whole range of directions in which the question might take us. I will loosely organize the discussion under three headings: "Inside/Outside," "The Limits of Formalization," and "Two Versions of the Real (Judith Butler and Slavoj Žižek)."

Inside/Outside

First, concerning the idea that the real is "outside" the symbolic. Jacques-Alain Miller developed the term *extimité* from Lacan, suggesting that the real is not exactly "outside," but is a kind of "excluded interior," or an "intimate exterior."[1] In *Seminar VII*, for example, in the chapter "On the Moral Law," Lacan says of the "thing": "*das Ding* is at the center only in the sense that it is excluded" (SVII, 71). And again, in the chapter "The Object and the Thing," he speaks of what is "excluded in the interior" (SVII, 101), noting that this exclusion presents us with a "gap" in the symbolic order—something that escapes the law—"a gap once again at the level of *das Ding*," which indicates that we can "no longer rely on the Father's guarantee" (SVII, 100). However much one may stress the notorious "law of the father" in Lacan, it is clear that the symbolic order is not the whole story, and that the relation between the symbolic and the real (or between language and *das Ding*) involves a certain failure of the law. We must therefore take account of this element that "escapes" the symbolic order, or renders it "incomplete." The problem remains as to how exactly this "excluded object" should be conceived. We can already see, however, that it is not simply "outside" the structure, but is missing *from* the structure, excluded from within. So the question is: Just how we are to understand this "belonging" and "not belonging" to structure, this "intimate alterity" of the real?

TOPOLOGY

Lacan often drew on topology in his attempts to describe this peculiar "extimate" relation between the symbolic and the real. One could thus approach the question in geometrical terms, for the usual relation between "inside" and "outside" that exists in Euclidean space (a circle, for example, has a clearly defined interior and exterior) is disrupted by topological figures such as the Klein bottle or the torus (the figure shaped like a doughnut, structured around a central hole). Even with the Mobius strip, which has only one side, the usual intuitive relation between inside and outside is disrupted. Lacan's use of these structures was more technical and precise. Juan-David Nasio argues that each of these topological figures is meant to address a specific problem within psychoanalytic theory.[2] Thus: (1) the torus describes the relation between demand and desire; (2) the Mobius strip describes the relation between the subject and speech; (3) the Klein bottle describes the relation between the master-signifier and the

Other; and (4) the cross-cap describes the structure of fantasy, where we find the subject's relation to the object.[3]

BEING-TOWARD-DEATH

Without developing these points in detail, it is easy to see this material at work in Lacan's text. Even in the familiar "Rome Discourse," Lacan says that the human being's relation to death is unlike the "natural" relation to biological death, and that death is not a simple "event," a moment "in" chronological time, but rather the very opening of time, its condition of possibility. Instead of being placed at the end of a temporal sequence, as a final moment in biological time, the relation-to-death is placed at the origin, and understood as the giving of human time, the opening of possibility, of time as a finite relation to the future and the past, structured by anticipation and memory. Death thus involves a peculiar link between the symbolic and the real, presenting us with a sort of hole or void in the structure of meaning—a void that is not a deficiency, but virtually the opposite, an absolute condition of meaning. The human relation-to-death (discussed in such detail by Heidegger) is thus in some sense at the "origin" of the symbolic order—not represented "in" language, or entirely captured by the symbolic rituals that seek to contain it, but rather "primordial" to language: "So when we wish to attain in the subject . . . what is primordial to the birth of symbols, we find it in death" (E, 105). The topological reference to a "missing" center (added to the text in 1966) follows: "To say that this mortal meaning reveals in speech a center exterior to language is more than a metaphor; it manifests a structure . . . it corresponds rather to the relational group that symbolic logic designates topologically as an annulus." He adds, "If I wished to give an intuitive representation of it . . . I should call on the three-dimensional form of the torus" (E, 105). In short, one can easily see that the relation between the symbolic and the real cannot be approached if one begins with a dichotomy between inside and outside. It is rather a matter of a void within the structure. This is of course what the theory of lack in Lacan tries to address. And this is why those for whom lack is foreclosed—those who lack lack—are in some sense deprived of access to language.

THE STRUCTURE OF THE BODY

Lacan's topological formulations may seem esoteric, and many commentators have ridiculed them, denouncing his "pseudo-mathematical" interests as chicanery or mysticism or intellectual posing. But if one thinks for a moment about the body—about the peculiar structure of the body, and all the discussions in Freud about the limit of the body, the difficulty of containing the body within its skin, or of determining what is inside and outside the body (the "relation to the object," the mechanisms of "projection" and "introjection," etc.), it becomes obvious that the space of the body is not really elucidated by Euclidean geometry. The body is not easily closed within itself, as a circle is closed with respect to the outside. The body does not occupy space as a natural object does. When it comes to the body, the relations of interior and exterior are more complex and enigmatic than one would suspect if one began by regarding the body as an "extended substance" in Cartesian space, or by presupposing that space is structured by Euclidean dimensions, and that the "place" of the body can be delimited in the same way that the natural object can be located by spatial coordinates in Euclidean geometry. So the discussion of topology may seem esoteric, but it addresses problems that are obviously fundamental to psychoanalysis. Freud speaks, for example, of the orifices of the body as points of exchange with the outside—points where the limit of the body is most obscure, where the relation between the inside and outside of the body is unstable and problematic. All the analytic problems having to do with "incorporation," "mourning," "abjection," and the "object-relation"—even the themes of aggression and love, and the entire question of the relation to the other—can be put in terms of the inside and outside of the body.

FROM THE "IMAGINARY BODY" TO THE SYMBOLIC CONTAINMENT OF THE VOID

These observations are very brief, but they should be enough to indicate that the "body" in psychoanalysis is not simply an imaginary body. To be sure, Freud speaks of the ego as a "bodily ego," and Lacan says that the body is an "imaginary body." This bears not only on the "space" of the body, but on "external" space as well: in the "Mirror Stage," he notes that the imaginary order allows the world of objects to appear, calling it "the threshold of the visible world."[4] But discussions of the "imaginary body" have tended to obscure the fact that the symbolic and the real also play a crucial role in the constitution of the body. Furthermore, if we speak of the body as "imaginary," we will tend to regard the symbolic as if it were a purely linguistic matter, a domain of speech and representation, and not a matter of our embodiment as well. I remember visiting a clinic in Boston once—a halfway house for schizophrenics. Many of the patients had specific materials—scarves or string or favorite hats—that they would attach to their bodies. Without these things, they became extremely anxious and refused to go outside, as if the body were not unified without this external prop. The body does not automatically cohere by nature: it holds itself together as one entity, and is able to move through space, not naturally, with the physical coherence of an objective thing, but only with the help of imaginary and symbolic props that give space and time their consistency. So we could say that the relation between the real and the symbolic—the formation of a "structure" that also includes the real as an "interior exclusion"—allows the body to move, and gives coherence to "external space." This human space—the space of desire and human movement—cannot be grasped in terms of Euclidean space, and the space of the body therefore cannot be adequately conceived through the usual geometry of inside and outside. Thus, while we are often told that the body is an imaginary body for Lacan, the constitution of the body also depends on the inscription of the void, the symbolic containment of lack.[5]

DEMAND AND DESIRE

The relation between the symbolic and the real can also cast light on the distinction between demand and desire. In a famous—but still notoriously obscure—passage in "The Meaning of the Phallus," Lacan distinguishes between demand and desire, calling desire an "absolute condition": "for the unconditioned element of demand," he writes, "desire substitutes the absolute condition" (E, 287). Demand is "unconditioned" in the sense that it simply designates the general "deviation" by which human demand comes to be separated from animal need (which is "conditioned" by the requirements of survival and reproduction). We thus have a "deviation in man's needs from the fact that he speaks . . . insofar as his needs are subjected to demand" (E, 286). This has a clear impact on the object-relation: for unlike the object of need, the object of demand is symbolic and is therefore subject to metonymic displacement, losing its natural specificity in a movement along the signifying chain that makes the object a "substitute," a signifier of the other's recognition. In Lacan's words, "demand annuls (*aufhebt*) the particularity of everything that can be granted by transmuting it into a proof of love" (E, 286). Demand is thus not only perpetually displaced, but also projected to infinity, always seeking "something more." As Marx also says, human life loses its foundation in nature, in a movement of "excess production" (the arena of "supply and demand") that goes beyond all biological need and has no natural limitation.

Consequently, at the symbolic level of demand, there is a further requirement for a limit," and it is precisely desire that emerges as this limit, to the infinite displacement of demand, giving a finite shape to the otherwise endless play of symbolic substitution. Thus, as Lacan says in "Direction of the Treatment," "Desire is produced in the beyond of demand" (E, 265; see also SVIII, 246) and introduces a limit to the displacement of the signifier. As Derrida also notes in "Structure, Sign, and Play," the free play of the signifier is *in principle* unlimited, but *in fact* is always brought to a certain tentative closure, and thereby grounded in a peculiar "center." "And as always," Derrida writes, this "point at which the substitution of contents, elements, or terms is no longer possible . . . expresses the force of a desire."[6] We can also see here why Lacan claims that although the "particularity" of the object of need is lost when we pass to the level of symbolic displacement ("demand annuls [*aufhebt*] the particularity of everything that can be granted"), he also insists that "the particularity thus abolished should reappear beyond demand" (E, 286). Thus, the "reversal" or transformation that characterizes the shift from demand to desire is accomplished precisely by the institution of a lack, a void or "obliteration" that is not symbolic, that escapes the dialectical movement of "productive negation," but is nevertheless constitutive of the subject. This void, therefore, has an effect: it leaves a remainder, a relic that is regarded as a power—"the force of a desire": "By a reversal that is not simply the negation of a negation, the power of pure loss arises from the relic of an obliteration" (E, 287).[7] We thus return to the "mortal center" of the "Rome Discourse"—as if language were opened by a mark of death that haunts it, but cannot be inscribed or reduced to a symbolic phenomenon. This not only explains the link between "death" and "desire," but also suggests why Lacan claims, in "The Meaning of the Phallus," that psychoanalysis goes beyond Hegel precisely insofar as it is able to give theoretical precision to an element of lack that is not dialectical—a lack that is not inscribed in the movement of symbolic production, but rather makes it possible. This is the "absolute condition" that "reverses" the "unconditioned" character of demand, allowing it to acquire a local habitation and a name.

THE "INVENTION" OF THE BODY

Before we close this initial "topological" approach to the problem, the historical aspect of these remarks should also be stressed. It is often said that psychoanalysis is simply ahistorical and that it promotes a "structuralist" position, a version of the "law" that is inattentive to different social and historical conditions. At least three points should be stressed in this regard. First, "classical" structuralism was in no way simply ahistorical (as Piaget pointed out, and as Derek Attridge has emphasized).[8] Rather, it sought to elaborate a model of historical transformation that would not immediately have recourse to the familiar, diachronic, and quasi-evolutionary models of history that had characterized the philology of the nineteenth century. For Saussure, it is obvious that there are "living" and "dead" languages, and the "laws" of the symbolic order do not ignore this fact; they simply seek to account for shifts and displacements in the structure—for what one might call the historicality of language—without automatically presupposing a "natural" time of "growth" and "decay." Second, if—having recognized the historical dimension of structuralism—one then turns from the strictly structural conception of the law (Saussure and Lévi-Strauss) to Lacan's concern with the relation between the symbolic and the real, one can see the problem of the real as precisely an additional temporal problem—since it bears on the incompleteness and thus the destabilization of the law. As Slavoj Žižek has rightly said, psychoanalysis is not simply "ahistorical," but it is "antihistoricist," insofar as it entails a conception of time that differs from the historically linear, chronologically sequential time of "history" as we usually understand it. Third—to return to our initial problematic—if one recalls that topology was invented by Leibniz in the late seventeenth century, as *analysis situs* (a theory of "place" that cannot be formulated in terms of "space"), one might be led to consider that the Freudian theory of the body could only emerge after the "classical," Euclidean conception of space had been challenged. In short, psychoanalysis is not simply ahistorical; on the contrary, it explicitly engages the question of the historical conditions of its own emergence. Indeed, as the reference to Leibniz suggests, Lacan, like many "postmodern" thinkers, is profoundly engaged with the Enlightenment, as a historical moment whose "end" we are still experiencing.

The body in psychoanalysis is thus conceivable only on the basis of a certain history. This is why Lacan talks so much about "measurement" and "science" and "Kepler" and "Copernicus." Even without going into Lacan's account of the history of science, one can see that the relation between the real and the symbolic is concerned with the theory of space (or rather, "place"), and is such that the real is something like an "interior exclusion"—not simply outside, entirely unrelated to the structure or completely foreign, but—quite the opposite—"contained" by the particular structure that excludes it, like an internal void. Many writers have recently taken up this problem—notably Irigaray, in her article on Aristotle's theory of place, but also Heidegger, whose famous analysis of the jug is intriguing here, since he insists that the jug is not an object in Euclidean dimensions, but rather a structure that contains the void. As Heidegger says, the "gift" and "sacrifice" that one encounters in the face of the "thing" cannot be understood unless we see that the jug is not reducible to an "object" in Cartesian space ("the jug differs from an object," he writes in "The Thing").⁹ As with the real in Lacan, the void or nothing that is given a place by the jug is not a natural void (nature abhors a vacuum), but an unnatural "nothingness," a "lack" that arises only *through* the structure, and only for the being who speaks: it is a lack that is produced in the symbolic order.

The Limits of Formalization

Let us now leave these topological matters aside and take another approach to the question. We have seen that the real is neither inside nor outside the symbolic, but is more like an "internal void." This can be clarified through topological figures, but we could also put the question in a more general way, as a question concerning the limits of formalization. This would oblige us to clarify the way in which psychoanalysis goes beyond structuralism. Many people condemn Lacanian psychoanalysis for being trapped in structuralism, committed to a "science" of the subject and a doctrine of the "law" that claims to be universal, and does not adequately attend to the contingent historical and cultural specificity of human existence. There is indeed a commitment to a kind of logic or formalization in Lacan, and an emphasis on the law of the symbolic, but one must recognize it as an effort to theorize the *limit* of the law, the incompleteness of the law, the fact that the law is not all, and that it always malfunctions. Slavoj Žižek has insisted upon this point more than anything else in his writing. In *For They Know Not What They Do*, he claims that the link between Hegel and Lacan should be seen in this way: "Hegel knows very well that every attempt at rational totalization ultimately fails . . . his wager is located at another level . . . the possibility of 'making a system' out of the very series of failed totalizations . . . to discern the strange 'logic' that regulates the process."¹⁰ The task is therefore to grasp what Derrida has called "the law of the law," the logic that governs the malfunction of the law, showing us why the classical position of structuralism is unstable and allowing us to see in a clear, "rational," and quasi-logical way what Lacan calls the "mystical limit of the most rational discourse in the world" (E, 124). In this sense, Lacan is a "post-structuralist": the real can be understood as a concept that was developed in order to define in a clear way how there is always an element that does not belong within the structure, an excluded element that escapes the law, but that can nevertheless be approached in a precise theoretical fashion.

CAUSE AND LAW

At this point, we could also take up the question of causality. To ask how the real, if it is outside the symbolic order, can possibly have an effect on the symbolic, it seems to me, is to express the position of classical structuralism (and perhaps the position of natural science, which aims to treat objects apart from language and representation). If we think of cause in terms of the usual scientific model—in terms of a "lawful" sequence of causes and effects ("the same cause always produces the same effect")—then we may suppose a *continuity* between law and cause. If we can account for the cause of a phenomenon (e.g., the cause of disease), we have begun to elaborate the laws that govern it. It is precisely here that Lacan introduces a "discontinuity": there is a "cause," he says (in the first chapter of *Seminar XI*), only where there is a *failure* of the law. To speak of the "cause of desire" is always to speak of a certain excess or deficiency in the relation between the subject and the Other, a lack that cannot be grasped at the level of the signifying chain. From here we could obviously go on to explore the very complex question of whether psychoanalysis is a science or not, and how it can claim to be scientific while questioning the usual notion of causality. And yet, many thinkers in the phenomenological tradition have followed Husserl in arguing that the scientific attitude is a construction that cannot simply be taken for granted as a starting point, but must be explored in its philosophical presuppositions and its historical conditions of emergence. Lacan addresses these issues explicitly in *Seminar XI*, where he asks, not whether psychoanalysis is a "science," but what science would have to be in order to account for the cause as a disruption of the law. This is the problem of the "subject," the problem of a desire that is normally excluded by science: "Can this question be left outside the limits of our field, as it is in effect in the sciences?" (SXI, 9).

THE OTHER AND THE OBJECT

For Lacan, the very concept of the subject cannot be understood without this split between cause and law. We thus circle back to the limits of formalization. If we start with the Saussurean position, we can elaborate the law, but we will not reach the cause. According to Saussure, the laws of the symbolic order function internally, on the basis of the relations between the elements, which are defined diacritically in reference to each other, and not to any outside. From this perspective, one can indeed claim that a closed structure can be defined by internal laws. As Piaget has shown, this is correct from the standpoint of Saussure: it is impossible to understand the structure, or indeed any of its elements (e.g., a particular signifier), except on the basis of the whole and the internal relations among its elements. It would be a mistake, from Saussure's perspective, to regard a particular signifier as having its cause outside the system—as though the signifier were based upon designation, and could be derived from outside, grounded in an external "reality" that it represents. On the contrary, we must recognize that the whole is greater than the sum of the parts: the system is not an atomistic accumulation and cannot be derived from its elements considered individually. (Foucault makes the same point in *The Order of Things*, locating this shift in priority from designation to system at the end of the Enlightenment: "in the Classical age, languages had a grammar because they had the power to represent; now they represent on the basis of that grammar."[11] On this basis, the entire philosophical problematic of "clear and distinct ideas" is replaced by a doctrine of "expression," "inheritance," and "national identity.") Contrary to common sense, the system is not built up, piece by piece, on the basis of designation, but rather the reverse: the very possibility of naming is derived from the system itself, which is thereby presupposed, since it makes meaning and designation possible. The entire system can thus be regarded as the "cause of itself." A quasi-theological view, no doubt, in which one cannot seek further into the "origins," since the system is always already in place, arising, as it were, in the beginning.

From Lacan's point of view, this is not altogether incorrect, and it is indeed the case that we cannot derive language "naturalistically," on the basis of designation ("there is no Other of the Other"). But we cannot stop with this observation: we must go on to note the incompleteness of the system, the fact that the Other functions only by the exclusion of a peculiar object, such that the smooth, consistent functioning of the law is disrupted, destabilized by what Lacan calls the "cause"—among other things, the "cause of desire," which is not the "object of desire" (in the sense of an actual thing outside language), but rather the "object-cause of desire," the lack that gives rise to desire, and yet is not present in the symbolic order, or situated at the level of signifiers. Lacan makes this explicit in "The Meaning of the Phallus" when he notes that if we may use structural linguistics to clarify Freudian doctrine, we must also recognize that Freud introduces a problem of lack that goes well beyond Saussure: "during the past seven years," he writes, "I have been led to certain results: essentially, to promulgate as necessary to any articulation of analytic phenomena the notion of the signifier, as opposed to the signified, in modern linguistic analysis. Freud could not take this notion, which postdates him, into account, but I would claim that Freud's discovery . . . could not fail to anticipate its formulas" (E, 284).

We must not stop here, however, as if Freud simply refers us to the structuralist theory of language, for Lacan adds: "Conversely, it is Freud's discovery that gives to the signifier/signified opposition the full extent of its implications," by raising the question of a certain outside, or an interior exclusion that has effects on the body which linguistics does not try to address. As he puts it in "Subversion of the Subject": "If *linguistics* enables us to see the signifier as the determinant of the signified, *analysis* reveals the truth of this relation by making 'holes' in the meaning . . . of its discourse" (E, 299, my emphasis). With this reference to "'holes' in the meaning," we see the step that takes Lacan beyond classical structuralism, to the limits of formalization, the element of the real that escapes symbolic closure. The cause is therefore outside the law as Saussure presents it.

THE SUBJECT AND THE REAL

This notion of cause should also allow us to situate the place of the subject as real, and not simply as symbolic. We often hear that for Lacan, the subject is "constituted in the symbolic order," but the subject is not entirely symbolic (as is suggested by some accounts of "discursive construction"). If we think of the autonomous sequence of signifiers as governed by the "internal" laws of the symbolic order, the diacritical relations between the elements (S_1-S_2-S_3), we can consider the "subject" ($\$$) as a "missing link," a place that is marked, and that can be located *through* the symbolic, but does not actually belong to the chain of signifiers (S_1-S_2-[$\$$]-S_3). We must be careful here to note the peculiar status of this subject, which is partly symbolic and partly real. In Freud, this place of the subject can be located in specific symbolic phenomena—the lapsus, the dream, free association, and so on—which reveal the repressed unconscious thought. We find here the symbolic aspect of the unconscious, where certain slips of the tongue indicate a discontinuity in the chain of signifiers, a disruption of conscious discourse, and a sign of unconscious desire. This is consistent with the famous Lacanian thesis that "the unconscious of the subject is the discourse of the Other." We must be careful, however, not to reduce the unconscious to a purely symbolic phenomenon. We must stress that although the "place" of the missing link is marked or "filled in" by certain symbolic formations, the subject does not belong to the chain, but indicates a point of non-integration or malfunction. This is why Lacan insists on the bar that divides the subject (\$): the subject of the unconscious is represented in the symbolic order (through the dream, or free association, or other symbolic forms), but in such a way that something of the "being" of the subject remains excluded—"absent" or "barred," but nevertheless "real"—and not without a certain force, an ability to have effects. In "Subversion of the Subject," Lacan says, "we must bring everything back to the function of the cut in discourse . . . a bar between the signifier and signified," adding: "This cut in the signifying chain alone verifies the structure of the subject as discontinuity in the real" (E, 299).

FORMATIONS OF THE UNCONSCIOUS (\$), FORMATIONS OF FANTASY (\$ ◊ A)

We thus see more clearly how the "object a" emerges in Lacanian theory: Lacan introduces the object a precisely in order to distinguish between the subject as real and the subject as manifested through the symbolic order. Thus, among all the mathemes and formulae that we find in Lacan, we can take our bearings—as Marie-Hélène Brousse has suggested—from two basic forms: generally speaking, the *formations of the unconscious* (the lapsus, dream, symptom, parapraxis, etc.) reveal the subject in a symbolic form (the unconscious as discourse of the Other), whereas the *formations of fantasy*, by contrast, provide us with a relation between this subject and the object a—the peculiar object that does not appear in the signifying chain, but that marks a point of pathological attachment, bound to the "real" of the body, a point of libidinal stasis where desire is lost.[12] Accordingly, we find these two aspects of the subject linked together in the formula for fantasy (\$ ◊ a), which concerns the relation that binds the split subject of the symbolic order (\$) to a certain real element (a) that exceeds the symbolic order. In a manner that is similar to fantasy, the "object of the drive" designates a point of bodily *jouissance*, a "libidinal attachment" that does not appear at the level of the signifier and is irreducible to the symbolic order. This is why Freud speaks of the silence of the death drive—the fact that (unlike other symptomatic formations) it does not emerge in speech and cannot be resolved through free association. We must stress here the peculiar status of the object, for the object of the drive, as real, is not a matter of biological instinct ("it is not introduced as the original food . . . the origin of the oral drive"; SXI, 180), but it is also irreducible to language, since it concerns a "remainder" or "excess" that escapes the symbolic law ("this object, which is in fact simply the presence of a hollow, a void," Lacan says, "can be occupied, Freud tells us, by any object'" SXI, 180). It is therefore not a matter of a "prelinguistic" material that is simply outside language and prior to it. It is rather a question, as Judith Butler has said, of the particular materialization of the object—the specific "occupation" of the void being unique to the individual subject.[13] The problem is therefore to define the relation between the Other (the symbolic order) and this object that is "outside" the law. And we can regard this problem in terms of the limits of formalization—that is, in terms of a certain failure of the law.

A NEW DIVISION: FREE ASSOCIATION AND TRANSFERENCE

Once this distinction between the symbolic and the real has emerged, we are led to a radical shift in psychoanalytic theory—a sudden division between transference and free association. At first, in the period of the "Rome Discourse" (which is perhaps canonical for the secondary literature), Lacan relied heavily on the symbolic order, stressing the difference between the imaginary (the ego) and the symbolic (the "subject divided by language"). The great battle against ego psychology was thus presented as a "return to Freud," a return to the unconscious, presented as a "discourse of the Other." The subject was marked by a split that could not be overcome, though the ego always tended to conceal this division, in the name of imaginary unity. This argument is condensed into "schema L." In this account, analysis could be presented in a classical Freudian manner, as grounded in free association, which would reveal the discourse of the Other in the symbolic form of symptoms, dreams, the lapsus, parapraxis, and so on. The difficulty arose when the symbolic order encountered an impasse, something that was in principle beyond the reach of symbolization (the "silent work" of the death drive). This is where we first find

Lacan claiming that the transference is no longer simply a symbolic matter, an intersubjective relation governed by speech and aiming at the discourse of the Other. Instead, the transference suddenly presents us with an object—something outside the symbolic order—an object that marks a point of impasse, a sort of "affective tie" that stands as a limit to symbolization. Freud spoke of this when he characterized the transference as a form of love and noted that this "love" could actually be an impediment to the patient—an impasse for analysis rather than a means. The crucial point for Lacan is thus to recognize that this dimension of "transference-love" (identification with the object) presents us with a form of identification that is *opposed* to symbolic identification.

We thus reach a split between free association and the transference, a split between the symbolic and the real. In *Seminar XI* Lacan is explicit, insisting that we must now confront something "beyond" the symbolic order, "precisely what one tends most to avoid in the analysis of the transference" (SXI, 149): "In advancing this proposition, I find myself in a problematic position—for what have I taught about the unconscious? The unconscious is constituted by the effects of speech . . . the unconscious is structured like a language. . . . And yet this teaching has had, in its approach, an end that I have called transferential" (SXI, 149). We are now faced with a dimension of bodily experience that cannot be reduced to the symbolic order, a problematic division between language and sexuality. Lacan returns here to Freud's persistent claim that the unconscious always has to do with sexuality—that "the reality of the unconscious is a sexual reality." In spite of his emphasis on language, Lacan cannot ignore this claim, since "at every opportunity, Freud defended his formula . . . with tooth and nail" (SXI, 150). This is a crucial shift in Lacan's work: if the classical method of "free association" once provided access to the unconscious (as a symbolic phenomenon), it now appears that some aspect of the transference disrupts that process and works against the very meaning and interpretation that free association was intended to support. In Lacan's words: "the unconscious, if it is what I say it is," can be characterized as "a play of the signifier" (SXI, 130), and the relation to the analyst should allow this play to unfold. And yet, we must now recognize that "the transference is the means by which the communication of the unconscious is interrupted, by which the unconscious closes up again. . . . I want to stress this question because it is the dividing line between the correct and incorrect interpretation of the transference" (SXI, 130). The same claim marks the very beginning of the seminar as a whole, so its importance is unmistakable. There Lacan rejects "the hermeneutic demand," which characterizes "what we nowadays call the human sciences" (SXI, 7). In explicit contrast to this hermeneutic demand, we find psychoanalysis insisting on the limit of the symbolic order, a certain dimension of the real, an aspect of the unconscious that is linked to the body and sexuality, and not to the symbolic order. Viewed in this light, the first sentence of *Seminar XI* (written afterward, in 1976), could not be more of a challenge: "When the space of a lapsus no longer carries any meaning (or interpretation), then only is one sure that one is in the unconscious" (SXI, vii).

AGAINST HERMENEUTICS

A similar shift can be found in Freud. Initially, it seemed to Freud that free association, being a relatively loose and uncensored mode of speech, would allow the unconscious to emerge, permitting analysis to gather up unconscious associations and construct the logic of this "Other" discourse in which the subject's destiny was written. But as Freud himself observed, there often comes a point at which analysis encounters something "unspeakable," a center that cannot be reached by analysis:

> There is often a passage in even the most thoroughly interpreted dream which has to be left obscure; this is because we become aware during the work of interpretation that at that point there is a tangle of dream-thoughts which cannot be unravelled and which moreover adds nothing to our knowledge of the content of the dream. This is the dream's navel, the spot where it reaches down into the unknown. (SE 5:525)

We have here precisely the relation between the symbolic and the real. Faced with this absent center, analysis is suddenly confronted with the prospect of becoming interminable. The transference, guided by free association and a symbolic conception of the unconscious (as discourse of the Other), is suddenly insufficient. Something else must come to pass, some nonsymbolic element must be grasped, if analysis is to reach its end. The aporetic point described by Freud—the nodal point that resists symbolization and "adds nothing to our knowledge"—leads Lacan to the concept of the object a, which can be understood as a point of identification that is *opposed* to symbolic identification. As he says in *Seminar XI*: "what eludes the subject is the fact that his syntax is in relation with the unconscious reserve. When the subject tells his story, something acts, in a latent way, that governs this syntax and makes it more and more condensed. Condensed in relation to what? In relation to what Freud, at the beginning of his description of psychical resistance, calls a nucleus" (SXI, 68). Some analysts regard this "psychical resistance" as a phenomenon of the ego, calling it a "defense" and suggesting that analysis must "break down the resistance" and reveal the unconscious. In Lacan's view, however, such a procedure amounts to imaginary warfare between egos. He therefore insists that "we must distinguish between the resistance of the subject and that first resistance of discourse, when the discourse proceeds towards the condensation around the nucleus." This nucleus is not a "content" or "meaning" that might be reached through the symbolic order, if only the ego were not "resisting." On the contrary: "The nucleus must be designated as belonging to the real" (SXI, 68). The fundamental issue of *Seminar XI* could be reduced to this single point, where it is a question of elaborating the limit of the law, the peculiar relation between the symbolic subject and the subject in the real. All of the chapters—on the gaze, on sexuality, on the transference, and so on—could be seen as different perspectives on this single problem.

IDENTIFICATION WITH THE OBJECT

The object a thus emerges in Lacanian theory at the moment when the symbolic law no longer has the final word. This is the point at which we can "no longer rely on the Father's guarantee" (SVII, 101). We are thus led to what Jacques-Alain Miller calls "the formula of the second paternal metaphor," which "corresponds point by point to the formula of the name-of-the-father," but which adds a twist that "forces us to operate with the inexistence and the inconsistency of the Other."[14] In fact, Miller locates this moment in the development of Lacan's thought between *Seminars VII* and *VIII* (the ethics and transference seminars). In the former, we find "the opposition between *das Ding*, the Thing, and the Other," but it is "worked out enigmatically" and remains "wrapped in mystery"; in the transference seminar, however, "this opposition is transformed into a relation," giving us "a revolution in Lacan's teaching."[15] However one may date this shift in Lacan's work, the question it entails is clear enough. We must now regard the transference as bearing on a certain "affective tie," a certain "libidinal investment," a dimension of "identification" that cannot be reached by the symbolic work of free association—an "attachment" to an "object" of *jouissance* that is not reducible to the symbolic order and is linked to the patient's suffering—to the symptom, and the body, insofar as they are irreducible to the symbolic order. This is where the question of sexuality (of the drive and libido) emerges in a certain "beyond" of language. In the seminar of 1974–75 called *R.S.I.*, he will take this question up in terms of affect. "What is the affect of existing?" (FS, 166); "What is it, of the unconscious, which makes for ex-istence? It is what I underline with the support of the symptom" (FS, 166). "In all this," he adds, "what is irreducible is not an effect of language" (FS, 165).

THE "END" OF ANALYSIS

The question of identification—to be precise, identification with the object, as distinct from symbolic identification—introduces a limit to the process of symbolization. If something about the transference suddenly distinguishes itself from the labor of free association, it is because the endless labor of speech (the "hermeneutic demand") cannot reach the "rock of castration," the point of pathological attachment that binds the subject to a suffering that will not be relinquished. If analysis is suddenly faced with the prospect of becoming "interminable"—if it cannot simply proceed by resting on free association—this means that the "end" of analysis requires a certain "separation" between the subject and the object a, insofar as that object is understood to entail a bodily *jouissance* that works *against desire*, a "suffering" akin to what Freud called the death drive. *Seminar XI* closes on this very topic: "The transference operates in the direction of bringing demand back to identification" (SXI, 274), that is to say, by revealing the link between the unending series of demands and the singular point of identification that underlies them. But the "end" of analysis requires a move "in a direction that is the exact opposite of identification" (SXI, 274), a direction that amounts to the destitution of the subject. This act of "crossing the plane of identification is possible," Lacan says, and it is what one might call the "sacrificial" dimension of psychoanalysis. It is therefore the "loss" of this pathological attachment that marks the terminal point of analysis: "the fundamental mainspring of the analytic operation," Lacan writes, "is the maintenance of the distance between the I—identification—and the *a*" (SXI, 273). These details are perhaps somewhat technical, and warrant further discussion, particularly with respect to the problem of the relation between the "symbolic order" and "sexuality," but I will not pursue them here. I have discussed the problem in "Vital Signs" (following some remarks by Russell Grigg), where I have tried to show how the limit of the symbolic order (and the question of sexuality) has consequences for Lacan's reading of the case of Anna O.[16]

APORETIC SCIENCES

Let us now turn from the internal affairs of psychoanalysis and try to sketch the intellectual horizon it shares with some other domains. Our remarks should be sufficient to show that the unconscious cannot be reduced to a purely symbolic phenomenon, and that the theory of sexuality and *jouissance* will only be understood if the relation between the symbolic and the real is grasped—in such a way, moreover, that we do not simply return to familiar arguments about the real of sexuality as a natural phenomenon, a libidinal force that is simply outside language. It is often said that Lacanian theory places too much emphasis on the law and the symbolic order, and we have suggested that this is not the case. But if we refer to the real (to sexuality and the drive), does this mean that we are now returning to a "prelinguistic reality," a "natural" aspect of the body that is outside the symbolic order? Is this evidence of the biological essentialism that is often attributed to psychoanalysis, in spite of its apparent emphasis on the symbolic order? This is what many readers have concluded, and yet "everyone knows" that Lacan rejects the biological account of sexuality. In what sense is the real "outside" the symbolic order, if it is not an "external reality" or a "prelinguistic" domain of sexuality? This is the point at which the logical aspect of psychoanalysis and the limit of formalization becomes especially important. They allow us to elaborate the real, not as a prelinguistic reality that would be outside the symbolic order, but in terms of a lack that arises within the symbolic order. The object a is this element put forth by Lacan, not as an object "in reality," an external thing that is somehow beyond representation, but as a term that designates a logical impasse. Jacques-Alain Miller has this problem in mind when he writes that, with the object a, we are dealing with a certain limit to presentation, but a limit that cannot be grasped by a direct approach to reality: "If there were an ontic in psychoanalysis, it would be the ontic of the object a. But this is precisely the road not taken by Lacan. . . . Where does the object a come from in Lacan? It comes from the partial object of Karl Abraham, that is, from a corporeal consistency. The interesting thing is to see that Lacan transforms this corporeal consistency into a logical consistency."[17] Without following the theory of the body further here, we can nevertheless see that the general form of the question can be posed in terms of the limits of formalization, thereby recognizing that psychoanalysis is not in fact committed to the law in the manner of classical structuralist thought—in the tradition of Saussure and Lévi-Strauss. In view of this, we might try to make this aporetic point more concrete by referring to a paradox that takes a similar form in various disciplines.

INCEST

In anthropology, the incest taboo is not simply a law, but a logical aporia: it functions as a sort of nodal point where the symbolic and the real are linked together. As is well known, the incest taboo presents us with a peculiar contradiction: on the one hand, it is a prohibition, a cultural institution that imposes family relations and kinship structures upon what would otherwise be the state of nature; on the other hand, however, this law, because of its universality, is also defined as something natural, since it cannot be ascribed to a particular social group or located in a single historical period. Lévi-Strauss and others have stressed the paradox or scandal of the incest taboo in just this way: "It constitutes a rule," Lévi-Strauss says, "but a rule which, alone among all the social rules, possesses at the same time a universal character." Citing this passage in "Structure, Sign and Play," Derrida has stressed that this impasse should not be reduced to a mere contradiction, but must be given its own theoretical precision. It is not a question of eliminating ambiguity by determining, once and for all, whether this law is "cultural" or "natural"—whether it is "really" a human invention (a symbolic law) , or a biological principle that insures genetic distribution (a natural mechanism). The scandalous or paradoxical character of the incest prohibition is not an ambiguity to be eliminated, but must rather be taken as the actual positive content of the concept itself: it suggests that, properly speaking, the incest taboo must be situated prior to the division between nature and culture. In Derrida's words, "The incest prohibition is no longer a scandal one meets with or comes up against in the domain of traditional concepts; it is something which escapes these concepts and certainly precedes them—probably as the condition of their possibility."[18] Like the nodal point of the dream, the incest taboo thus isolates a singular point that "reaches down into the unknown," a point that "has to be left obscure," that cannot be interpreted ("adds nothing to our knowledge of the content") and yet is absolutely indispensable to the organization of the dream. We thus return to the limit of formalization, an impasse in the symbolic system of cultural laws, but on which, far from being a mistake, is curiously imperative, irrevocable, and necessary—as if it were somehow integral to the law itself.

The crucial point, however—and the connection between this "logical" impasse and the object a—is to recognize that this scandal somehow materializes itself. The prohibition is not only a paradox; it has the additional characteristic that it condenses itself into an enigmatic "thing"—what Freud calls the "taboo object." Is this not the crucial point of *Totem and Taboo*, this peculiar relation between the symbolic system of totemism (the system of the name), and the taboo object that somehow accompanies it? Indeed, as Derrida points out in speaking of the limits of formalization, it is not simply a matter of aporias; if we are confronted with an impasse in the concepts of nature and culture, "something which escapes these concepts," it is because "there is something missing."[19] This missing object entails a certain materialization, but it cannot be clarified by a simple empiricism, a simple reference to presymbolic reality. As Derrida notes, in fact, there are two ways of asserting the impossibility of formalization: "totalization can be judged impossible in the classical style." This would consist in pointing to an empirical diversity that cannot be grasped by a single law or system, an external wealth of historical differences that cannot be mastered by any theoretical glance. The other way consists in recognizing the intrinsic incompleteness of the theoretical gaze itself, the fact that the law is always contaminated by a "stain" that escapes the system:

> if totalization no longer has any meaning, it is not because the infiniteness of a field cannot be covered by a finite glance or a finite discourse, but because the nature of the field—that is, language and a finite language—excludes totalization . . . instead of being an inexhaustible field, as in the classical hypothesis, instead of being too large, there is something missing from it: a center which arrests and grounds the play of substitutions.[20]

Psychoanalysis can be described as the theory that tries to grasp the bodily consequences of this fact, the physical effects of this missing object on the structure of the body. It is not a theory aimed at describing the connections between a supposedly biological "sexuality" and the symbolic codes that are imposed upon this original "nature," but rather a theory that aims to understand the corporeal materialization of this impasse, the concrete somatic effects of this excluded object that accompanies the law of language.

THE GOLD STANDARD

In economics, a similar nodal point might be found that seems to be both inside and outside the structure. If one speaks of money as a symbolic order, a conventional system of representation governed by certain internal laws, a formalist or structuralist account would say that it is not a question of what a particular amount of money will buy (what it "represents"), but a question of purely internal relations. Precisely as with the signifier in Saussure's account, we are concerned not with the relation between the sign and reality, but with the "internal affairs" of the symbolic order—with relations between signifiers, and not with what the signifier represents outside the system. Accordingly, "ten dollars" is not defined by what it will buy, or by its relation to external reality. That is a purely contingent and constantly changing relation—today it will buy three loaves of bread, but next year it only serves as change to ride the bus. If we wish to define ten dollars "scientifically," we must therefore take a formalist perspective and say ten dollars is "half of twenty," or "twice five," and then we have a constant measure, in which the definition is given not by any (contingent) external reference, but rather by a (lawful) diacritical analysis, which places it in relation to the other elements in the system.

Nevertheless, there is a point at which the structure is, paradoxically, attached to the very reality it is supposed to exclude. Although "ten dollars" has no fixed or necessary relation to anything outside the system, but should rather be defined internally, in relation to five dollars or twenty, the system itself is said to rest on a "gold standard," a "natural" basis that guarantees or supports the structure. "Gold is thus both natural and symbolic—or perhaps neither, since it has no natural value in itself, and yet also no place within the system of money that we exchange. On the one hand, it is a pure convention: unlike bread (which we *need*), gold has no value in itself, but is entirely symbolic (a pure signifier without any use value). On the other hand, it is not an element within the symbolic system of money, something we might define in relation to other elements: instead of being a signifier in the chain (S_1-S_2-S_3), it is a "ground," a gold "reserve" that stands outside the system of exchange, giving value to the symbolic elements—whose purely formal relations are supposed to operate precisely by excluding any such outside. We are faced here with the same enigma we encounter in the incest taboo. And again, it would be a mistake to think that we have simply found a contradiction or inconsistency in the concept; we should rather be led to recognize this scandalous and paradoxical character of the object (gold), not as a confusion that might be removed (e.g., when we finally come to our senses and realize that gold is merely symbolic), but as its positive content: it is to be understood (in Derrida's words) precisely as "something which no longer tolerates the nature/culture opposition."[21] Gold thus functions as a kind of nodal point, a paradoxical element that is neither inside nor outside the structure.

SUPPLEMENTARITY

At this point, however, we must again (as with sexuality and libido) be careful not to define this external element too naively. If it seems at first glance that gold is a natural basis for monetary value, the bullion in the bank that guarantees the purely symbolic money that circulates in exchange; if gold presents itself as the one element that is not symbolic, but has value in itself and thus serves as a ground (insofar as money represents it); this view is precisely what we must reject, for like the nodal point in the dream, it would not have its peculiar function except through the system that it is naively thought to support. The enigma of gold as a "quilting point" is that it has no value in itself, but *acquires* its status as a "natural value" from the system itself, not in the sense that it is simply an element within the system, another symbolic phenomenon that might be placed at the same level as the money that circulates in the market, but in the sense that it is a "surplus-effect," a "product" of the system that expels it from the chain of representations, and buries it in the earth, where it can be "found again." Strictly speaking, therefore, the natural and foundational character of gold, the fact that it was already there, apparently preceding the monetary system and providing it with an external ground, is an illusion, but a necessary illusion, one that the system, in spite of its apparent autonomy, evidently requires. As a result, it cannot be a question of simply denouncing this illusion and asserting the "purely symbolic" character of "value," its arbitrary, conventional, or constructed character. The task is rather to understand just how the system, which at first appeared to be autonomous, governed by purely conventional and internal laws, nevertheless requires this peculiar object and requires that it have precisely this enigmatically "natural" status, this apparent and illusory "exteriority."

In *Tarrying with the Negative*, Slavoj Žižek suggests that this peculiar aspect of the object, as a surplus effect of the system, a product that is not simply symbolic, but concerns an excluded object that must take on the illusion of naturalness (of "already-being-there-before," so that it can be "found again"), can be clarified by reference to a famous passage from the *Critique of Pure Reason*, a passage from the "Transcendental Dialectic" where Kant speaks of "delusion"—not of empirical delusion (a mistaken impression of the senses, which can always be corrected), nor, indeed, of merely logical error (which consists in the commitment of formal fallacies, a "lack of attention to the logical rule," A296/B353), but of an illusion proper to reason itself. It is *proper* to reason in the sense that, as Kant says, it "does not cease even after it has been detected and its invalidity clearly revealed" (A297/B353). It is thus not an ambiguity to be avoided, but "a *natural* and inevitable *illusion*," an "unavoidable dialectic" that is "inseparable from human reason" and that "will not cease to play tricks with reason . . . even after its deceptiveness has been exposed" (A298/B354). It is not that reason (the "symbolic order") falls into contradiction by some error that might be removed; rather, reason would itself be, as Kant says, "the seat of transcendental illusion." But how is the Lacanian object *a* related to this illusion? How are we to understand the claim that Kant recognizes not only that the idea of "totality" gives rise to contradiction, but also that it is attended by a peculiar surplus-object? For this (the "sublime object") is what the antinomies of Kant's "dialectical illusion" imply, according to Žižek. The point can be clarified by reference to sexual difference. Žižek argues that, for Kant, "there is no way for us to imagine the universe as a Whole; that is, as soon as we do it, we obtain two antinomical, mutually exclusive versions," two propositions that cannot be maintained at the same time. In Lacan, moreover, this structure is precisely what we find in the symbolic division between the sexes: it is not a division into two halves of a single species, or two complementary parts, which together might comprise the whole of "humanity." On the contrary, the division between the sexes makes them "supplementary." (Lacan: "Note that I said *supplementary*. Had I said *complementary*, where would we be! We'd fall right back into the all"; FS, 144). In Žižek's words, "the antagonistic tension which defines sexuality is not the polar opposition of two cosmic forces (yin/yang, etc.), but a certain crack which prevents us from imagining the universe as a Whole. Sexuality points towards the supreme ontological scandal."[22] The status of the "object" is thus clarified, for if an object appears to fill this gap, offering to guarantee a harmonious relation between the sexes (sometimes this object is the child, which "sutures" the parental bond), it can only do so as the prohibited object, the product of "dialectical illusion." We thus see more clearly the relation between the logical aporia that accompanies the symbolic order (the real of incest or gold) and the object a.

THE TIME OF THE OBJECT

Before we close this discussion of the limits of formalization, we must stress the peculiar temporality of this object. We have identified the peculiar character of the prohibited or incestuous "object": unlike the abstract "signifiers" that circulate in the community, gold is a product or effect of the system, but a symbolic effect whose precise character is to materialize itself, separating itself from all the other elements of exchange, in order to appear as if it existed before the system ever came into being and as if it possessed its value "by nature." Its function is to dissimulate, to veil itself—to hide its own nature, we might say, if it were not for the fact that its nature is just this hiding of itself. We must therefore link the paradoxical or contradictory character of the object to the peculiar time that governs it. It is not enough to stress the contradictory character of this object—the paradoxical fact that it belongs to both "nature" and "culture" (or more precisely, to neither, since it precedes this very division)—or to recognize that this paradox is not an ambiguity to be removed, but rather constitutive of the object itself. We must also recognize that its peculiar temporality is such that it comes into being through the system, but in such a way that it must have been there "before," so that the system might emerge on its basis. This is why the incest taboo always refers us to an earlier "state of nature," a time of unrestricted sexuality that was supposedly limited "once upon a time," when the law was imposed and a certain object suddenly came to be prohibited. Since the taboo object is not a prelinguistic reality, but the placeholder of a lack that only comes into being through the law, we are forced to recognize the purely illusory character of this supposed past, as a past that was never present. This temporal aspect of the taboo object was clearly identified by Lacan in *Television* when he wrote that "the Oedipus myth is an attempt to give epic form to the operation of a structure" (T, 30, translation modified). If we now wish to clarify the relation between this object and the system of representation in Freudian terms, we might say that gold is, in relation to the system of money, not so much a representation, as the "representation of representation," the "primal signifier" that grounds signification, but whose essential feature is that it had no such status as ground prior to the system which is said to be based upon it. In short, gold is the "Name-of-the Father": as the "quilting-point" of the system, it is not one signifier among others, but the signifier of signifiers, the ground of exchange that appears to precede symbolization and guarantee its basis in nature, but is in fact a by-product of the structure itself—not an element in the structure of exchange, but a peculiar object that comes into being to "veil" the lack that inhabits the structure. Needless to say, the phallus has precisely this status in Lacan. The phallus is a veil.

THE PHALLUS

Setting out from the limits of formalization thus allows us to see why the most common debate over the phallus is fundamentally misleading. It is often said that the concept of the phallus confronts us with a crucial ambiguity: on the one hand, the phallus is a signifier, and as such demonstrates the symbolic construction of sexual difference; on the other hand, the phallus is by no means arbitrary, a purely symbolic function, since it clearly refers to anatomy. We are thus led into a familiar debate, in which some readers defend Lacan, asserting that the phallus is a signifier and that psychoanalysis rejects any biological account of sexual difference, while other readers insist that, despite protests to the contrary, the phallus is the one element in the theory that unmistakably implicates psychoanalysis in a return to biology, perpetuating the essentialism of sexual difference and securing a certain privilege for the male and a corresponding lack for the female. Numerous accounts of psychoanalysis vigorously defend both these positions, but in fact neither is accurate, and the entire polemic could be seen as actually concealing the theory it pretends to address. The phallus is not biological and does not refer to prelinguistic reality, but neither is it purely symbolic—one signifier among others, an element contained within the system. As a signifier of lack, it marks the impossible point of intersection between the symbolic and the real, the introduction of a lack that allows the mobilization of signifiers to begin their work of substitution, a lack which is the "absolute condition" of desire, but that "can be occupied, Freud tells us, by any object" (SXI, 180). The phallus is this veil ("it can play its role only when veiled"; E, 288), the singular mark of signification itself, the paradoxical signifier of signifiers which (like gold) functions only through a substitution that dissimulates, allowing it to appear in imaginary clothing, like "gold," a natural anatomical ground guaranteeing signification—a materialization that, in presenting itself as "already-there-before," veils its status as a surplus-effect, a non-natural lack in the structure that has been filled in by this extimate object. Like gold and incest, then, it cannot be a question of finally determining whether the phallus belongs to "nature" or "culture," to the order of biology or the order of the signifier. Such efforts will only circumvent the logic of the nodal point that this paradoxical concept is intended to articulate. And insofar as the phallus is also bound up with the imaginary body, one can see that the concept requires clarification in all three registers: as imaginary, symbolic and real. To ask whether the phallus is biological or symbolic is thus to refuse the very issue it addresses.

MATERIAL APORETICS

We have stressed the fact that this paradox is not simply a question of a logical contradiction, a term that belongs to both nature and culture—or, more precisely, that escapes this very distinction—or only a question of time, but also a question of a certain materiality. Gold is also an object, unlike the signifiers that are said to represent it, but also unlike the purely natural things that might be said to exist independently of any language. Need we add here that in the incest taboo, we are also faced with a certain materialization of the taboo object, the thing that is excluded from the totemic order of the name? And is not psychoanalysis the theory that endeavors to articulate the consequences of such materialization in terms of our bodily existence? Discussions of Lacan that insist on the linguistic or symbolic character of his theory (whether to denounce or to celebrate it) serve only to conceal this enigmatic logic of the body. Our general claim is thus given some concrete clarification: every effort to establish a structure on its own terms, by reference to purely internal relations (money, kinship, language), will encounter a point at which the system touches on something outside itself, something that has a paradoxical status, being simultaneously symbolic and yet also excluded from the system. The real in Lacan is a concept that tries to address this enigma. Readers of Derrida will of course recognize that many of the fundamental Derridean terms— the "trace," the "supplement," and so on—touch on precisely the same problem, the limit of formalization, an element that founds the structure while being at the same time excluded from it. One day, someone who knows something about both these writers will develop these issues in more detail.

TWO VERSIONS OF THE REAL

Let us now attempt a final approach to the question by distinguishing two versions of the real. This will allow us to develop the concept in slightly more detail. One of the difficulties with the concept of the real in Lacan is that it appears in several different forms as his work unfolds. Without exploring all the detailed transformations, let us simply isolate the most important development in his use of the term. It is this: initially, the real seems to refer to a presymbolic reality, a realm of "immediate being" that is never accessible in itself, but only appears through the mediation of imaginary and symbolic representation (in this case, it tends to correspond to the common meaning of "reality"); later, however, the term seems to designate a lack, an element that is missing from within the symbolic order, in which case the real can only be understood as an effect of the symbolic order itself. One might thus speak of a "presymbolic real" and a "postsymbolic real." In the first case, the real precedes the symbolic and exists independently; in the second case, the real is a product of the symbolic order, a residue or surplus-effect that exists or comes into being only as a result of the symbolic operation that excludes it. It is perhaps this very duality in the concept that leads to the question of whether the real is inside or outside the symbolic order.

A PARENTHESIS ON "BEING"

These two versions of the real also imply two different modes of being. In the first case, one can say the real "exists" independently, and then go on to ask whether we can have any knowledge of it independent of our representations. But in the second case, we are led to speak of the "being of lack"—thereby initiating a whole series of apparently paradoxical claims about the "being" of what "is not," reminiscent, perhaps, of theological disputes concerning the existence of God. As Lacan says in *Seminar XI*, "when speaking of this gap one is dealing with an ontological function," and yet, "it does not lend itself to ontology" (SXI, 29). In distinguishing these two versions of the real, we must therefore recognize two different "modes" of being, since the existence of the presymbolic real is not the same as the being of the lack (or the "lack-in-being") that characterizes the postsymbolic real. Anyone who has read Heidegger knows how complex these questions concerning existence and being can be. One has only to think of Heidegger's account of Kant's thesis that "Being is not a real predicate"—a thesis discussed by Moustafa Safouan in *Pleasure and Being*—to see how many philosophical issues weigh on the discourse of psychoanalysis.[23] Apart from the question of whether (and in what mode") the real "exists"—"inside" or "outside" the symbolic—it may also be necessary to distinguish between real, imaginary, and symbolic modes of existence. On a first approximation, one might say that the imaginary is a dimension of "seeming," the symbolic of "meaning," and the real of "being" (though, as we have suggested, this last term can be divided further, into two forms). If, moreover, we recall Lacan's claim that "the real is the impossible," we would have to consider the other categories of modal logic as well. Lacan seems to have followed Heidegger to some extent in speaking of the "impossible," the "contingent," the "necessary," and the "possible."[24]

"REALITY" AND "LACK"

The significance of the distinction between these two versions of the real should thus be clear: we know that the concept of lack is central to Lacanian theory and that it cannot be adequately grasped in terms of the "symbolic," since it is closely bound up with the category of the real. Much of the secondary literature on Lacan, however, characterizes the real as a prediscursive reality that is mediated by representation—the reality that is always lost whenever we represent it. This does in fact capture some aspects of Lacan's work, but if we wish to understand the relation between the real and lack, it is not sufficient, for as Tim Dean has argued, the concept of lack points us in the direction of a void that cannot be understood by reference to prediscursive reality.[25] Thus, even if there is some validity in regarding the real as a dimension of immediate existence that is always filtered through imaginary and symbolic representations of it, we will be able to grasp the concept of lack only if we turn to the real in its second version, as an effect of the symbolic order, in which case we can no longer regard it as prelinguistic.[26] Let us therefore consider these two versions of the real more closely.

THE "PRE-SYMBOLIC" REAL

The first version of the real—the presymbolic real—provides the more familiar account. One often hears that, according to Lacan, the real is "organized" or "represented" through images and words that do not actually capture the real, but always misrepresent it. Human life is thus subject to a fundamental and irremediable misunderstanding, such that the real is always already lost—figured or disfigured in some manner. Such a conception, however, makes it difficult to understand what Freud means by the "reality principle" or "reality-testing," and it completely obscures the concept of lack, since the real, understood as a prediscursive reality, is "full." Nevertheless, Lacan himself sometimes used the term in this way, and it cannot be entirely rejected. We thus face an apparent conflict between the prediscursive real (which is "full"), and the real as a lack that arises *through* the symbolic order. One recalls the Lacanian dictum, based on our first version, that "nothing is lacking in the real" (a phrase often cited in reference to the supposed "castration" of women, which, in this account, is not real but strictly imaginary castration). One can already see here that *symbolic* castration (lack) cannot be understood through this account of the imaginary and real, which circumvents language in order to enter a debate between imaginary lack and a reality in which nothing is lacking. Let us develop the first version somewhat further, to see why it has played such a prominent role in the secondary literature—for despite its deficiencies, it has a number of virtues, and Lacan's own text provides some justification for it.

In the first version, the real is construed as a domain of immediate experience, a level of brute reality that never reaches consciousness without being filtered through representation—by memory, by the ego, or by various internal neurological pathways that mediate and organize our sensory experience. This is a familiar motif in Freud, who often speaks of "consciousness" and even of "bodily experience" (sensory stimuli) as being fashioned or channeled by past experiences, anticipation, projection, and other forms of representation, which allow *some aspects* of our experience to become "present" to us, while others are not registered, and therefore remain "absent," even though they are "real." A correlation would thus be made between two different modes of presence (namely, imaginary and symbolic), and, in contrast to these, a real that remains absent insofar as it is inaccessible. Robert Samuels uses this notion of the real when he speaks of the subject as the "existential Subject," that is to say, the subject in its brute existence prior to imaginary and symbolic formation.[27] The real subject (S) would thus designate what Lacan in the essay on psychosis calls a level of "ineffable, stupid existence" (E, 193). This notation, in which "S" designates the subject "in the real," is useful insofar as it encourages us to separate real, imaginary, and symbolic definitions of the subject—distinguishing the subject as "real" (S), from the ego as formed in the imaginary (the "a" of schema L, which designates the *moi* as a correlate of the image or alter ego), distinguishing both of these in turn from "$"—the "split subject," or the "subject of the signifier."

Richard Boothby's book *Death and Desire* gives an excellent account of this argument, in which the real is a dimension of immediate existence or prediscursive reality that is never actually available to us as such, but only appears *through* the intervention of the imaginary or the symbolic.[28] He shows how Lacan's theory of the imaginary—and above all of the imaginary body—allows us to understand what Freud means when he says that even sensory experience and bodily excitations do not provide direct contact with the real, since even our most concrete, bodily experience or perception is organized and shaped through the imaginary, which "translates" or "represents" the real, thereby also distorting it. As Boothby says, the imaginary is a dimension of narcissism that maintains its own world by defending itself against the real, recognizing only those aspects of the real that accord with the interests of the ego. Boothby stresses the imaginary, but one could also speak of the symbolic here, as another level of representation that organizes the real, presenting it by translating or mediating it. As Lacan says, "the symbol is the murder of the thing"; it mediates our contact with the real, negating the thing and replacing it with a representation, and thus with a substitute. It is important to recognize that imaginary and symbolic presentation (or representation) do not function in the same way, but in any case, the concept of the real as an immediate or prediscursive reality is clear. Eventually, we must come to see why Lacan gave up this notion, why he came to regard this account as inadequate and was obliged to develop a different conception of the real. But let us not go too quickly.

THE "RETURN" OF THE REAL

It is important to observe that, in this view, the real is not absolutely lost: on the contrary, one can speak of the real as sometimes "asserting itself" or disrupting the systems of representation that have been set up to encode and process it. As Boothby suggests, certain bodily experiences can be characterized as real if they threaten or oppose the imaginary system of the subject: the narcissistic structure refuses or defends itself against the real, which is excluded, but which nevertheless sometimes returns, disrupting the structure by asserting itself. This is in keeping with Freud's observations in the *Project for a Scientific Psychology* (SE 1:283–397), where he notes that the bodily apparatus, its neurological pathways, act partly by blocking certain stimuli, which are in some sense felt, but not actually registered by the subject. One can then regard the sudden rupture of these neurological blocking mechanisms as an "encounter with the real." A number of Freud's metaphors appear to work this way, as if the "system" of the body were a system of "pressure" and "release" in which a particular threshold must be crossed before the real is allowed to register. The advantage of this account is that it allows us to see that the body is not a *natural* system of rivers and dams, governed by a biological force of pressure and release, but is rather an imaginary system, in which force is the expressly nonbiological force of representation. Such an account allows us to explain the "return of the real" as a disruptive or traumatic event while also showing us why the "body" in psychoanalysis is not a biological system. This is why Boothby insists on the imaginary structure of the body, and on the fact that the energy Freud speaks of is not a natural or physical energy, but rather "psychic energy"—whatever that means. As Freud often says, "We would give much to understand more about these things."

BEYOND MIMESIS

This is the most common understanding of the real, but it has one great disadvantage, in that it tends to equate the real with prelinguistic reality. On the basis of this conception, psychoanalysis is immediately drawn back into a number of traditional questions about mimesis. Starting with the idea that there is a symbolic order, or indeed an imaginary system of representation, we may ask whether it is possible to have access to an *outside reality*, but we will never be able to clarify the *concept of the real*. We will be able to enter a whole series of familiar debates about representation in which two alternatives appear to dominate. Some (the "postmodernists") say that "everything is symbolic": we have no access to "reality" in itself, for reality is always given *through* some historically specific discursive formation; it is not a question of reality, but only of different symbolic systems, different representations, which compete with each other, and which succeed in becoming "true" because they are persuasive (rhetoric), or because they are formulated by those in power (politics), or because they have the authority of "tradition" (history), or for some other reason—in short, "there is no metalanguage," no discourse that can ground itself in a nondiscursive "external reality," since the only thing "outside" discourse is . . . more discourse. Others (the "positivists") say that, despite these symbolic codes, there is a "reality" that asserts itself, or presents itself to us: we may try to ignore it, or refuse to give it any symbolic importance, or construct certain "fantasies" that seek to circumvent it, or highlight only certain of its features, but it is still the case that symbolic systems have a more or less adequate purchase on reality, and that some discourses are more true than others. These arguments are familiar, but they will not take us very far toward understanding Lacan.

REALITY AND THE REAL

This is why, if we wish to understand Lacan, we must distinguish between "reality" and the "real" (thereby moving toward our second version). In "The Freudian Thing," for example, Lacan explicitly refers to Heidegger when he discusses the classical definition of "true" representation (*adaequatio rei et intellectus*, the correct correspondence between the idea or word and the thing), saying that the Freudian account of "truth" cannot be grasped in terms of the problem of "adequate correspondence." Freud's truth cannot be approached in terms of true and false representations or in terms of the symbolic order and reality, for truth is linked to the real, and not to reality. Lacan even coined a word to suggest the link between truth and the real—*le vréel* (a term that has been attributed to Kristeva, but that came from Lacan). To address the relation between the symbolic and the real is therefore quite different from engaging in the task of distinguishing between "reality" and the symbolic or imaginary world of the subject.

Let us note, however, that the distinction between "reality" and the "real" must be made in a specific way, according to Lacan. It is perfectly possible to accept the distinction between reality and the real while sustaining the first version of the real (as a prediscursive reality). In this case, reality is defined, not as an unknowable, external domain, independent of our representations, but precisely as the product of representation. Our reality is imaginary and symbolic, and the real is *what is missing from reality*—the "outside" that escapes our representations (the *Ding-an-sich*). The real thus remains an inaccessible, prediscursive reality, while reality is understood as a symbolic or imaginary construction. Many commentaries have taken this line of argument, distinguishing the real and reality while nevertheless maintaining our first version. As Samuel Weber writes, "the notion of reality implied in the imaginary should in no way be confused with Lacan's concept of the 'real.' . . . In Lacan, as in Peirce, the 'real' is defined by its resistance, which includes resistance to representation, including cognition. It is, therefore, in a certain sense at the furthest remove from the imaginary."[29] If we turn to Jonathan Scott Lee, we find the same distinction: "All language allows us to speak of is the 'reality' constituted by the system of the symbolic. . . . Because 'there is no metalanguage,' the real perpetually eludes our discourse."[30] The same conclusion appears to be drawn by Mikkel Borch-Jacobsen, who expresses profound reservations about Lacan's apparent "nihilism," and writes that the "truth" ultimately affirmed by Lacan is that we have no access to the "real," but are condemned to live in a domain of subjective "reality," a domain of subjective "truth": "Lacan's 'truth,' no matter how unfathomable and repressed, remains nonetheless the truth of a desire—that is, of a *subject*. It could hardly be otherwise in psychoanalysis. Isn't the patient invited to recount *himself*—that is, to reveal himself to himself in autorepresentation?"[31] The real is thus a prediscursive reality that is always already lost (a thesis tediously familiar to us, Borch-Jacobsen says, from a certain existentialism): "Thus the 'real,' as Kojève taught, is abolished as soon as it is spoken."[32] Or, in another passage: "for Lacan—agreeing, on this point, with Kojève's teaching—truth is essentially distinct from reality. Better yet, truth *is opposed* to reality [since] the subject speaks himself by negating, or "nihilating" the "Real."[33] The peculiarity of this formulation is that it seems to *equate* the real and reality, but this is simply because we are to understand "reality" not as the constructed reality of the subject (what Borch-Jacobsen here calls the subject's "truth"), but as the external reality that is always already lost. In all these cases, we can distinguish between a real (or prediscursive reality) that remains outside representation, and reality as constituted by the subject, while retaining the first conception, in which the real is an external domain that precedes representation and remains unknown.

"THE INNERMOST CORE OF THE IMAGINARY"

How, then, are we to pass beyond the familiar problem of true and false representations, the classical problem of mimesis, the dichotomy between a prediscursive reality (which is permanently lost, or which occasionally returns in the form of a traumatic disruption of the representational system), and the network of imaginary or symbolic representations which either capture or simply replace that reality? How are we to move to our second conception in which we arrive at the concept of lack—a void that is not reducible to the imaginary or symbolic (that remains absent from representation), and yet does not exist in external reality? Clearly, the real, insofar as it is connected with lack, can only be grasped through this second formulation, as a postsymbolic phenomenon, a void that arises *through* the symbolic order, as an effect of the symbolic order which is nevertheless irreducible to the imaginary or symbolic.

At this point, we can return to the question of the trauma, the return of the real, in order to see why the first conception of the real is inadequate. One might well say that certain experiences or "encounters with the real" (momentary ruptures of our defenses) are traumatic or disruptive, but this is not simply due to their "nature"—as if it were a direct, unmediated encounter with some traumatic "reality." The disruptive character of the real, regarded as a dimension of experience that disturbs the order of representation, is not due to the real in itself, as a prediscursive domain, but is due to the fact that it is unfamiliar. The real is traumatic because there has been no sufficient symbolic or imaginary network in place for representing it. It is traumatic, not in itself, but only in relation to the established order of representation. We must return here to Samuel Weber's formulation. If he claims (following our first version) that "the 'real' is defined by its resistance, which includes resistance to representation" and that "it is, therefore, in a certain sense at the furthest remove from the imaginary," he immediately adds a curious twist: "At the same time, one could with equal justification describe it as residing at the innermost core of the imaginary."[34] Obviously, the Freudian concept of repression, as something "contained" (in every sense) by the subject's representational system, would come closer to this conception of the real as an "innermost core," rather than an autonomous "external reality." Consequently, the real, even if we wish to characterize it along the lines of our initial approach, as a disruptive element that asserts itself and threatens the usual expectations of the ego, cannot be understood as preexisting reality, but must rather be understood as an "innermost core," an "inside" that only acquires its repressed or traumatic character in relation to the familiar order of representation. As early as the "Rome Discourse," Lacan stressed this aspect of the trauma, distinguishing it from any simple external event: "to say of psychoanalysis or of history that, considered as sciences, they are both sciences of the particular, does not mean that the facts they deal with are purely accidental . . . [or] reducible to the brute aspect of the trauma" (E, 51).

In "The Story of Louise," Michèle Montrelay provides a remarkable account of a traumatic event, one that obliges us to see the real not as prediscursive, but as an effect of symbolization. She speaks of the onset of a phobia, describing it as a particular moment in the history of the subject, a "moment" or "event," however, which is not a simple "present," and which consists, not in the immediate experience of some traumatic "reality," but in an experience in which two chains of signifiers, previously kept apart, are suddenly made to intersect, in such a way, moreover, that in place of "meaning," a hole is produced. "This hole opened by the phobia is situated in space like a fault around which all roads would open . . . except that all of a sudden the ground vanishes."[35] Instead of a metaphor, a spark of meaning, something impossible suddenly emerges from this intersection of signifiers, a hole or cut in the universe of meaning, a cut that is linked to an obscure knowledge that Louise suddenly acquires about her father—a forbidden knowledge that remains excluded the moment it appears: "knowing is contained not in the revelation of the "content" of a representation, but in a new and impossible conjunction of signifiers. Two signifying chains created a cut or break. That is, they marked the place of an impossible passage. . . . The chains, suddenly brought into proximity, created a short-circuit."[36] An additional observation is necessary here, if we are to grasp the object, as well as this cut in the symbolic universe. We must also note that the phobia dates from this moment, this symbolic intersection, this Oedipal crossing of the roads, which is to be understood, not simply as producing a hole in meaning, but as having an additional effect. Such is the genesis of the "phobic object" in the story of Louise: a fish has come to fill the place of the void that has suddenly opened at the subject's feet, giving it a "local habitation," a specific place among all the things spread out across the extended surface of the world—a place that is prohibited and can no longer be crossed. (Other places become contaminated, too, for thereafter, Louise will no longer enter the library, where her father taught her to read.) One day, Louise, who was preparing dinner in the kitchen with her mother (the domestic space is not a matter of indifference), goes to the dining room and watches while this fish-object (its eye still looking up) is transferred to the father's plate: "Louise, who was watching the fish cooking without saying anything, begins to scream. Nameless terror. She refuses to eat. The fish phobia has declared itself."[37] The daughter, who had always been clever and mature, becomes dizzy and speechless, to the bewilderment of her parents. She can no longer occupy space as before. As Lacan says in "The Agency of the Letter": "Between the enigmatic signifier of the sexual trauma and the term that is substituted for it in an actual signifying chain there passes the spark that fixes in a symptom the signification inaccessible to the conscious subject . . . a symptom being a metaphor in which flesh or function is taken as a signifying element" (E, 166). The traumatic "fact" or "event" in psychoanalysis thus acquires its status not as an encounter with some autonomous, preexisting reality, but only through the network of representation in relation to which the particular thing in question acquires a traumatic status.

RETROACTIVE TRAUMA

The trauma can therefore no longer be understood as a simple brute reality that is difficult to integrate into our symbolic universe. Žižek notes this when he corrects his own account of the trauma in *For They Know Not What They Do*. In a "first presentation," he referred to the trauma as a sudden, disruptive experience of reality that is not easily placed within our symbolic universe. But this notion is soon modified: "when we spoke of the symbolic integration of a trauma," he writes:

> we omitted a crucial detail: the logic of Freud's notion of the "deferred action" does not consist in the subsequent "gentrification" of a traumatic encounter by means of its transformation into a normal component of our symbolic universe, but in almost the exact opposite of it—something which was at first perceived as a meaningless, neutral event changes retroactively, after the advent of a new symbolic network . . . into a trauma that cannot be integrated.[38]

Thus, in place of a presymbolic reality that we might regard as traumatic and that we must eventually accommodate into our symbolic universe, we have a trauma that emerges retroactively, as an effect of symbolization. One might think here of contemporary efforts to rewrite the literary canon: for many years, most literary critics regarded the canon as "full," as a list of "great names," but after a shift in the symbolic universe (which consisted in acknowledging that there might possibly be women who also happened to be writers—*mirabile dictu*), the past suddenly appeared as traumatic, as false and slanted and full of holes—holding great vacancies that needed to be occupied. Here, the traumatic event must be clearly recognized for what it is—not the immediate contact with an external reality, the simple encounter with a historical reality, the discovery of women writers, but a new signification that has retroactive effects on the past.

Obviously, this model of the event does not fit the popular examples of traumatic events—the brute experience of violence or war that must gradually be given a place in the symbolic universe. In this second version, where the structure of symbolic retroaction is stressed, we are in fact closer to the sort of trauma induced by Foucault, whose writings have the effect of making a neat, coherent, and familiar past (the "grand narrative") suddenly emerge as mad, deceptive, and fictional—and thus in need of reconfiguration. This is why I have argued that Foucault's work cannot be understood as a historicist description of the past in all its archaeological strangeness and contingency, but must rather be understood as aiming to produce effects by negotiating the relation between the symbolic and the real.[39]

Given this account of the trauma, we are led to shift our account of the real slightly and to ask, not so much about the real "in itself"—the direct, unmediated reality that is always distorted by representation—but about the *relation between* the real and the order of representation (symbolic or imaginary). It thus becomes clear that our initial view of the real as a prediscursive reality cannot be entirely precise, since the real only acquires its unfamiliar and disruptive status in relation to the symbolic and imaginary. Even without considering the temporal factor of retroaction introduced by Žižek, or the peculiar event-structure of the symbolic overlapping whose truth effects are discussed by Montrelay, we can already see in the account given by Boothby that the disruptive emergence of a real that violates the normal order of the ego—the sudden rupture of neurological pathways—cannot be characterized simply as a moment of contact with external reality. As Boothby suggests, the real is constituted in relation to representation, and thus appears as an "innermost core of the imaginary" (or symbolic) itself. We must therefore drop the idea that the real is presymbolic, that it is an unreachable reality that exists prior to language (the first version), and recognize that the imaginary, the symbolic, and the real are mutually constitutive—like the rings in the Borromean knot, which provide us with a synchronic and equiprimordial structure linking the imaginary, the symbolic, and the real in a single set of relations.

THE "POST-SYMBOLIC" REAL

We are thus brought to a second account of the real in Lacan, in which it is no longer regarded as a prelinguistic domain that is never available to us or that occasionally returns to disrupt our representations. In its post-symbolic form, the real designates something that only exists as a result of symbolization. In this view, the symbolic order is structured in such a way that it produces a kind of excess, a remainder or surplus-effect, that is not at all equivalent to reality, but is, rather, an effect of the symbolic order, though not reducible to it. This refinement of the concept of the real is one of the major interests of Lacanian theory. At this point, however, a new complication arises (we have seen it already in the phobic object), for with this second version of the real, two related problems are now introduced: first, we are faced with a concept of lack, a void that cannot be clarified by references to prediscursive reality (which is "full"), and second, we are faced with the production of an object, a surplus-effect in which the symbolic order gives rise to a certain excess it cannot adequately contain. The real, in this second formulation, would therefore seem to be simultaneously too little and too much—something missing, but also a certain materialization. The object a is Lacan's effort to resolve this issue: it is a construction that seeks to address the link between the void and this excess by establishing a relation between lack and this peculiar surplus-effect. Before turning to this enigmatic splitting within the second conception of the real, let us characterize the postsymbolic version more precisely.

BUTLER AND ŽIŽEK

In distinguishing these two versions of the real, we may cast light not only on Lacan, but also on some recent discussions of Lacanian theory. Consider Judith Butler's *Bodies That Matter*, which contains a chapter called "Arguing with the Real." In this chapter, Butler touches on both versions of the real when she observes, in reference to Žižek, that it is unclear whether the real is to be understood as a prediscursive, material realm, a hard kernel located outside symbolization, or whether it is to be understood as a product of the symbolic order, "an effect of the law," in which case we would be concerned, not so much with a material real, but rather with a lack. Such is the ambiguity Butler points to in Žižek's work, noting that the real appears in two forms, as both rock and lack. She writes: "the 'real' that is a 'rock' or a 'kernel' or sometimes a substance is also, and sometimes within the same sentence, 'a loss' [or] a 'negativity.'"[40] According to Butler, we thus find a certain equivocation: the concept of the real "appears to slide from substance to dissolution." As "substance," the real would seem to implicate Lacan in a reference to prediscursive reality.[41] Lacanian theory would thus cut against the grain of most "postmodernism," for if we assert the "discursive construction of reality," stressing its contingent, historical formation, the real would seem to be a limit, an external domain that is untouched by symbolization. But as "loss" or "negativity," the real would seem to bring Lacan closer to the thesis that reality is discursively constructed, though with the additional complication that the real implies a lack that remains in some enigmatic way irreducible to the symbolic—beyond discourse, though not simply prediscursive. In view of our distinction between two versions of the real, we might see this sliding from substance to dissolution not as confusion or self-contradiction, but as the simultaneous articulation of two forms of the real.

BEYOND "DISCURSIVE" POSTMODERNISM

In her discussion of Žižek and the real, Butler focuses on the fact that the concept of the real amounts to a critique of the "postmodern" thesis asserting the discursive construction of reality. This is indeed the crucial point and the crux of all of Butler's critiques of Lacanian theory. She notes that the real presents us with a limit to discourse: "Žižek begins his critique of what he calls 'poststructuralism' through the invocation of a certain kind of matter, a 'rock' or 'kernel' that not only resists symbolization and discourse, but is precisely what poststructuralism, in his account, itself resists and endeavors to dissolve."[42] At this point, however, the distinction between our two versions of the real is crucial: we must ask whether Žižek's critique of "poststructuralism"—conceived (rightly or wrongly) as a theory of discursive construction—amounts to a naive appeal to prediscursive reality (a rock or substance) or whether it concerns the failure or incompleteness of the symbolic order (a certain lack or negativity). In the latter case, as I have suggested, the Lacanian account of the real would be very close to certain questions formulated by Foucault and Derrida concerning the limits of formalization—the supplement, or transgression, or madness, for example. It is because of this second possibility, moreover, that Butler does not simply reject the concept of the real (as a naive appeal to "reality"), insisting on an equally naive account of the "discursive construction of reality" (a thesis that has often been wrongly attributed to her).

On the contrary, she regards the concept of the real as a genuine contribution, an effort to address a problem that contemporary theory has to confront if it is to pass beyond certain inadequate formulations of "cultural construction." For those of us who wish to insist upon an antifoundation-alist approach and develop the claims of a postmodern tradition that rec-ognizes the contingent formation of the subject, the concept of the real is not a stumbling block or a naive reference to "reality" that must be re-jected, according to Butler, but rather a concept, or a theoretical difficulty, that must be confronted and adequately developed. The question of the body and "sexuality" is one arena in which this issue is particularly impor-tant, and which psychoanalytic theory has done much to develop in a clear way, since the body and sexuality oblige us to recognize the limits of sym-bolic construction without, however, appealing to any presymbolic reality. If psychoanalysis has taken on an increasing urgency today, it is precisely for this reason, for psychoanalysis has perhaps the clearest conception of the real of the body as a material dimension of the flesh that exceeds repre-sentation, yet does not automatically refer us to a "natural" domain of "preexisting reality." As I have suggested in "The Epoch of the Body," debates concerning whether psychoanalysis amounts to a form of biologi-cal essentialism or whether it asserts the historical construction of sexuality only conceal the theoretical difficulty that psychoanalysis seeks to address.[43]

Thus, Butler does not simply reject the real. On the contrary, the im-portance of this element beyond the symbolic is unmistakable, since it is crucial to recognize the limit of discursive construction, what Butler calls the "failure of discursive performativity to finally and fully establish the identity to which it refers."[44] Thus, she agrees that "the category of the real is needed," and notes that if Žižek is right to be "opposed to post-structuralist accounts of discursivity," it is because we must provide a more adequate account of what remains "outside" discourse, what is "fore-closed" from the symbolic order—since "what is refused or repudiated in the formation of the subject continues to determine that subject."[45] Yet, while stressing its importance, she focuses on the ambiguous status of this "outside," this foreclosed element, which remains paradoxical insofar as it is difficult to say whether it is a prediscursive rock or kernel that is simply beyond representation, or an effect of language itself, a lack that would be produced by the symbolic order, instead of simply preceding it. Butler thus identifies a certain wavering, an apparent duality in the concept, a "vacillation between substance and its dissolution" that is evident in the fact that the real is simultaneously "figured as the 'rock' and the 'lack.'"[46] Whatever the details of the discussion between Žižek and Butler may be,

I have tried to suggest that this difficulty can be clarified by distinguishing between two quite different conceptions of the real, a presymbolic real, and a postsymbolic real, which would take us in the direction of lack.

THE ANATOMY OF CRITICISM

On the basis of Butler's remarks, in fact, one might even undertake an "anatomy of criticism," a map of contemporary responses to postmodernism, distinguishing "two interpretations of interpretation" in contemporary cultural theory.[47] One is a reactive response, which has gained force recently and which amounts to a "return to reality"—in the form of a call for concrete historical and empirical research, a virulent rejection of "theory" (which is more and more characterized in terms of "French influences" and regarded as "foreign"), and also in the rise of genetic and biological explanations of consciousness, behavior, and sexuality. The other response is an effort to pass "through" postmodernism, to correct certain deficiencies in the theory of discursive construction, and—without returning to the "good old days" in which discourses were thought to be true when they secured nondiscursive foundations for themselves, without appealing to a subject or a human nature that might be regarded as independent of historically contingent discourses or practices—to develop an account of the limit and insufficiency of discourse, thereby doing justice to the concrete historical effects of symbolic life, not by disregarding language in favor of a "return to the empirical," but by recognizing the material effects of the malfunction of the symbolic order itself. This is precisely what is at stake in psychoanalysis, particularly with respect to the "body." In speaking of the "real" of the body, psychoanalysis does not simply endorse a return to biology or to a prelinguistic reality (the reality presupposed by biomedical discourse, which focuses on the *organism* and not the *body*). If, however, the "body" in psychoanalysis is distinguished from the organism, it is not because it is simply a discursive construction or a product of language, but because it is a peculiar structure or phenomenon that is not governed by nature, but is at the same time irreducible to the symbolic order.

THE OBJECT—"PROHIBITED" OR "LOST"?

Let us now take a final step. Having distinguished two versions of the real, we must now return to the problem noted earlier, namely, the fact that the second, postsymbolic conception of the real gives rise to two different, apparently paradoxical or contradictory results, since it leads us to speak not only of lack, but also of a certain remainder or excess. As a peculiar remainder, the real is a surplus-effect of the symbolic order—a product that cannot be explained by reference to prediscursive reality, but that is also distinct from the idea of a void or lack. We have indicated that the object a is Lacan's attempt to provide a theoretical resolution to this problem, by establishing a relation between lack and this peculiar remainder. Is this not in fact the paradox of the term itself, the object a, which allows us to speak of an object of lack?

In order to clarify this final point, let us return to the argument of Robert Samuels, who speaks of the "subject in the Real" as an "existential" subject, prior to any imaginary or symbolic mediation—the purely hypothetical and always already lost subject of "unmediated existence." With this "subject in the real," we would seem to return to our first version of the real, a level of immediate reality that is never accessible as such. Beginning with this prediscursive conception, Samuels argues for a link between the real in Lacan, and the Freudian account of autoeroticism and infantile sexuality. He establishes this link by suggesting that a primitive, more or less chaotic, polymorphous and undifferentiated infantile sexuality comes to be ordered and unified by the formation of the "imaginary body." We can therefore regard consciousness, narcissism, the ego, and the body (as imaginary), as a set of related functions that impose unity upon the real of infantile sexuality. As Samuels puts it, we have an "ideal form of unity that gives the subject the possibility of organizing its perceptions and sensations through the development of a unified bodily image."[48] There are good grounds for this link between the real (thus understood) and infantile sexuality in Freud, who writes in "On Narcissism": "We are bound to suppose that a unity comparable to the ego can exist in the individual from the start; the ego has to be developed. The auto-erotic instincts, however, are there from the very first; so there must be something added to auto-eroticism—a new psychical action—in order to bring about narcissism" (SE, 14:76–77). In this view, the "real" subject of "existence" and infantile autoeroticism is an original state that is lost with the arrival of the imaginary body and lost again (twice, like Eurydice) with the advent of symbolic mediation. But this prediscursive conception of infantile sexuality will soon be complicated.

Later, in a chapter on *Totem and Taboo*, Samuels returns to this formulation, but in a way that raises the question of the possible "resurgence" of the real in the unconscious, what he also regards as a form of incestuous desire outside the symbolic law: "in the position of the Real," he writes, we find "the subject of the unconscious and infantile sexuality who exists outside the symbolic order."[49] One often hears that the Lacanian unconscious is simply a "symbolic" phenomenon, the "discourse of the Other," but by stressing the subject of the unconscious as real, Samuels indicates that he is concerned here with something beyond the symbolic order, something that concerns the body, a sort of remnant or "trace" of infantile sexuality that persists in the unconscious, in spite of the symbolic law. It is this persistence of the real, this trait of incestuous desire within or beyond the advent of the symbolic order that we need to clarify, and that will lead Samuels to shift from our first version of the real to a second version (though he does not mark the shift in the manner we are suggesting). We must now ask whether the real that "returns" beyond the law, after the imaginary and symbolic have lost it, is the same as the origin, the initial infantile state, or whether this trait or trace that exceeds the symbolic order is not rather a product, an effect of the law itself—in which case we can call it "infantile" only by a certain metaphorical displacement, a ruse that pretends to locate this incestuous desire *before* the law, when it is in fact a product of the law itself. The consequences are obviously decisive: if we believe that "infantile sexuality" is a prediscursive state of existence that is gradually organized and made lawful by representation (what Foucault calls the "repressive hypothesis"), we may regard the return of infantile sexuality as a sort of liberation. But if the return is in fact a product of the law, and not a prediscursive state of nature, then this trait of incestuous desire can only be an effect of the law itself—not a form of liberation or the restitution of a natural origin, but a surplus-effect of the symbolic order itself. This is in fact Lacan's thesis, developed in particular when he speaks of *père-version*, a "turning toward the father," a "trait of perversion" that accompanies the father of the law. In this view, something in the very operation of the law splits the paternal function into two incompatible parts, one of which bears on the inevitability of symbolic mediation, while the other bears on a certain "trait of perversion" that— far from designating a resurgence of "natural" sexuality—in fact designates a suffering that accompanies the law itself. This is what the concept of *jouissance* seeks to address.

THE INCESTUOUS OBJECT

This is also the point at which we must introduce the concept of the object a, as a lack that entails a surplus-effect, a certain materialization. According

to Samuels, this persistence of the real of infantile sexuality within or beyond the law, is precisely what Lacan addresses in terms of the relation
between the symbolic order and the object a. Thus, in addition to distinguishing between the subject as real and symbolic (S and $)—while recog-
nizing, of course, the ego as imaginary—we must also confront the
problem of the object, as that which allows us to give concrete, bodily
specificity to the dimension of incestuous desire that remains alongside,
or in excess of, the lawful desire that characterizes the symbolic order.
Samuels makes this additional development quite clear in his discussion of
Totem and Taboo: we not only have an opposition between the symbolic
subject (who enters into lawful kinship relations, governed by exogamy
and symbolic exchange) and what Samuels calls "the Real subject of the
unconscious who rejects the law of the father"; we must also develop a
conception of the object, the prohibited object that somehow "returns"
despite the symbolic law, or rather comes into existence through it. As
Samuels puts it: "Implied by this dialectic between incest and exogamy is
the persistence of an incestuous object in the unconscious of the subject."[50]
Such is the relation not simply between the real and symbolic subjects, but
between the Other (symbolic law) and the object a. As the prohibited object, the lost object, the taboo object, or the object of lack (and these may
not be identical), the object a allows us to locate "the Real subject of the
unconscious who rejects the law of the father and presents the existence
of incest within the structure."[51] The polymorphous perversity of infantile
sexuality is thus designated as a real that is lost with the advent of the
imaginary body, renounced when the subject passes through the mediating
structure of the symbolic law, and yet a "trace" or remnant of this lost
world remains and is embodied in the form of the object a. Obviously, the
concept of the "trace" in Derrida, as a past that was never present, bears
a close resemblance to this Lacanian concept and calls for further
examination.

Thus far, Samuels's account appears to coincide with our first version
of the real: in speaking of an "existential subject" (S) that is distinguished
from the ego and the "split subject" of the symbolic order ($), he seems
to rely on the idea of a prediscursive real, prior to its having been filtered
and organized by representation. This is the real of infantile sexuality and
immediate existence, which is always already lost, repressed or mediated
by the imaginary, and by the symbolic order. The problem arises, however, of the possible resurgence of the real, which is lost, but nevertheless
able to return within the symbolic order and somehow present itself—as a

traumatic return of the repressed, as a momentary breakdown of representation that is due to a sort of direct contact with an unfamiliar reality, or in some other form of "presentation" that remains to be clarified. According to Samuels, the object a in Lacan designates precisely this element, a real that is not *represented* in symbolic or imaginary form, but is nevertheless *presented* somehow. It is not a past that has been lost, but something that presents itself in the present: "The object (a) represents the presence of an unsymbolized Real element within the structure of the symbolic order itself."[52] Obviously other writers have taken up this disruptive presentation, a certain "concrete" remainder that exceeds symbolization—as Kristeva does, for example, with the "Semiotic" and as Kant does with the sublime, which is the experience of an excess that disrupts both sensory and conceptual presentation, that cannot be contained by images or concepts, that disrupts the very faculty of presentation (the imagination), and yet somehow presents itself. At this point, the real is no longer a domain of immediate existence, a prediscursive "reality" that is always already lost, but a peculiar "presence" within the symbolic order itself.

This is where matters become complicated, and we are confronted with a certain paradox. For one thing (to put the point in a logical or structural way), it is difficult to say that the object a is a presence, or that (in Samuels's words) it "represents" something like infantile sexuality, if we have claimed that all presence and all representation are imaginary or symbolic and that the real is inaccessible, always already lost, impossible, or absent. If the symbolic law means that all of the subject's experience and desire is organized through representation—if the most concrete content of our bodily experience is given to us through an imaginary unity that is in turn filtered through the symbolic order—then the object a would be an element that does not fit within the imaginary or symbolic structure, that is abjected from the order of images and words, but nevertheless persists in "presenting itself." This is the structural aspect of the problem: the object a is *a presence that does not belong to the system of presentation*, an element that appears without appearing, emerging "inside" the structure without belonging to the structure. As Samuels points out, we thus face "the paradox of the analytic attempt to Symbolize that which cannot be Symbolized."[53]

Despite this apparent paradox, we should not be too quick to dismiss the question on logical grounds: we should perhaps be prepared to consider the possibility of a real that is beyond representation, an aspect of the subject that is outside the symbolic order, but would somehow present itself or have an effect on the system of representation. Freud appears to have something like this in mind when he speaks of unconscious "residues," that remain present without the subject being aware of them, residues which have an effect on the subject's life, even when they are excluded from the field of representation. Butler appears to have something similar in mind when she writes that we must not reduce the subject to a purely symbolic effect or regard the subject as a "discursive construction": "Žižek is surely right that the subject is not the unilateral effect of prior discourses, and that the process of subjectivation outlined by Foucault is in need of psychoanalytic rethinking."[54] But if the concept of the real is indispensable, we cannot ignore the problem of its presentation. As I have indicated, Jacques-Alain Miller's approach to this difficulty is a logical one, insofar as he does not take an ontic approach to the object, but claims that the object is a construction, a concept that arises as a way of addressing the structural impasses of the symbolic order. As an object, however, it is not simply a logical issue, but should allow us to give concrete, bodily specificity to this aporia without appealing to a prediscursive conception of the object. Obviously, the relation between Lacanian theory and object-relations theory is extremely complex at this point. It is clear, however, that we can no longer sustain the first version of the real as a domain of immediacy that is always already lost and that we must instead consider the object as an unsymbolized real element within the structure of the symbolic order itself.

If we turn from the structural to the temporal aspects of the return of the real, we can put the paradox in a slightly different form. In this case, it is not simply a matter of representing what is beyond representation, or of presenting the unpresentable. It is rather a question of the return of an original state within a structure that was supposed to reconfigure, prohibit, or transcend it. The example of infantile sexuality is particularly important here, for if we begin by characterizing the real as a "primitive" domain of disorganized polymorphous experience—if we claim that the ego and narcissism are imposed (together with the structure of language) upon the original chaos of the "real" body, in such a way that this "original experience" is lost—then the question concerns the return, in the present, of a lost origin. At this point, a temporal twist is given to our paradox, for it is clear that *what returns* is not the same as this supposedly original state. What returns, "within" the system of representation (as a rupture or unsymbolized element), is not, in fact, an initial condition of infantile sexuality—the memory of a past that is somehow preserved in all its archaeological purity—but rather a trait that emerges *from* the symbolic order, and yet *presents itself as* the remnant of a past that has been lost. We now see more clearly why the object a can only be understood in terms of our second version of the real, but also why it appears to be conceivable in terms of the first version: this trace, designated as the object a, is not the origin, a leftover that remains from the past, or the "return" of an original state, but the temporal paradox in which we find the return of something that did not originally exist, but only emerged "after the fact" (*nachträglich*) as an *effect* of symbolization. Its apparently "original" status is thus strictly mythical. For the "thing" first came into being only when it "returned," hiding itself or disguising itself as an origin, while it is in fact a product of the symbolic order, an effect of the law itself.

We are thus brought to our final observation: the importance of this second, temporal formulation is that it obliges us to recognize a *split* between the object a and the real understood as an initial, presymbolic condition. Samuels puts the point as follows. Speaking of unconscious "fixations"—what Freud calls "the incestuous fixations of libido" (SE, 13:17)—Samuels writes: "The fixation is *not the existence of infantile sexuality (jouissance) itself, but rather a rem(a)inder* of the primitive Real within the structure of the symbolic order."[55] The conclusion is clear: we now have a split between the "primitive" real of an original infantile sexuality, and the "rem(a)inder" that appears in the present, within the symbolic order. As Samuels puts it, "There must be a separation between what Lacan calls the primitive Real of *jouissance* [infantile sexuality], which is placed logically before the Symbolic order of language and law, and the post-Symbolic form of the Real, which is embodied by the object (a)."[56] That remainder, the object a, is no longer identical with the original *jouissance* it is said to embody or represent. The object a is, rather, a product, the concrete materialization of an element of transgression or *jouissance* that does not submit to the symbolic law, but that, far from being an original state, a moment of natural immediacy, is precisely a product of the law, a surplus-effect of the symbolic order, which disguises itself as an origin. Where the first version of the real allows us to maintain the illusion of a lost immediacy (together with the hope of its possible return, through "affect," or "transgression," or "liberation," or in some other way), the second account, based on the object a, recognizes this state of immediacy not only as a myth, a retroactive construction, but also as a peculiar materialization, a product of the symbolic order itself.

We thus see more clearly what the status of the "prohibition" is in psychoanalysis. It is not an interdiction that prohibits a possible pleasure, compelling us to accept the standards of civilized behavior, but rather a "no" that veils an impossibility. It does not banish us from a state of nature, but rather erects (the word is used advisedly) a barrier to cover what is originally lacking. The object a is therefore not so much a piece of infantile sexuality that remains latent in the subject in spite of the laws of civilization, a piece of libido that refused to sign the social contact, a biological Id that resists the symbolic law, but rather a construction that accompanies the law itself—the trace of a past that was never present as such, but only comes into being when it returns. Lacan touched on this difficulty in the "Rome Discourse" when he observed that the traumatic event is not an original reality (the "brute aspect of the trauma") that might be located in the past, but a later condensation or "precipitation" of the subject, and that psychoanalysis is a science of "conjecture" in this precise sense, since it has to construct the object rather than simply discover it. Freud drew a similar conclusion about the peculiar, conjectural status of the prohibited object when he observed that, when primitive tribes are asked about their "taboos" and "prohibitions," it is difficult to get a clear grasp on the object that is prohibited, since every account always already falls back on symbolic rituals and other presentations that amount to misrepresentation. As Freud remarks in his brilliantly offhand way, these "primitive" cultures are in fact "already very ancient civilizations."

The "taboo object" is not a thing that is itself dangerous or contaminating, but a representation, a symbolic form, a ritualized displacement of a terror that, in itself, remains "unknown" and "obscure," like the nodal point of the dream. Thus, when we ask about the reason for the prohibition—why this particular thing has been chosen as the forbidden act or object—we reach what we might call an "original displacement." In Lacanian terms, the taboo object is a veil thrown over a void. This brings us to the strictest definition of the prohibition: what is prohibited is actually impossible or originally lost, but the prohibition produces the illusion of a possible possession—either in a mythical past or in a promised future. The prohibition (and perhaps morality as well) thus reveals its status as a veil. We pretend to restrict ourselves, or to elaborate ethical standards of civilization, in order to refuse what is in fact unavailable—the very structure of the veil that Žižek sees in Wittgenstein's famous conclusion to the *Tractatus*: "what we cannot speak of, we must leave in silence." Why, it might be asked, is it necessary to *prohibit* what in fact cannot be said? Because "that is the law." As Freud observes, the "primitive" tribes make this original displacement especially clear: "even primitive people have not retained the original forms of those institutions nor the conditions which gave rise to them; so that we have nothing whatever but hypotheses to fall back upon, as a substitute for the observation which we are without" (SE, 13:109). The prohibited object thus acquires a *strictly mythical status*: it is not a thing that was once possessed (in infancy or prehistory), but a thing that came into existence through the law, as the lost object. The idea that this object was once possessed is strictly a retroactive fantasy—but an illusion that is inseparable from the symbolic order itself and does not cease to have effects, even when its nonexistence has been demonstrated. We must therefore recognize its postsymbolic status, but also do justice to its ability to create the illusion that this object derives from an origin, that it somehow represents a past that was once possessed (not only in the patient's past, but also in the past that always haunts theoretical work as well, including psychoanalytic theories of "infancy," "maternity," and other "origins").

CHAPTER 2

The Atrocity of Desire: Of Love and Beauty in Lacan's *Antigone*

It is a maxim among men that when an exploit has been accomplished it must not remain hidden in silence. What it requires is the divine melody of praising verses.

—PINDAR, *Nemean Odes*

It was then, perhaps, that some individual, in the exigency of his long-ing, may have been moved to free himself from the group and take over the father's part. He who did this was the first epic poet; and the advance was achieved in his imagination. . . . He invented the heroic myth. . . . The myth, then, is the step by which the individual emerges from group psychology. . . . The poet who had taken this step and had in this way set himself free from the group in his imagination, is nevertheless able . . . to find his way back to it in reality. For he goes and relates to the group his hero's deeds which he himself has invented.

—FREUD, *Group Psychology*

Transmission: Of Love and Beauty

When so much of the story is already known, when the content or action is already defined as mythic, in the sense that it belongs to ancient his-tory—to the stories by which we identify ourselves as a group, a people, and a community—when the events are part of a narrative that we have already heard a thousand times, and interpreted anew with every genera-tion, we may as well begin without rehearsal, without setting the stage too much, as if the drama were already at an end, its destiny played out long ago, before we were even born, leaving us simply to bear witness, to reflect on one or two details, in their supreme and somewhat esoteric isolation.

Beginning thus, by making a cut in the highly complex and overdetermined symbolic network, we might be able to detach a few elements, in order to see how the story looks when it is gathered once again around these somewhat eccentric, but in no way simply arbitrary features.

To begin, therefore, let me simply isolate two elements in Lacan's reading of *Antigone*, two features, which are also two relations. One of these takes place on the stage, within the action of the play; the other takes place between this action and the audience who come to witness its unfolding. Within the play, it is a question of Antigone's relation to her brother, and the strange desire or fate, the compulsion or responsibility, that binds her to her brother—more precisely (since there are two), to that brother who is dead but not yet buried, that singular and irreplaceable brother towards whom Antigone alone is able, or willing, or compelled to act [*egō dē de taphon chōsous' adelphō philtatō poreusomai*, 80–81].[1] If Antigone is, for Lacan, the figure who "does not give up on her desire," if she represents desire in its most radical and stubborn persistence ("perseverance," Lacan says, using a word that explicitly calls attention to the father),[2] if she is the heroine of the tragedy, who assumes, on her own, the absolute responsibility (SVII, 88) for this work of mourning—an act of burial that also entails the assumption of her ownmost being-toward-death—if she chooses her fate with unwavering clarity from the opening lines of the play, all these features would come to rest, according to Lacan, on the singular relation that binds her to her brother, this particular brother, a troubling and even wounded attachment, which all the commentaries have found disturbing, some to the point of wanting to excise from the play the famous lines in which she proclaims this singular bond, in language that cannot any longer be contained, according to Lacan, by the famous Hegelian account of the antagonism between the family and the state.[3] Her link to her brother would thus be the decisive point that allows us to gather up all the other details—Antigone's status as the tragic heroine, the ethical nature of her position, her persistence in her desire, her relation to death, and so on. How, then, are we to understand this singular, triumphant, and catastrophic attachment? Lacan insists upon one word: *love*. "Antigone is the heroine," Lacan says (SVII, 262). "She's the one who shows the way of the gods. She's the one . . . who is made for love rather than for hate" (SVII, 262; see Sophocles, line 523). Again Heidegger comes to mind, insofar as "hesitation" is a crucial category for the account of that mode of being wherein Dasein flees from its own destiny, through "indecision," "procrastination," and "hesitation"—temporal relations that could be correlated with Lacan's account of these terms in his note on "temporal tension" and "intersubjective time."[4]

The way of the gods is the way of love, and Antigone is guided by their unwritten law (SVII, 278; line 454), which not only binds her to her brother, but governs the entire course of the dramatic action, determining Antigone's relation to every other figure within it: to Creon, Haemon, Ismene, her father, and thus to politics, marriage, family, and even the unfortunate past, the evil that descends from Oedipus (*ap Oidipou kakōn*, line 2), transmitting across the generations the legacy of a crime that she did not commit, but that she (the child of incest) chooses to assume as her own, as her own destiny or fate.[5] She announces her decision in terms of love in the opening lines of the play, using the word *philia*, which she repeats in many places. And after her condemnation, when she is about to be "shut up in a tomb" (SVII, 280), cast aside unburied and unmourned, the third choral ode tells us that she goes forth like a goddess and a warrior, and that her face is radiant and shining. She is *ta ekphainestata*, Lacan says, the most shining and manifest (from *phaino* and *phainomenon*: she is the shining of the "Thing," in Lacan's vocabulary), and what shows in her eyes is love, according to the chorus, which uses the words *Erōs* and *Aphrodita* (lines 781–90). In the vocabulary that runs from *philia* to *Erōs*, then, we are asked to see, not a set of discrete definitions—a familiar contradiction between erotic and brotherly love, or between friendship and passion—but a movement of exposition and clarification.[6] The purity of her love for her brother (*philia*), and the filial piety that supports her act of mourning are thus revealed, in the end, to be a desire (*Erōs*), which is to be understood not only as a *power* (the power to act: "I did the deed," she says, "and I won't say otherwise," line 443), but also as evidence that a "moment of decision" has been reached ("It is time," she says to her sister in the opening lines of the play, "for you to show whether you are noble and well-born or not," line 38).[7] It is this desire, this singular, mysterious, and somewhat troubling power, whose divine aspect (*Aphrodita*) shines forth, made visible in her face as "beauty." The first relation, then, would be marked out as follows:

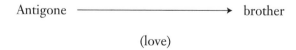

Antigone ———————————————→ brother

(love)

The second feature that concerns us is located in the relation between the action of the play and the audience that bears witness to that action. If Antigone is not only the heroine, but the heroine *for us*, if it is she who most of all attracts our attention and rouses our emotions, if we are drawn toward her in a kind of horrified captivation that both attracts and repels, moving us forward in pity even as we recoil in fear, then she is the principal focus of what Aristotle calls *katharsis*, that obscure but crucial experience of "emotion" which is definitive of tragedy as such. It is an open question as to how we should understand this "affect" or "emotion"—not only in the Greek context (where "pity" and "fear" already belong to a terminology and an interpretive apparatus imposed by Aristotle on an experience and an aesthetic structure whose meaning, as Jean-Pierre Vernant has argued, may have been profoundly different in the time of Sophocles), but also in the context of psychoanalysis (where the "cathartic method" has a long and complicated history, and where "affect" is but poorly understood).[8] Freud repeatedly insists on this difficulty. Speaking of the difference between anxiety and other "feelings," for example, he writes: "Anxiety, then, is in the first place something that is felt. We call it an affective state, although we are also ignorant of what an affect is" (SE, 20:132). Without entering into this difficulty in any detail, we can at least say that, whether one interprets *katharsis* on the model of medical purging, or as a quasi-religious purification, or indeed in some other way—for Lacan will reject both views (SVII, 244–45, 312)—this "experience" or "subjective effect" is a defining feature of tragedy as such, understood as an *aesthetic* phenomenon, a feature that (as Kant also says) distinguishes the work of art from cognitive and moral phenomena, as well as from immediate or everyday experience (as the classical notion of "aesthetic distance" also suggests). Though we cannot develop the point here, it is worth noting that the question of transmission runs persistently through this seminar, in connection, no doubt, with the transmission of psychoanalysis, as well as with historical transmission in general. "With the category of the beautiful," Lacan writes, "Kant says that only the example—which doesn't mean the object—is capable of assuring its transmission" (257). And again, "Freud finds no other path adapted to the transmission of the rationalist Moses' message than that of darkness; in other words, this message is linked, through repression, to the murder of the Great Man. And it is precisely in this way, Freud tells us, that it can be transmitted and maintained" (174). It is this transmission that we have tried to mark in the epigraph from Freud, which speaks of a certain creative work, by means of which the individual—radically detached from the group—produces a mythical discourse that can be articulated and given over to the community—as is clearly the case with Antigone.[9]

For the distinctively aesthetic experience of tragedy, everything thus depends on our relation to the figure of the hero in her captivating presence: the proper accomplishment of tragedy, its very capacity to fulfill its function as a work of art, comes to rest on this link of fascination and horror that binds us to Antigone. All the other features of the drama—the pronouncements of the chorus, the stupid and brutal application of Creon's edict, the logic of the plot, and the entire sequence of stages in which Antigone's movement toward death is slowly unfolded, from the entreaties of Haemon, to the warnings of Teiresias, to the final destructive events—all this radiates outward, according to Lacan, from the single and decisive point of Antigone herself, insofar as she works upon us, drawing the audience into a gradual experience, which is neither the "ordinary" experience of immediate reality, nor the "philosophical" experience of thinking and conceptual reflection, but rather the experience of catharsis, in which one passes through a highly controlled relation to pity and fear, a relation that would seem to be paradoxically traumatic and tranquilizing—disturbing and yet somehow also pacifying. All the features of tragedy thus seem to find their center in this unique attachment, this bond that is far from simply pleasurable, but that draws us inexorably towards Antigone. How are we to understand this bond, this singular and somewhat troubling attachment? Like Antigone's bond with her brother, our attraction to her would also be troubling, because, as Aristotle says, it is strange that we humans should take pleasure in the representation of death, that we should turn ourselves toward death when an animal would simply turn away in fear. What, then, is our attachment to Antigone? Lacan insists upon one word: *beauty*. It is the sheer radiance of Antigone, the uncanny power of her image, what Lacan calls "her unbearable splendor" (SVII, 247), that draws the audience to her. "Antigone," Lacan says, "reveals to us the line of sight that defines desire. This line of sight focuses on an image that possesses a mystery which up to now has never been articulated . . . that image is at the center of tragedy . . . the fascinating image of Antigone herself" (SVII, 247).[10]

The second relation, our link to the image of Antigone, could thus be marked out as follows:

(beauty)

We are faced here with an image that cannot be immediately raised to the level of the concept, or drawn into the strife between opposing principles. To isolate this image, according to Lacan, is therefore to go beyond the famous "conflict between the two divided powers of ethical substance."[11] Lacan insists upon this point, in explicit opposition to Hegel: "over and beyond the question of family and country," he says, "over and beyond the moralizing arguments, it is Antigone herself who fascinates us, Antigone in her unbearable splendor. She has a quality that both attracts and startles us in the sense of intimidates us; this terrible, self-willed victim disturbs us" (SVII, 247). "It is in connection with this power of attraction that we should look for the true sense, the true mystery, the true significance of tragedy" (SVII, 247).

We must open a parenthesis at this point, for the translation is not right here. Lacan says that Antigone has a quality "qui nous reteint et à la fois nous interdit" (SVII, 290), a quality that holds us back, that restrains and at the same time prohibits us (*interdit* also means "stuns").[12] The text thus says neither "attracts" nor "startles." It is rather a question of *prohibition* (like a force imposed from without: the father's "no"), but at the same time of *holding* or *restraint* (like an internalized sense of conscience, not an external prohibition but a capacity to "hold oneself back"), which Lacan will later develop in terms of the categories of "modesty" and "shame" (characteristics conspicuously lacking in Creon, whose law knows no restraint). This peculiar intersection between the image and the law, revealed by the figure of Antigone, is what authorizes Lacan to connect beauty and desire—terms that one might expect to be opposed to one another, insofar as the image, and the imaginary attachments of narcissism, are usually taken to be distinct from the symbolic dimension of desire. The peculiar condensation of imaginary and symbolic functions manifested in the image of Antigone—the fact that an imaginary support now seems to supplement and perhaps even modify Lacan's conception of the law—thus opens a decisive meditation on aesthetic phenomena.[13] The paradoxical character of this unexpected relation between the image and the law, moreover, is that beauty does not simply *arouse* desire, as common sense might lead us to suppose (this is Plato's worry about art in relation to enthusiasm, as well as Kant's concern, the entire discourse on "disinterestedness" being a protracted effort to temper or refine the arousal of our merely sensuous "appetite" on behalf of a proper "reflective judgment"); on the contrary, in this seminar on ethics, beauty moves from the imaginary register and now has the function of a veil, which restrains and even prohibits. Lacan thus speaks of "the extinction or tempering of desire through the effect of beauty" (SVII, 249): "It is when passing through that zone that the beam of desire is both reflected and refracted till it ends up giving us that most strange and most profound of effects, which is *the effect of beauty on desire*" (SVII, 248, my emphasis).

In short, something is happening to the concept of the imaginary in Lacan's thought: it is as if the image of Antigone were suddenly able to function at the level of the law, yet without being a name or a signifier, or as if, in the face of this "terrible beauty," we were confronted with a "no" that not only *forbids* (*qui nous interdit*), but also holds or protects (*qui nous reteint*), in the sense that this image does not simply interdict, with the celebrated "negativity" of the signifier (which "murders the thing"), but rather provides a support, a "form," and a "presence" that restrain us, so that the image of Antigone would function not like a mirror (in the imaginary) but like a veil—an image aligned with the concepts of shame, humility, or modesty: "I should like to introduce here," Lacan writes, "as a parallel to the function of the beautiful, another function . . . a sense of shame" (SVII, 298). One might recall that, for Lacan, the phallus is also a veil, a point of intersection between the image and the law, whose imaginary character—if one should reduce it to this level—is profoundly misleading. Such a reduction allows the boy, for example, to believe that he is not castrated, just as it allows the girl to believe that something is deficient, or that something anatomical has been lost. One might wish, therefore, to leap from this sublime image of Antigone to the phallus (as if the woman were always a stand-in for the phallus), but Lacan will not move so quickly: "Do the fantasm of the phallus and the beauty of the human image find their legitimate place at the same level? Or is there, on the contrary, an imperceptible distinction, an irreducible difference, between them?" (SVII, 299). Let us leave these questions as they are and take up our thread again. It is enough to have a glimpse of what is at stake in the development of Lacan's thought, as we follow his account of *Antigone*.

We have isolated two relations and two terms: we have Antigone's relation to her brother and our relation to Antigone, the first defined by love, the second by beauty. The love that draws her toward her brother is the crucial feature underlying her status as the tragic heroine and the subject of desire, while her beauty is the decisive element that allows us in turn to be drawn toward her in pity and fear.

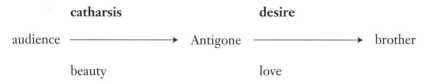

We can thus take another step, for it now becomes clear that these two relations are themselves related: it is love that allows or compels her to assume her fate in such a way that we in turn come to be fascinated with her radiant image, captivated and drawn through the experience of tragedy. These two relations are linked to one another, in a curious process of *transmission or translation*: if her love for her brother allows Lacan to define her as the heroine of desire, it is *this same desire* that shines forth in her face and makes her the object of fascination for us, the unbearable image that draws us through the experience of catharsis that is the crucial and defining feature of tragedy. These two attachments—of love and beauty—are thus linked to one another, as if her love for her brother were somehow handed over to us: a gift in the form of tragic experience.

The Sublime Image

Let us look more closely at these two relations, focusing for the moment on this image. It should be clear that, in addition to its peculiar force, its power to move the audience towards catharsis, this image also has effects within the action of the play. "Nothing is more moving," Lacan says, "than that *himeros enarges*, than the desire that visibly emanates from the eyelids of this admirable girl" (SVII, 281; he is citing line 796 in the third choral ode). *Enarges* means "visible," manifest and clear; it also means "appearing in bodily form," and it is used in this sense (e.g., by Homer) to designate the times when the gods take on a corporeal shape.[14] *Himeros* means "desire" or "love," but it also means "longing," yearning in tears and grief. It indicates a link between desire and mourning, and Lacan insists that it is only after Antigone has given voice to a long lament for everything that she is giving up—a lament that some commentators have regarded as a mistake, since it seems to compromise the unity of her character, which has thus far been so steadfast and unrelenting (SVII, 280)—it is only after this lamentation that she appears in such a light that the chorus in turn is able to lament, to raise a cry about her suffering, and to look on the law of the city as something that suddenly appears unjust. "Antigone," Lacan says:

> will lament that . . . she will never have any children, that she will never know a conjugal bed . . . that she is departing *ataphos*, without a tomb . . . without a dwelling place. . . . And it is *from this same place* that the image of Antigone appears before us as something that causes the Chorus to lose its head . . . [that] makes the just appear unjust, and makes the Chorus transgress all limits, including casting aside any respect it might have for the edicts of the city. Nothing is more moving than that *himeros enarges*, than the desire that visibly emanates from the eyelids of this admirable girl. (SVII, 280–81, my emphasis)

This unexpected relation between the image and the law, in which desire shines forth with this effect upon the city, making the just appear unjust, should allow us to clarify an earlier question, for if Antigone's love for her brother has largely been expressed in terms of *philia* during the course of the play, this *philia* is transformed, and shines forth in her eyes as the divine power of *Erōs* (she is *amachos . . . theos Aphrodita*, the chorus tells us, "the invincible goddess Aphrodite," lines 781–800), *precisely at the moment of a speech that gives voice to mourning*. This moment of mourning not only marks the transformation of *philia* into *Erōs* and highlights the peculiar divinity of her image, its sublime and blinding radiance, but at the same time brings into view the singular *transmission* of her act, its capacity to reach beyond itself, disrupting the world of the chorus and the city, with all the political effects that this entails.[15]

We must therefore stress not only the shift from *philia* to *Erōs*, within the domain of Antigone's "love" or "desire" (two terms that are clearly undergoing considerable analysis in this seminar: previously opposed to one another, the first imaginary, the second symbolic, they are now in close proximity, though by no means synonymous); we must also attend to the link between action and speech, the peculiar logic that binds Antigone's deed (the solitary act of burial that is grounded in her desire), to the *memorial* of that deed, the testimony she gives in the form of her lament. For this memorial ("My journey's done. One last fond, lingering look I take"; 809–10) does not simply *record* her loss, in the sheer passivity of historical documentation. On the contrary: Antigone's speech must be understood as the *completion* of her deed ("I did the deed, and I won't say otherwise"), as the proper accomplishment and fulfillment of an act that, as Carol Jacobs has noted, is relentlessly marked by Sophocles as taking place "in secret" and in "silence," without leaving any trace—so that only her words can complete the event, unfolding her act by bestowing upon it the full weight of its tragic consequence, and the power of its effect upon the city.[16] What is given, transmitted, and accomplished by her speech must thus be understood as integral to the domain of her action itself.

This is also what our epigraph from Pindar tells us, stressing the peculiar relation between speech and action, which is at the same time a relation between the human and the divine: "It is a maxim among men that when an exploit has been accomplished it must not be covered in the earth with silence. What it requires is the divine melody of praising verses." A complex relation is thereby announced, not only between speech and silence, or the exploits of men and the divine melody of the gods, but also between the word and the deed, for human action, and in particular heroic action, great and important action, with common or public significance (the kind that is represented in tragedy, as Aristotle observes), is not enough in itself, but requires speech for its completion: for "when an exploit has been accomplished," it runs the risk of remaining unfulfilled, hidden and left in obscurity, deprived of its public value, its capacity to signify to others. Without the complement of "praising verses" (*kauchas*) it cannot enter into tradition, where it will be repeated and handed down from one generation to the next, and thus able to forge a link between the past and the future. Without "the divine melody of praising verses," the deed remains silent ("covered in the earth"), a great exploit, to be sure, but powerless with respect to time. In the relationship between word and deed, then, Pindar does not pretend that there are no actions but only words; he does not say that everything comes down to the signifier, or that language "creates reality." There are deeds, apart from all speech, and even great deeds, that have their greatness, their character as exploits, apart from any narrative and reportage. But these deeds cannot live without the word; they remain buried, entombed in the silent earth (*chamai siga kalupsai*), without the song of praise that lifts them up beyond the sphere of human agency and its heroic exploits, and colors them with the "divine melody" (*thespesia*) that gives them life beyond the moment. And only in this way, through the support of a song that puts human action into contact with the divine, is human action able to lift itself beyond itself and become public and communal—an action that goes beyond itself as action ("exploit" or "accomplishment") and passes into the order of time, the order of myth and tradition. Without this supplement of song, the deed is dead and silent. Great deeds must therefore be completed, accompanied on their journey beyond the veil of silence, whose shroud would otherwise keep them buried in the earth (like Antigone, entombed away from the light). And this accompaniment is not itself a human action, another exploit, but rather a song that humans make as a gift (*kauchas aoida pros prosphoros*), hoping to find their mortal verses graced by a "divine melody" (*thespesia*)—as if the "praising verses," already detached from the order of deeds and identified as a matter of speech, were nevertheless insufficient in themselves (as human speech), and sought, beyond themselves, the accompaniment of a "divine melody." Such is the double edge of this phrase, the "divine melody *of* praising verses," which is a "requirement," and perhaps even a law—the law that governs human action and human speech, which "must not" remain hidden, but "requires" (as if with a strange imperative) not only praising verses, but verses that sing of those deeds in such a way that they (the verses and the deeds) become open to the complement of the gods, just as Antigone's deed was accompanied by the protective cloud of divine dust. Only in this way, through the verses that accompany the heroic deed, is human action able to receive the gift that is not human, that is neither human action nor human speech, but "the divine melody of praising verses." With Pindar's oracular help, we may grasp somewhat more clearly, perhaps, something of what the chorus hears when it witnesses the lament of Antigone and calls her divine and born of the gods (*alla theos toi kai theogennēs*; line 832).[17]

The moment of mourning is thus the fulfillment of her deed, which thereby acquires a peculiar fecundity within the city-state, turning *philia* into *Erōs*, and allowing the divine aspect of Antigone's love for her brother to be "manifested" before the chorus, in its full and terrible atrocity (a word that, as Lacan points out, derives from *ate*: blindness, delusion, bewilderment, recklessness, ruin, pestilence, doom, and abomination). Such is the peculiar power of desire, beyond all calculation or willful intention—for, as we shall see, Antigone buries her brother simply because she must, and not because she seeks to prove a point to anyone else, or because she aims at some useful or calculated political end.

Lacan is not alone in remarking on the curious character of this transformation, in which Antigone's heroic act—a solitary act, undertaken solely for itself, and in the reckless fury of a ruinous devotion—somehow reaches beyond itself, rebounding upon the city precisely at the moment of mourning, a moment that turns the head of the chorus, causing it to weep in turn and leading it to see the law of Creon for what it is—namely, an arbitrary brutality that exceeds the bounds of justice. The chorus like-wise elaborates this passage from *philia* to *Erōs*, and the correlated link between her blinding image and its power to move, to turn our heads and our judgment: Antigone, the chorus says, is *daimonion teras* (line 375), a "strange vision," according to the Loeb translation. She suddenly appears as *daimonion*, a half-goddess Lacan says (SVII, 281) (born of the gods, *alla theos toi kai theogennēs*; line 832), "daemonic" and *teras*, "strange," more precisely, "monstrous," *teras* meaning a sign, a wonder, a marvel or a por-tent, but also a monster or monstrosity (a meaning carried in the English *teratology*). She is monstrous, in the sense of *to deinotaton*, the most won-drous of all the many wonders on the earth—in the words of the first choral ode so famously discussed by Heidegger in the *Introduction to Meta-physics* (*polla ta deina kouden anthrōpou deinoteron pelei*; line 332, "of all that is strange on the earth, none is stranger than man").[18] Thus, if this blinding light—one might even say this "gaze"—that moves the chorus is *Erōs* (and even *theos Aphrodita*, the "goddess that looks forth from the eyes of the girl"; line 800), it is *this same light* that makes Antigone the object of fasci-nation and power for us, the moving force of catharsis.[19] In short, while the force of her image is clear throughout the play, and while her stubborn willfulness is captivating from the outset, even the sign of an almost divine power, it is only when she begins to mourn her own loss that her image begins to have this additional effect, this political effect, such that the chorus now *begins to see* the law of the city as unjust. Such is the curious and subtle relation between the image and the law, or between the appar-ently distinct domains of beauty and justice. And such is also the link of transmission between her love for her brother and the power of her image over us.

Psychoanalysis and Art

Love and beauty—these are the two elements that concern us. And we may as well acknowledge the somewhat eccentric nature of the decision that would isolate these particular features, when there are grander and more cataclysmic things that might be discussed. In the technical vocabu-lary of tragedy, "love" and "beauty" are not the first or the most obvious words. To be sure, Lacan does not avoid the fateful, agonistic features of the play—the tyrannical fury of Creon, who pursues his enemy even after death, or the final lament of Antigone, who despite her unwavering com-mitment knows very well what she will have to sacrifice. The grand and more obviously tragic themes are not absent, then, but it should strike us as somewhat unorthodox that Lacan allows these two features to have such organizing force, in relation to the other components of the tragedy—particularly in relation to the historically canonized debate between the two great ethical principles (family and state, *dike* and *nomos*) that have organized the reception of the play.

We may therefore be justified in suspecting that the choice of these elements—whatever light they may shed on tragedy—has a close connection to Lacan's own thinking, at this particular moment in his work, about matters internal to psychoanalytic theory. If he turns to *Antigone* in order to speak (somewhat perversely, it might be said) of love and beauty, we should be prepared to understand this choice at least in part from within the development of Lacan's own thought. From this standpoint, we may venture the following explanation: problems have arisen in the theory of psychoanalysis, and these somewhat unexpected features of *Antigone* are offered as a step forward. If this is so, it should be possible to show precisely what these problems are, and thereby grasp more clearly the reasons for Lacan's defiantly eccentric treatment of the play. At the same time, however, if his remarks have a legitimate bearing on tragedy itself, it should also be possible to show how these features (whatever they may mean for psychoanalysis) also contribute to the classical treatment of tragedy as an aesthetic phenomenon. The proof that Lacan's reading *also* aims to engage the text at this literary and philosophical level can be found in his discussion of other commentators—Goethe and Bernfeld, to be sure, but above all Aristotle, Kant, and Hegel, his rivals not (or not only) in terms of what they may teach us about psychoanalysis, but in terms of their contribution to the history of aesthetics.

Love and beauty can thus open to a double analysis. To put the point somewhat schematically, we may say that Lacan's treatment of the beautiful (the image of Antigone, *l'éclat d'Antigone*) is both a revision of the theory of the imaginary (a treatment of the image that will eventually—four years later, in *Seminar XI*—culminate in the concept of the gaze, which is no longer a purely imaginary phenomenon), and also a mediation on aesthetics, and more precisely, on Kant's treatment of the beautiful in *The Critique of Judgment* and Aristotle's discussion of catharsis in the *Poetics* (an experience in which pleasure and pain are mixed, and which, for Lacan, is primarily grounded in the sublimely veiled image of Antigone). And as for love (the nodal point of Antigone's relation to her brother), it is likewise approached by Lacan both as a development within psychoanalysis and, more precisely, as a new account of the "object relation" (the corpse of Polyneices, which Antigone devotedly covers with a veil of dust), and also as a contribution to the theory of tragedy. In particular, it offers a reflection on the status of the tragic hero and on the "law"—or perhaps the blindness, delusion, or recklessness (*ate*)—that governs her heroic action (and it is here that Lacan's engagement with Hegel takes on particular importance).

Our diagram can thus be elaborated further. Suspending for a moment the psychoanalytic axis of the argument (the imaginary, the gaze, and the libidinal relation to the object), let us focus only on the link between Lacan's account and the philosophical tradition (on the one hand, Aristotle and Kant, on the other hand, Hegel, and the laws that orient the hero in relation to the family and the state):

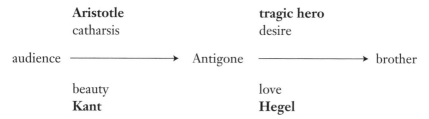

The difficulty with such a linkage between Aristotle and Kant will not be lost on readers. Lacan seems to yoke together two incompatible views, not only combining "ancient" and "modern" aesthetics (a historical question that dominates this seminar), but also forcing together a passive and contemplative theory of "rest" and "disinterestedness," organized around the "pure form" of the image (Kant), with a more active and affective theory of "emotion," in which the passions of the soul are mobilized (Aristotle). The difficulty is clear: our relation to the figure of Antigone is at once "cathartic" and "disinterested."

Furthermore, in a second contradiction (and we now factor in the psychoanalytic axis of the argument), this peculiar, Kanto-Aristotelian "experience" of the audience—apparently unique to the aesthetic domain—would at the same time have a bearing on the psychoanalytic experience, since the kind of emotion or affect that is proper to psychoanalysis, the engagement of desire that it (like art) entails, is not like the emotion one feels in everyday life, but occurs within a horizon of deliberate artifice, a specific and highly controlled discursive operation. In analysis, emotion is not engaged at the level of immediate experience, but (like the mythical material presented in tragic drama) is remembered, repeated, and worked over again, in a deliberate labor of symbolization (*Durcharbeiten*). Like tragedy, the analytic setting presents us not with the unfolding of a real event, but with a representation of some kind, a repeated or reduplicated experience, recalled from ancient times and staged or mediated by language. Like artistic representation, the analytic experience is in fact a genre, a discursive form whose setting is governed by a series of highly determined (though performatively malleable) rules and techniques—a form whose *Poetics* one might almost write. The twin concepts of the beautiful and catharsis, specifically confined by the philosophers to the region of art—since tragedy requires its own treatise, distinct from the *Ethics* and *Metaphysics*, just as the "reflective" judgment of taste cannot be confused with the "determinate" judgments of pure and practical reason—would thus isolate a strictly "aesthetic" domain, which nevertheless, without losing its specificity, and indeed precisely by maintaining it, also has a bearing on the domain of psychoanalysis and the uniquely analytic experience. Thus, in addition to the peculiar yoking of Aristotle and Kant, we are faced with a curious intersection between aesthetic and analytic experience, both being defined as distinct from moral and cognitive experience, as well as from the immediate experience of reality. It is this protracted encounter with tragedy, then, that gives Lacan the means to rethink both affect and the imaginary, and it is this conceptual trajectory that will lead to the concept of the gaze and allow him to develop the question of affect through a complex account of the relation between desire and *jouissance*. With the factors in mind, we might add to our diagram as follows:

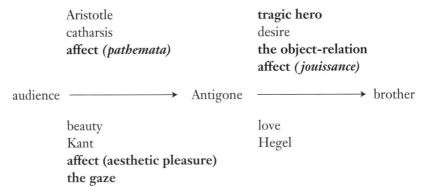

Again, these developments are more than we can outline in such a brief account (and clearly the question of affect proliferates in this reading, since it is by no means identical in each instance), but even these superficial remarks should allow us to grasp in a general way both what Lacan claims to contribute to the analysis of tragedy and what tragedy contributes to the development of Lacanian theory.

We have sketched the outlines of a conjunction between aesthetics and psychoanalysis, around the concepts of beauty and catharsis. The problematic is clearly enormous, involving as it does both Aristotle and Kant, and we can do no more than hint at its basic features here. But the direction for further work is at least indicated, according to our schema, as follows. (1) With respect to the beautiful image of Antigone, two lines of thought would be necessary: (a) one that would explore Lacan's introduction of sublime features into the concept of the beautiful (in direct violation of Kant's third *Critique*), and (b) another that would explore the transformation of the imaginary and its sudden relation not only to the law (the symbolic order), but also to a certain "blinding" or "divine" or "invisible" dimension, an enigmatic center that Lacan develops under the heading of the "Thing," that unsymbolizable and terrifying fragment of the real that Antigone's image somehow contains (as the body of Socrates will be said to contain the *agalma* in Lacan's seminar of the very next year, in his reading of Plato's *Symposium*). (2) With respect to the problem of catharsis, two directions could also be taken: (a) one that would develop the meaning of "affect" in tragedy (which is neither a medical purging nor a quasi-religious purgation and that leads Lacan into a lengthy discussion of Dionysian music [244–46], in which he distinguishes the "frenzy" of musical excitement from the kind of emotion involved in "pity" and "fear," the former generating "enthusiasts" [*enthousiastikoi*], and thereby recalling Kant's equally concerted effort to purge aesthetic pleasure of all merely "impassioned" feeling), and (b) another that would develop the slowly emerging category of *jouissance* in the discourse of Lacanian psychoanalysis, an affective dimension of suffering that takes us beyond the pleasure principle ("What is this pleasure to which one returns after a crisis that occurs in another dimension, a crisis that sometimes threatens pleasure?"; SVII, 246). Without following these indications further, let us now turn to the question of love.

With Heidegger, against Hegel (Or, the Hero and the Ordinary Man)

We have said that these two elements—love and beauty—cannot be grasped, according to Lacan, in terms of the Hegelian reading in which two opposing principles or laws would be brought into conflict. At first glance, it is not clear how Lacan can sustain this claim. When Antigone defends her right to act on behalf of Polyneices, does she not speak of the "unwritten laws," which contradict the laws of the city? Is this not precisely an opposition of principles, an opposition between *dike* and *nomos*, divine and human law? And is not the image of Antigone the very index of her divinity? Is it not the *manifestation* of that higher law, a principle she incarnates for all to see? Nevertheless, Lacan refuses to situate these two issues at the level of the "concept." For him, it is not a question of two opposing laws or principles, and if he insists upon love and the image, it is precisely insofar as these two phenomena cannot be grasped at the level of the symbolic order, with its dyadic oppositions between you and me, good and evil, presence and absence, Fort and Da. For Antigone, this game of meaning is at an end. What remains is the stark truth: there is *just enough time* for her to do what she must do.

Since we have touched on the question of beauty and its peculiar relation to the functions of prohibition, shame, and the veil, let us consider love more closely. Antigone's love cannot be grasped in terms of opposing principles or laws. The asymmetry between love and law is explicit in Lacan's account: Creon is *punishing* Antigone, he is setting his will against hers. Creon is punishing Antigone—that's what he thinks—but she is not *being punished*. We are faced with a crucial asymmetry, and not a simple "opposition between antagonists": for Antigone, this is no struggle to the death, no rivalry between master and slave. These terms (like passivity and activity) cannot define the true relation between these characters, even if it expresses Creon's perspective (and in fact, Lacan will argue, following Freud, that "activity" and "passivity" only serve to *mask* the truth of sexual difference, providing it with an imaginary cover). Thus, Antigone is not being punished, but is already "beyond the law" in some sense, having already passed "over the line"; she is in that zone where nothing can touch her now, or make her hesitate for an instant.[20] The "moment of decision" has passed, for her. Thus, if Creon is engaged in a contest of wills, an agon that situates him clearly in the narcissistic register—and the threats to his ego are conspicuously displayed ("I won't be beaten by a woman," etc.)—it will take somewhat greater effort to capture the precise nature of Antigone's singular and sovereign position. But her supreme disengagement is evident: she does not resist Creon's will, but neither is she submissive. Neither obedient (like Ismene) nor defiant (as Creon believes), she is, we might say, "disinterested," and this disinterestedness shows in her face as beauty.[21] In Freudian language we can say that whereas Creon, the imaginary father, exercises his power in a display of phallic aggression (SVII, 249), she is neither the dutiful daughter nor the defiant, rebellious outlaw—the hysteric who seeks to demonstrate that the place of the master is empty. Antigone's desire is thus placed beyond imaginary rivalry, beyond the game of power that defines the action of the king and marks him as a narcissist who cannot perform his symbolic function ("I'll show them who's in charge," etc.). For her, all these imaginary games have lost their meaning: she simply does what has to be done, with the awesome indifference of one who sees the situation for what it is.

Let us look at the question of the hero more closely, in order to see what is at stake in Lacan's effort to detach the tragic hero from the circuit of Hegelian mastery. Lacan distinguishes Oedipus and Lear in just the way that we have distinguished Antigone and Creon. In each case the former has passed into a peculiar space between life and death, Oedipus being—at least in *Colonus* (the play Lacan focuses on)—the one who finally has assumed his destiny, "who goes so far as . . . true being-for-death" (SVII, 309), even if it leaves him nothing but "the true and indivisible disappearance that is his" (SVII, 310). In this moment, then, Oedipus is *no longer being punished*. If, at first, his blinding and exile appear to be the punishment that would properly follow his crime, balancing his transgression with a correct measure of lawful retribution, we must recognize that in *Colonus* Oedipus himself no longer sees things this way. However it may seem to the chorus or the spectators (or to moralizing readers who wish to find some lesson of justice in the text), Oedipus himself has now passed into a zone that is no longer defined by punishment: "Entry into that zone for him is constituted as a renunciation of goods and of power that is supposed to be a punishment, but is not, in fact, one" (SVII, 310). This is why, for Lacan, the text of *Oedipus at Colonus* is so important (see SVII, 272 and 285), dwelling as it does on the long unfolding of this peculiar moment, this interval of the *Augenblick*, this moment "between two deaths," when Oedipus is symbolically dead, but without having mortally expired. In *Oedipus the King*, the hero is still dominated by the desire for truth; he is still the detective, the figure aspiring to know, in whom philosophers find their prototype. But something else emerges during the time that Antigone leads him by the hand toward his sacred place of rest, a time that is no longer governed by the distribution of goods, or the promised equilibrium of truth and justice. In this space, there is *just enough time* for a few things: above all, for words to mark the great act of passage into this zone that has just taken place. Before death, before the passage into the tomb, there is just enough time to memorialize this step that takes him from the calculated order of punishment and retribution to the zone between two deaths. It is that space and that time, attained by Oedipus at the very end, which Antigone occupies from the very outset of the play, without hesitation, in a stunning assumption of her fate: "Have you heard, dear sister, what fate comes down to us now from our unfortunate father?" That zone, she says in effect, is now ours to inhabit if we dare.

As for Lear, this passage beyond "the time of the king" (in Derrida's phrase) is too narrow for him to navigate: he remains trapped in the order of goods, counting the number of his retainers, a "tragic figure" in the peculiar sense that—like Hamlet, perhaps—he is unable to rise to the height of the tragic hero, which means unable to act, unable to accomplish any exploit. "Hamlet is by no means a drama of the importance of thought in relation to action. . . . I don't believe that the drama of Hamlet is to be found in such a divergence between action and thought nor in the problem of the extinction of his desire. I tried to show that Hamlet's strange apathy belongs *to the sphere of action itself*" (SVII, 251, my emphasis). Like Lear's, Hamlet's action falls short of properly tragic action, having been captured in a prolonged moment of hesitation that Antigone surpasses from the outset. And as with Antigone, so also with Hamlet the question of "action" is understood in terms of a certain relation to the father. If Hamlet's trait is "apathy," Lacan says, "we will find its origin in a relationship to the mother's desire and to the father's knowledge of his own death" (SVII, 251). This is why we must understand Antigone's fate, and the atrocity of her desire, in terms of her assumption of what comes to her from her father, and indeed from her mother—her desire being "her own" (*eigentlich*) precisely through this relation to the desire of the Other. The act, and even what we might call the "freedom" to act, which comes in a "moment of decision," is thus configured for the subject (Antigone or Hamlet, Oedipus or Lear), not as an isolated, psychological capacity of "subjectivity," but in terms of a peculiar "fate"—the atrocity of a bond linking the subject to the desire of the Other. Such is the difference between the act and its suspension, between the *Augenblick* that passes through anxiety, and the time of hesitation that turns away in fear. Thus, following his remarks about Oedipus's final moment in Colonus, in which (like Antigone) he is no longer attached to the demands of crime and punishment, Lacan writes: "I showed you the reverse and derisory side of this topology . . . in connection with poor Lear, who doesn't understand a thing and who makes the ocean and the earth echo because he tried to enter the same region in a salutary way with everyone agreeing. He appears in the end as still not having understood a thing and holding dead in his arms the object of his love, who is, of course, misrecognized by him" (SVII, 310). Such is also the difference between Antigone, who follows her father in this respect, and Creon, who shares with Lear the stubborn expectation that he can measure the injustice of the world, and who likewise sacrifices love to this demand.

This is the difference between the "hero" and the "ordinary man," discussed by Freud in *Group Psychology*. Something opens up here about the status of the "subject" as such, in these remarks about the "tragic hero"—the "truly" tragic hero as contrasted with the subject who "tragically" falls short of this position. In order to clarify this final point concerning the status of the tragic hero, let us take as our guide David Grene, whose introductory remarks to a translation of *Antigone* commonly used for teaching undergraduates will help to focus these questions, above all, the simple question: Who is the hero of the tragedy? The answer to this question is obviously "Antigone," but this has not kept certain commentators from asserting that Creon is the tragic hero of the play. In his introduction, Grene tells us confidently that *Antigone* contains all the elements of a classic Greek tragedy, such as recognition, *peripeteia*, *hubris*, *hamartia*, and so on.[22] Like *Oedipus the King*, he says, *Antigone* is a play about a great and noble king who makes a bad decision, who blindly and in stubborn self-assurance goes beyond the proper limits of human judgment, with the best intentions, only to find that he has unwittingly committed a terrible crime. The hero of Sophocles' play is therefore obviously Creon: it is Creon who plays the noble leader of the state, Creon who makes a bad decision, Creon whose pride leads him to assert this position with inflexible rigidity, Creon who suffers a reversal of fortune, Creon who undergoes *anagnorisis* and comes to recognize his mistake, and so on. The evidence is so compelling that one wonders why Sophocles was foolish enough to name the play *Antigone*. Obviously it should have been called *Creon*.

My first reaction to Grene's remarks was to ask: "How could anyone be so blind?" It is obviously Antigone who fascinates us, who compels our attention and demands an explanation. Creon is a functionary, a bureaucrat, a somewhat tedious and boorish administrator whose life requires almost no attention. Antigone is obviously the heroine. Taking his model from *Oedipus the king* and applying it in a strictly Aristotelian fashion, Grene draws a line straight from Oedipus to Creon—two kings who come to ruin on the basis of their own actions. And yet, Sophocles makes it perfectly clear that the line must be drawn from Oedipus to Antigone and that the fate of Oedipus is handed to Antigone, passing from father to daughter.

Such was the analogy Freud used to characterize the passing of psychoanalysis to his daughter Anna. Yet we should not dismiss Grene's remarks too quickly, even if they clearly amount to a mistake. We should perhaps ask why Sophocles has written this play in such a way that Creon can appear to play this role. If so many features usually attributed to the tragic hero are easily associated with Creon, this does not mean that Creon is the hero, but it does mean that we must ask why Sophocles has put things together in this manner. It is as if Creon functioned as a kind of screen or a ruse, assuming a position that absorbs into itself some of the central features of the tragic hero, so that Antigone now stands out in a stark and radical singularity, shorn of all these features, and yet nevertheless able to function as the heroine.

The analytical genius of Sophocles—the manner in which the history of tragedy is being comprehended in this play—is unmistakable: with Creon as a semblance, a calculated assemblage of traditional features, Antigone now captures the essence of the hero, its purest distillation, unencumbered by the traits and attributes that normally accompany this figure. We are asked to consider this, because it is a striking fact that Antigone goes through no change of heart. She comes to no recognition, undergoes no change of fortune, and exhibits no blindness, but only a severe and lucid clarity about what she has to do. She is stubborn, perhaps, or, rather, persistent, but this persistence is not the rigid fixity of Creon's inflexible edict, or the dogmatic self-assurance that Oedipus shares with Creon. It is, rather, the persistence of a desire that she simply cannot yield. Lacan points all this out. Consider pity and fear, for example. Goethe, he says, took the peculiar position of seeing pity and fear "in the action itself" and not in the audience. This contradicts Aristotle and displays a certain perversity on Goethe's part, but it at least leads us to notice something about the subjective positions of Creon and Antigone. "At first glance," Lacan says, "of the two protagonists, Creon and Antigone, neither one seems to feel fear or pity" (SVII, 258). But this is only at first glance. Lacan continues: "at least one of the protagonists *right through to the end* feels neither fear nor pity, and that is Antigone. That is why, among other things, she is the real hero. Creon, on the other hand, is moved by fear *towards the end*" (SVII, 258, my emphasis). Lacan thus sees that Sophocles presents us with a question as to who is "the real hero," and he distinguishes Creon's fear, his personal concern—what we might call his *concern for himself*, his *care for himself*—from Antigone's terrible indifference, her detachment from pity and fear, her almost inhuman resoluteness. It is this resoluteness that makes her the true heroine. It is the same with *hamartia*: *hamartia* (blindness) is usually attached to the hero of tragedy; in Oedipus, for example, blindness, or ignorance, or some error of judgment makes him unaware of what he is doing and thereby also makes possible *anagnorisis*, the moment of recognition in which things are suddenly made clear. Here again *Antigone* is unique. "I would not have any difficulty finding *hamartia* in others of Sophocles' tragedies; it exists, it is affirmed. . . . [In *Antigone*, however,] *hamartia* does not appear at the level of the true hero, but at the level of Creon" (SVII, 259). It is Creon who is blind, who comes to a recognition, who is punished by the gods and who fears for himself, revealing to us a certain affective state, a recognizable human emotion. But all these things cannot grasp the essence of the tragic hero, which is revealed by Antigone alone. There is thus a kind of purification in this text, a peculiar work of separation in which many of the features or traits that normally go on the side of the hero are passed off onto a surrogate, a substitute who takes on these attributes, as if to demonstrate a difference between essence and attribute, true power and the *semblance* of power. One can therefore understand how Grene might take the bait, and conclude that Creon is the hero of the play. Sophocles has prepared this trap, this veil of appearances, for those who cannot see the essence of the tragedy, which is captured by Antigone alone.

If Creon is thus, despite this semblance of heroic traits, a bureaucrat, a functionary, an exemplar of *das Mann*, what then really "constitutes the difference between an ordinary man and a hero" (SVII, 321)? This difference "is more mysterious than one might think." "For the ordinary man the betrayal that almost always occurs sends him back to the service of goods." This is what happens to Ismene, and this is what Creon supports from the outset: a rule of the city according to a good that would extend its rule over everything—going beyond the limit, to rule even over death. The first choral ode is unmistakable on this point. Man is the most awesome creature, the most wondrous of all the many wondrous things. He rules over the earth and the sea, with the plow and the ship, and with his halter he rules over the horse and the bull, a master of cunning, with the singular power of speech, and the invention of civil society. And yet, he has found no cure for death, no way out, no way to flee from death. This is what Creon seems not to understand—precisely what is most wonderful, most terrible, and awesome—the very essence of being human. The chorus thus emphasizes the remarkable cleverness of man, but also the limit of finitude, and the peculiarly "aporetic" character of the human relation to death. According to the chorus (first aporia), the human being is *pantaporos aporos*, having many ways open to him and yet having no exit, no way out. *Poros* means way. As Heidegger says, commenting on these lines.

> *poros* means: passage through . . . transition to . . . path. Everywhere man makes
> himself a path; he ventures into all realms of the essent, of the overpowering
> power, and in so doing, he is flung out of all paths. Herein is disclosed the
> entire strangeness of this strangest of all creatures: not only that he tries the
> essent in the whole of its strangeness, not only that in so doing he *is* a violent
> one striving beyond his familiar sphere. No, beyond all this he becomes the
> strangest of all beings because, without issue on all paths, he is cast out of every
> relation to the familiar and befallen by *ate*, ruin, catastrophe.[23]

This is what *pantaporos aporos* means. It is, as Lacan says, an aporia: having all ways open, and having no way out. This (and not any clever invention) is what makes man the most strange, *to deinotaton*, the most wondrous of all beings.

In the same choral ode, we are given a second and similar formulation, another aporia, which neither Lacan nor Heidegger comments on, namely, that man is *amechanon mechanoen*—having techniques for everything, having skills and cunning for every situation, and yet *amechanon*, finally without means. For *amechanon*, the dictionary gives "wanting." Man is wanting, without means or resources, helpless, incapable and awkward, at a loss and unable to proceed. Having many skills, man is finally without help or remedy, brought face to face with impossibility, with a limit that cannot be crossed, the end of all possibility. This is what makes man the most strange, *to deinotaton*, the most wondrous of all beings. It is this aporetic limit that Antigone confronts and that Creon and Ismene ignore, one because of his commitment to the rational, ordering power of the will, the other because she gives herself over to this will and abandons her responsibility.

We thus see more clearly what it means when Lacan insists upon the radical asymmetry between Creon and Antigone, refusing the Hegelian debate between two opposed but dialectically intertwined principles.

When it comes to the conflict between family and state, Lacan insists that Goethe sees farther than Hegel: "It is not, for him [for Goethe], a question of a right opposed to a right, but of a wrong opposed to—what? To something else that is represented by Antigone. Let me tell you right away that it isn't simply the defense of the sacred rights of the dead and of the family" (SVII, 254). "Not simply," he says, for certainly Antigone may *also* support these rights, and he even says that she does so. But this is not the essential point. What matters is how she is *able* to do so—what *force* or *power* allows her to persist in her position, underlying whatever law we may believe she upholds. "It is not simply the defense of the sacred rights of the dead and of the family," Lacan says. "Antigone is borne along by a passion" (SVII, 254), and not by a law opposed to another law.

It is therefore not a matter of opposing principles, because even if Antigone speaks of "unwritten laws," in contrast to the written proclamation (*kereugma)* of Creon, these two cannot be situated at the same level. One might claim that Antigone appeals to *dike* in opposition to Creon's *nomos*, but Lacan is emphatic: "She denies that it is Zeus who ordered her to do it. . . . She pointedly distinguishes herself from *Dike*. 'You've got all that mixed up,' she says in effect . . . 'I'm not concerned with all these gods below'" (SVII, 278). Why does Lacan insist upon this somewhat eccentric reading, refusing to identify Antigone with the divine law? It is because Antigone cannot be understood if one regards her as *following* the law. She does not oppose one law to another, but is borne along by something that is *before the law as such*. What is *agrapta*, unwritten, is what cannot be placed at the level of any law. "The laws of the gods . . . are said to be *agrapta*," Lacan says. "Involved here is an invocation of something that is, in effect, of the order of law, but which is not developed in any signifying chain or in anything else" (SVII, 278). Like the beauty of Antigone, which is likewise "of the order of law," insofar as it has the power to restrain and even prohibit, but cannot be inscribed at the level of the concept or written in a general, transmissible form, so also Antigone's love cannot simply be placed in opposition to the law or proclamation asserted by Creon, as one force opposed to another. Her attachment to her brother thus follows an "unwritten law" in the sense that it is before the law as such, at the origin of the law—not in the sense of having chronological priority, but in the sense that the law itself harbors within it an origin that it cannot codify and distribute, an origin that can always be forgotten or betrayed, an aporetic origin that Antigone protects and that Creon cannot see.

   This is what binds Antigone to her brother, in a singular relation to the object of love, a bond that cannot be articulated at the level of the signifying chain or inscribed within the principle of pleasure—a bond so enigmatic that even when we seek to make it intelligible by taking refuge in the explanation that she indeed follows "another law," we are forced to acknowledge the fragility of the line that separates the ethical and pathological faces of her action—the enigmatic link that binds her unmistakably ethical decision, what one can only call her responsibility, to its compulsive, ferocious, destructive, and inhuman aspect—as if this other "law" to which she appeals were no longer a matter of the common world, but detached itself from the symbolic domain of communicable universality. Early in the seminar, in a chapter called "On the Moral Law," we find the following formulation: "*das Ding* . . . is the very correlative of the law of speech in its most primitive point of origin, and in the sense that this *Ding* was there from the beginning, that it was the first thing that separated itself from everything the subject began to name and articulate" (SVII, 83). This is why, two hundred pages later, Lacan says that we are concerned with "an invocation of something that is, in effect, *of the order of law, but which is not developed in any signifying chain*" (SVII, 278, my emphasis). Antigone's relation to her brother is thus *before* the law, not in the sense of a chronological priority, as something that would predate the law and exist autonomously, but in the sense that the law itself carries within it an origin that it shelters, but that it cannot articulate. Unspeakable, unwritten, and in excess of any justification she can give, any rendering of reason she may offer (and she makes these offerings too), the love that ties her to her brother is thus not chronologically prior to the law, but is on the contrary "of the order of law" and yet beyond the reach of the signifier.

   We are thus brought up against the (libidinal) relation to the object, the corpse of Polyneices, which commands Antigone beyond all commandment, beyond the "father's no," which Creon incarnates, and she protects this relation beyond all writing, all giving of accounts, in a singular attachment of love. If we have stressed, in passing, Antigone's enigmatic relation to time, it may now be somewhat clearer through the time of this "origin," insofar as this origin is not chronologically prior, because, being "of the order of law," it is only brought into being *through* the operation of the signifier, which nevertheless (as Creon shows) cannot grasp it by means of legislation.[24] The "unwritten law" is thus harbored within the law itself, "from the beginning," more like a Thing than a signifier, "the first thing that separated itself from everything the subject began to name

and articulate" (SVII, 83). Such is the unwritten law that marks her relation to Polyneices apart from any signifying chain. "Is the Law the
Thing?" Lacan asks. "Certainly not. Yet I can only know of the Thing by
means of the Law . . . for without the Law the Thing is dead" (SVII, 83).
Thus, if she claims responsibility for her brother beyond everything that
he has done, beyond all the qualities that can be attributed to him, beyond
the good or evil that he may have done, if she insists upon the necessity of
the act of burial simply as a memorial of his being, it is for reasons that
come *before what can be written* about him, but that paradoxically emerge
only *through the operation of the name*, which would thus designate without
predicating, or indicate without signifying, without linking the being of
the nominated to any differential or systemic chain: "Antigone," Lacan
says:

> invokes no other right than that one . . . the ineffaceable character of what
> is—ineffaceable, that is, from the moment when the emergent signifier freezes
> it like a fixed object in spite of the flood of possible transformations. . . . That
> purity, that separation of being from the characteristics of the historical drama
> he has lived through, is precisely the limit or the *ex nihilo* to which Antigone is
> attached. It is nothing more that the break that the very presence of language
> inaugurates in the life of man. (SVII, 279)

It is precisely the relation between the law of the city and this mysterious
origin, conspicuously ignored by Creon, but triumphantly exposed by
Antigone, that makes it possible for Sophocles to show us how Antigone's
singular commitment is able to have an unexpected effect on the world of
the chorus, overturning the entire order of political life.

On Power, Violence, and Speech

When it comes to Antigone's love, then, Lacan does not believe that the
essential point resides in a conflict between two laws or principles that
confront each other at the same level and lead to an opposition, dialectical
or otherwise. The essential point is, rather, Antigone's desire, her capacity
to persist in her desire, to remain responsible to the unwritten law of the
gods, which is the law of love. This is not a principle opposed to the state,
at the same level, or with the same claim to universality and social equilibrium. It is an earlier law, whose claims are made before the law, before
any written laws. Her persistence on this point not only makes her the

heroine, in contrast to Creon, who is just an ordinary man in this respect, but also allows her to isolate for us the very essence of being human, the most fateful and wondrous aporia of being human. Let us say, following Heidegger, that by persisting in her desire, she "becomes the strangest of all beings because, without issue on all paths," with no way out, "[s]he is cast out of every relation to the familiar and befallen by *ate*, ruin, catastrophe."[25] Here again, the relation to the father would seem to play an especially important role. For Antigone's *force* does not lie at the same level as the force of law, the force that Creon puts to work when he leaves Polyneices to decay like an animal, threatening to punish anyone who transgresses his edict. Antigone's power is not a counterforce at this same level. She is not defiant. She has no wish to contradict the law; she simply does what she must do. In Lacanian terms, we can say that she has no interest in competing with the father, no interest in any struggle with the imaginary father. Unlike her sister, she is indifferent to Creon's authority, neither defiant nor submissive. Her father is dead, and she has absolutely no interest in Creon; she is beyond the imaginary father.

In short, there is nothing rebellious about her decision, whatever Creon may think. Her choice comes from another place altogether. She does not wish to be subversive, she has no interest in opposing Creon, or entering into any agon with any rival (as Hegel might lead us to suppose). In this, Heidegger says, she brings to light the essential *power* of being human.[26] This *power* is not a *kraft*, like the craft of statesmanship, a *force* to be situated at the level of her abilities—her skill or technique, her knowledge or her will. Human cleverness has many virtues, it gives us many ways to go, but we know that all these ways are empty, they come to nothing in the face of death. "Man is *to deinotaton*," Heidegger says, "the strangest of the strange."[27] "On the one hand, *deinon* means the terrible," but "on the other hand *deinon* means *the powerful* in the sense of one who uses power, who not only disposes of power [*Gewalt*] but is *violent* [*gewalttätig*] insofar as the use of power is the basic trait not only of his action but also of his being-there. *Here we use the word violence in an essential sense* extending beyond the common usage of the word, as mere arbitrary brutality."[28] Her power is thus not opposed to the power of Creon. It is a more fundamental phenomenon, a law before the law, which is related to Creon's power not as a counterforce, but in the sense that Antigone's action alone allows us to see Creon's law for what it is, namely an "arbitrary brutality." She acts, to be sure, but this action cannot be understood at the level of Creon's edict, which is a mere "pronouncement"—a "proclamation" *kereugma* that has the police to back it up, but that does not really think the essence of action deeply enough.

In the case of Antigone, Heidegger says, "the use of power is the basic trait *not only of [her] action but also of [her] being-there.*"[29] With this action, grounded in her desire, the essence of human action is thought more deeply: it is not a question of skill or ability, or any application of the rational will, but something that shows the essence of her being there, her *Dasein* (just as Polyneices himself lays claim upon Antigone, according to Lacan, not for his actions, for what he has done, or for anything that can be written about him, but simply as a memorial of his being). Her act is dedicated to this alone, and it separates her action from the acts and pronouncements of Creon, which are those of an ordinary man, enforced by the police, but without the relation to power that we find in Antigone's action. This power, Heidegger says, "*can also be called violence,*" but only if we understand this word in a way that goes beyond arbitrary brutality. "Here we use the word violence in an essential sense."

Finally, let us recall that *hubris*, the Greek word that is so often translated as "pride" or even "sin," has nothing to do with these Christian notions. *Hubris* means violence. *Hubrizdo* means to commit an act of violence, but in a special sense, which belongs not to the sphere of human will, or to the exercise of brutality, but to the singular and more essential character of the tragic hero as such. This would complete the Sophoclean purification: Creon has fear, he makes a mistaken judgment and even comes to a certain recognition, but Antigone alone has this *hubris*, this demonic and awesome power, which has absolutely nothing to do with defiance, but which captures the essential strangeness of being human. "Man is *deinon*," Heidegger says, "first because he remains exposed within this overpowering power, because by his essence he belongs to being. But at the same time man is *deinon* because he is the violent one in the sense designated above. (He gathers the power and brings it to manifestness.)"[30] It is perhaps this manifestness that Lacan seeks to capture through his account of the beauty of Antigone.

At the end of *Seminar VII*, some weeks after he has finished the discussion of Antigone, in the concluding chapter of the seminar, Lacan returns to the question of the hero. If Antigone is the true heroine, even or especially in having been shorn of all the usual attributes, what really distinguishes her as such? According to Lacan, Creon, in his fear and his stubbornness, in his sense of being right and knowing the law, is not a hero but an ordinary man. "His language," Lacan says, "is in perfect conformity with what Kant calls . . . the language of practical reason" (SVII, 259). He wants "to promote the good of all" (SVII, 259), and this is all he really understands. "His error of judgment," Lacan says, "is to want to promote the good of all," and "to promote the good of all as *the law without limit*" (my emphasis). To say that one cannot at one and the same time honor those who protect the state and those who try to subvert it is to put forth a maxim that has a strictly Kantian form: "his refusal to allow a sepulcher for Polyneices" is grounded in "a maxim that can be given as a rule of reason with a universal validity" (SVII, 259). It doesn't matter what it costs, and the just ruler cannot think of who the person in question is or what the consequences will be: one simply has to follow the law, which is on the side of what is good. That is Creon's position, and he is not the hero of the tragedy. Consequently, Lacan says, if we recall "the ethical progression that, from Aristotle to Kant, leads us to make clear the identity of law and reason, doesn't the spectacle of tragedy reveal to us in anticipation the first objection?" (SVII, 259). Before the law, before the law of philosophy, before the entire historical project that leads from Aristotle through modernity, the ancient poet would already ("in anticipation") have brought to light the first objection. Thus, it is not that Antigone represents another conflicting maxim, a second moral law that cannot be harmonized with the first, as if it were a question of two competing principles. Antigone may indeed defend the law of the gods, and even explain law that she follows. But we cannot grasp this "law" that binds her to her object at the level of universality, which is the level Creon occupies. Rather, we must see that Creon has crossed a limit, he has gone beyond the limit that is proper for man, and it is this limit that Antigone defends ("he has crossed that famous limit," and "Antigone defends it"; SVII, 259). Lacan refers us again to Hamlet at this point, saying that Hamlet's reason for hesitating, when he has the opportunity to kill Claudius, has nothing to do with the famous indecision that has been attributed to him. It is not that Hamlet cannot make up his mind; it is, rather, that killing Claudius is not enough for him. He wants Claudius to suffer an eternity of hell. Like Creon in relation to his enemy, Hamlet pursues Claudius beyond life, beyond the world of the living, and wants to cheat death, to insure somehow that Claudius will not rest in peace, that he will not have confessed his sins, that he will not die with a clear conscience, so that he will continue to suffer even after he has been killed. Hamlet pursues his enemy beyond death, and this is why he cannot act (SVII, 251). He crosses the limit of what is right for humans, and this is what Creon does, in a very different way, in refusing to bury Polyneices. He goes beyond the limit of what is right, and it is this limit that Antigone defends.

We thus see more clearly the reasons for Lacan's refusal to place Antigone's desire within the framework of the Hegelian account, in dialectical opposition to Creon. For all his pride, his blindness, and his eventual recognition, Creon is an ordinary man and not a hero—a tyrannical man, to be sure, but not the hero of tragedy. This is the question that dominates the conclusion of the seminar. "Last time," Lacan says: "I opposed the hero to the ordinary man, and someone was upset by that. I do not distinguish between them as if they were two different human species. In each of us the path of the hero is traced, and it is precisely as an ordinary man that *one follows it to the end*" (SVII, 321, my emphasis). A path would therefore lead from the ordinary man to the hero, for they are not two different species. It is rather a matter of "following the path to the end." The motif is repeated by Lacan, with an insistence that is marked, but that never receives full elaboration: "We find ourselves brought back to following the path to the end" (SVII, 176). It is not impossible, however, to find the reason behind this repeated motif: it is quoted from a text by Freud that Lacan surely had by his side, the text *Group Psychology*, more precisely, the appendix on the artist, in which Freud remarks the peculiar way in which the artist, through the production of the aesthetic work, is not simply carried away from reality by his or her imagination, but is able to "find his way back" to reality—by which Freud means the human reality of the group and the community.

Transmission, translation: it is just this "finding her way back" that Antigone accomplishes *in the end*, in the "just enough time" that remains for her to speak, reaching out in lamentation before she enters the silent tomb, transforming the singular and unspeakable bond that ties her to her brother and handing it over in a moment of memorialization. So also the work of art communicates itself to others, and "the poet who had taken this step and had in this way set himself free from the group in his imagination, is nevertheless able . . . to find his way back to it in reality. For he goes and relates to the group his hero's deeds, which he himself has invented." The moment of decision, which casts the subject precipitously into the zone between two deaths, may take place in the instant of the *Augenblick*, the fragile time that exists between Oedipus's blinding and his death, a moment that opens at the limits of the human community, but it leaves *just enough time* for words to pass between Oedipus and his daughter, *just enough time* for Antigone—who has already made up her mind, and already reached her end—to say a few words to her sister and to turn the heads of the city elders. It is in this way, too, that the exploit is passed on from Antigone to us, in accordance with ancient wisdom—what spoke before the language of philosophy, telling us of the maxim among men that when an exploit has been accomplished, it must not remain hidden in silence. What it requires is the divine melody of praising verses.

CHAPTER 3

Emotion, Affect, Drive

I

In the opening sentence of "Mourning and Melancholia," Freud speaks of "the affect of mourning" (SE, 14:243). In the face of a death, the work of mourning brings with it a certain affective state. Accordingly, the word for mourning, *Trauer*, designates not only the activity of the mourner, but also the disposition or grief that accompanies it. *Trauer* is thus both the ritual activity (social or religious) that one undertakes in the face of a death and also the state of mind (mood, disposition, affective state—*Stimmung*, in Heidegger's vocabulary) that characterizes the one who mourns.

Freud notes that the position of *melancholia* should be distinguished from that of *mourning*. When the mourner withdraws from the world, unable for a time to continue with normal life, it is the loss of the object that causes suffering. The world has become suddenly poor. This is also true for the melancholic, for whom a beloved object has likewise been lost. But in the case of the melancholic, the loss of this object is intolerable and the object, instead of being altogether lost, is maintained within the subject, entombed within the ego, where it continues to live, with a life that brings suffering to the subject.

This suffering is different from what we find in the case of mourning. And we must therefore distinguish between the grief of the subject who mourns, a grief that I will call an emotion, for reasons that will become apparent, and the suffering of the ego in melancholia, which is perhaps something different from emotion. If Freud begins by speaking not simply of mourning, but of the "affect of mourning," it is perhaps because this affect will be a central clue to the difference that he finds in melancholia, where the ego suffers in a different way because the object remains alive within the ego. One consequence of this difference, for Freud, is that the ego is split in melancholia such that one part of the ego is deprived of the object of love in a way that is similar to mourning, while the other part of the ego, the part that has identified with the lost object, exhibits a series of distinctively melancholic conditions—conditions that Freud gathers together under the heading of self-reproach. "The patient represents his ego to us as worthless, incapable of any achievement and morally despicable. . . . He abases himself before everyone and commiserates with his own relatives for being connected with anyone so unworthy" (SE, 14:246). The melancholic exhibits "an extraordinary diminution in his self-regard, an impoverishment of his ego on a grand scale." This is the consequence of the internalization of the lost object, for Freud, who condenses the matter in a beautiful formulation: "In mourning it is the world that has become empty; in melancholia it is the ego itself" (SE, 14:246).

Now, most of the clinical literature on melancholia has taken up this feature of self-reproach, guilt, and even hatred, insofar as the splitting of the ego in melancholia allows the subject to hate in himself the object that has died and abandoned him. We have become familiar with this discussion in several contexts, perhaps most famously in discussions of the Holocaust, the AIDS pandemic, and other events that confront us with the problem of "survivor guilt." "The shadow of the object fell upon the ego," Freud says, "and the latter could henceforth be judged by a special agency as though it were an object, a forsaken object" (SE, 14:249). We know that this special agency is taken up elsewhere by Freud in his work on the ravages of the superego, which speaks in a voice that is not the voice of the subject, but that nevertheless commands the subject in an irrevocable and terrible way.[1] Most of the secondary literature, from Melanie Klein's work on love, guilt, and reparation to more recent work in trauma studies, has taken up this reference to guilt in the melancholic's relation to death. And one might think, from these discussions, that the affect of mourning—what I called the emotion of grief—is matched by an affect of melancholia, such as guilt or self-loathing or moral masochism. The recent turn in cultural studies to the problem of "emotion" might well follow the path of these commentaries, in which the terms *emotion* and *affect* are used interchangeably.[2] But perhaps mourning and melancholia are not situated at the same level, as two different emotional states, which we can call "grief" or "sorrow" on the one hand, and "guilt" or "self-reproach" on the other. Perhaps there is a more fundamental difference, one that obliges us to distinguish, not between two emotional states, but more fundamentally between *an emotion and an affect*.

To be sure, Freud did not make this distinction in his technical vocabulary, but one can see it emerge in his thinking, not only in this text, but across the entire course of his work. To put things in a somewhat formulaic way, we can say that affect and emotion are distinguished as a *charge of energy* is distinguished from an articulated and meaningful *relation to the other*. In Freud, particularly in the early theory of anxiety, this is expressed in the distinction between "accumulated tension" and "sexual desire," a distinction that is far more complex and murky than the commentaries have suggested.[3] But from this first approximation (in this case, a division between anxiety and desire), the issue is clear enough: in Lacan's terminology, it is a question of the border between the real and the symbolic. An affect presents us with a charge of *jouissance* and a dimension of bodily suffering that is quite distinct from an emotion, which entails, to be sure, a strong bodily dimension, but which maintains a symbolic link. It is precisely this link that is compromised in the case of melancholia where we find a symbolic rupture that leaves the subject vulnerable to the intrusion of a voice that forces the subject to expend his hatred on himself and to remain absent and withdrawn from the process of mourning (and all the sociality it entails), incapacitated by the *jouissance* of a symptom that we call self-reproach, in contrast to the mourner, who feels grief in connection with others who likewise grieve.[4]

We can take an additional step at this point, for the charge of *jouissance* that we see in the melancholic's self-castigation belongs to the register of the drive and sexuality, while the grief of the mourner belongs to the register of the ego and its pleasure and pain, and thus presents us with a very different form of suffering. Thus, when Lacan, speaking of the superego, says that "the voice of the Other should be considered an essential object," he means that the voice as an object of the drive is something peculiar, something that falls outside the order of speech and communal memory. The voice, then, cannot be reduced to the symbolic order, any more than the gaze can be reduced to the field of the imaginary (Y, 87). Contrary to appearance, the melancholic's relation to the voice is not a symbolic phenomenon, like the cry of mourning (in which even the most elemental wailing is understood as a form of speech or address), but is rather a matter of *jouissance* and the drive. This means that the self-reproach of the melancholic is not in fact an "emotion," properly speaking, but is rather what we must call an "affect," a charge of energy that signals the presence of the object, which Lacan calls the "object voice."

Freud himself points out that this is really a question about libido: in mourning, the subject's libido withdraws from the world, and the subject is for a time preoccupied with grief, given over to the labor of mourning, until the libido finds a way back to another object. In melancholia, Freud says, the libido does not simply withdraw, but rather is identified with the object and remains attached to that object, which is buried within the ego. It is *that portion of the libido*, Freud says, identified with the lost object, which is then able to turn on the ego with the vengeance of self-reproach. The voice that accuses and incriminates the subject, in this account, is nothing other than a discharge of libido, in contrast with the voice of the mourner, whose discourse and feeling of grief are a form of address to the other who is gone. How are we to understand the border that separates this dimension of affective petrification from the domain of emotional life, in which the relation to the other remains open?[5] What is the relation between the symbolic and the real of *jouissance*, and how might it lead us to distinguish between affect and emotion more clearly?

Let us note that this peculiar manifestation of the voice, understood as the mark of a rupture in the fabric of the symbolic order, also amounts to a retreat of the subject, a sort of fading, as Lacan suggests in *Television* when he notes that the "who" that is suddenly incarnated here, in this moment of melancholic capitulation, cannot be directly identified with the subject. On the contrary, the voice in melancholia poses a question ("Who speaks?"), and points to an internal differentiation, a geography of the subject that demands further elaboration, much as Freud did by suggesting that the ego is split in melancholia. In Lacan's words:

> The voice of the Other should be considered an essential object. . . . Its manifestations should be followed, as much in the realm of psychosis as at that extremity of normal functioning in the formation of the superego. . . . Here we can no longer elude the question: beyond he who speaks in the place of the Other, and who is the subject, what is it whose voice, each time he speaks, the subject takes? (T, 87)

In short, it is not only spectacular instances of psychotic delusion that reveal the ravaging function of the voice, as Freud revealed in his accounts of paranoia; the more familiar labyrinths of "normal functioning" also testify to the intrusion of the superego in its malicious and punishing form, and the collapse of the subject that ensues.

II

In order to clarify the status of the voice, not in relation to the usual rubric of paranoia, but in relation to the question of mourning, let us consider briefly the case of Hamlet. Hamlet cannot mourn. His famous incapacity to act and the long temporal suspension of his desire, the "madness" that dominates the play—feigned, to be sure, but also quite real—can be read as a failure of mourning, whereby Hamlet's status as a subject is compromised. But let us not conclude too quickly that this melancholic state is merely a personal characteristic, or a sign of his unique individual subjectivity. As Teresa Brennan insisted over many years, we should not be too quick to think of affect as a "personal" trait, confined to the autonomous ego. If Hamlet cannot mourn, this is not an internal psychological failure. It is the transmission of a parental structure: his mother, Gertrude, made no effort to symbolize the death of her husband, but took the funeral meats directly to the wedding ceremony, before they were even cold. His father, moreover, was struck down by poison—as Shakespeare carefully notes—before he was able to register any illness, or establish any relation to his own death (the very point that also prevents Hamlet from killing Claudius when the latter, by contrast, has just finished preparing his soul for the afterlife). As a result of this double breach in his relation to death, the father returns to haunt the memory of his son, to ask for a symbolization where none was given. "Remember me," says the ghost, and Hamlet's own subjectivity is all but wiped away:

> Remember thee!
> Yea, from the very table of my memory
> I'll wipe away all trivial and fond records
> All saws of books, all forms, all pressures past
> That youth and observation copied there
> *And thy commandment all alone shall live*
> *within the book and volume of my brain.* (1.5 772–78)

What are the consequences for Hamlet? According to Lacan, Hamlet abuses Ophelia, mistreats her, and proves unable to recognize her because the shadow of his father has fallen over him.[6] Love, and all the libidinal "relation to the object" that it entails, as we see in the case of Antigone, is compromised by a failure of mourning, a failure that will exact its toll. Hamlet's own ego, Lacan tells us, now contains the object, the paternal object that has not been properly buried, and as a result, his libidinal investment is withdrawn from the world—not for a publicly or commonly designated time in which mourning might take place, but withdrawn in accordance with another time, a period of suspended animation, filled with doubt, hesitation, and almost suicidal self-incrimination. At the limit of symbolic belonging, and filled with a *jouissance* that is not his own, suspended on the borders of the decision "to be or not to be," Hamlet is lost in melancholia. In melancholy, Freud says, the shadow of the object has fallen across the ego, and what this means is that the normal process of mourning, whereby the loss of the object is symbolized, fails to take place, and the lost object, in spite of its absence, remains alive, buried within the tomb of the ego itself, so that the libidinal movement to another object becomes impossible. Ophelia is abused, then, in connection with Hamlet's melancholy, and Lacan tells us that Ophelia herself is not herself, for Hamlet, and is no longer recognizable by him, but is only a figure for the mother, Gertrude, whose refusal or incapacity to mourn has made her an object of scorn and contempt, which finally overflows beyond Gertrude ("Frailty, thy name is woman"), displaced by Hamlet onto the innocent girl. Ophelia's destiny, and perhaps Hamlet's to some extent, already sketches the outline of Brennan's reading of a certain formation of "femininity," which is not only characterized by the reception of historical fall-out such as this—what Brennan thematizes as the "transmission of affect"—but which reaches its culmination in Ophelia's suicide, itself no longer intelligible, in this account, as a merely "personal" event.

If Lacan's reading of Hamlet is in essence a reading of the destiny of desire, however, what can we say about the unfolding of Hamlet's destiny, given this initial impasse? If the relation to the paternal object, abandoned and unwept, provokes a melancholic identification in which Hamlet's desire is compromised and he is struck by self-reproach, guilt, and the withdrawal of libido into the tomb of an ego that is no longer even his own, but rather the sacrificial tomb in which the object remains alive, then what can we say about Hamlet's destiny in the course of the drama? As Darian Leader has observed, Hamlet in the end finds it possible to love Ophelia again, and jumps into her grave with an agonized gesture, a genuine declaration of love that undoes the previous deceptive subterfuge and indirection of his earlier courtly demeanor, that contrived madness in which truth was only indirectly declared, and relations with others were swamped by paranoia and deceit. How is this later moment possible? How does Hamlet pass from his melancholic state to what we can only call an act of mourning? Recall that Laertes appears mourning his sister, grieving loudly and protesting her death. He declares his love, and Hamlet sees in the other a relation to the lost object that he cannot achieve by himself, but that he finds through his alter ego, who traces out for him the path of a libidinal investment that he could not attain by himself.[7]

We may believe today that mourning is a private event, a matter of personal sorrow that isolates each of us and that we must bear individually in silence, like all emotion, which would thus stand as the most intimate and individuated core of our experience, the least amenable to discourse, the least shared and communicable. Teresa Brennan has shown us a different path. Emotion, she argues, is always exchanged, as a bodily energy that exceeds the boundaries of the ego and indicates a primordial sociality that challenges the modern fantasy of the "autonomous ego." But if, as we have suggested, there is a difference between emotion and affect, if Freud claims that the status of the subject in mourning must be distinguished from the subject in melancholia, and if, indeed, Lacan's account leads us to distinguish between desire and *jouissance*, how might this distinction clarify or further the work that Brennan has left us?

For her, affect and emotion (since she makes no distinction between the two) are always social, primordially so, and cannot be adequately conceived as "personal" or "psychological" phenomena. Like Lacan, she insists on the relation between the interiority of psychic life and the institutional and discursive horizon in which it is formed. This is why, in *History after Lacan*, she argues—against the prevailing view at that time—that Lacan's theory of subject formation is not an isolated, structuralist, and therefore ahistorical theory (and structuralism was never ahistorical in this way), but is also a theory of history, and that, for Lacan, the contemporary experience of the ego is part of a broader theoretical and institutional development dating roughly from the seventeenth century, the scientific revolution, and the Enlightenment—what Jacques-Alain Miller, in the epigraph to Brennan's book, calls "the 'modern ego,' that is to say, the paranoic subject of scientific civilization . . . at the service of free enterprise." Her argument thus sets the analysis of Lacan in a broader theoretical and institutional horizon: she views the entire development of psychoanalysis as an emerging critique of the larger historical movement in which proper or normal subjectivity comes to be defined in terms of its capacity for individual, autonomous, self-conscious agency; and she argues that this model in turn must be understood against the background of scientific and economic rationality after the Renaissance. Brennan thereby opens important lines of communication between Lacan and other thinkers, where an oppositional reception had quite mistakenly separated Lacanian psychoanalysis from other historical, economic, and philosophical modes of thought (purportedly "historical" thinkers). In this way, Brennan forged several large and sweeping alliances between Lacan and other thinkers—particularly Marx, Heidegger, and feminist theorists—who in different ways had launched a similar critique of the "subject" of modernity, understood as an autonomous, productive subject of representation constructed on a masculine model of scientific rationality. That this model was a fantasy and did not provide an accurate account of our social and psychic life—that it was part of what she called "the ego's era," which concealed the primordially intersubjective dimension of our affective experience and obliged the outcast, the disenfranchised, and the unrecognized to bear the burden of hostility, aggression, or self-doubt that "proper" subjects could not tolerate within themselves—all this is part of the argument of *History after Lacan*, which claims that the modern ego could not have arisen without the institutional support of capital, class struggle, and private property. Without entering into the details of her argument, let us simply say here that she understands very well the profoundly intersubjective and even socioeconomic foundation of human affectivity, the contemporary forms of which she links, in *History after Lacan*, to the development of subjectivity in post-Enlightenment European thought. Since she was also one of the rare Marxist feminists to take psychoanalysis quite seriously, however, and since the details of Freudian thought were crucial to *The Interpretation of the Flesh*, let us pay our respects to the internal details of our psychoanalytic itinerary a little longer. Brennan did not distinguish between affect and emotion, and we are suggesting that such a distinction would have clarified the territory that she wished to explore.

III

We have said that the melancholic's self-castigation belongs to the register of the drive and sexuality, while the grief of the mourner belongs to the register of the ego and its pleasure and pain. In his text "The Instincts and Their Vicissitudes," written the same year as the text on mourning, Freud makes the same observation about the difference between the ego and the drive. Freud tells us, in effect, that an emotion is situated at the level of the ego and its relations to others, whereas the sexual instincts—*Triebe*, which Freud's English translation renders as "instincts," but which Lacanians translate as "drives"—have a different sort of object, which Karl Abraham calls a "partial object" and which Lacan develops in terms of the "object a."[8] When it comes to the instinct and its satisfaction, Freud says:

We might at a pinch say of an instinct that it "loves" the objects towards which it strives for purposes of satisfaction; but to say that an instinct "hates" an object strikes us as odd. Thus we become aware that the attitudes of love and hate cannot be made use of for the relations of instincts to their objects, but are reserved for the relations of the total ego to objects. (SE, 14:137)

What this means is that the emotions of love and hate can be situated at the level of the ego's relation to its objects (such as the other who is gone), but that the drive's relation to its object cannot really be described in terms of emotions like love and hate, which have a symbolically elaborated place. The energy of the drive and its peculiar "satisfaction" must therefore be distinguished from the "disposition" of the ego that we see in the emotions of love and hate.

One might object that Freud himself does not distinguish between affect and emotion, and in fact, at first glance, his vocabulary does not seem to support such a distinction. Indeed, he speaks of the "affect of mourning," where we are claiming that mourning entails "emotion," and that "affect," properly speaking, should be reserved for the distinctive form of suffering that we find in melancholia. Moreover, we have just spoken of the "guilt" of the melancholic, which (like the "grief" of the mourner) must surely be regarded as an emotion in some sense. No doubt. It is clear that emotion may arise in both mourning and melancholia, and it cannot be a matter of simply separating two domains into dyadic and opposite camps (emotion and affect, language and the body, mourning and melancholia—so many familiar tropes of tedious opposition). The relation between the symbolic and the real is not as simple as this. The point is not to claim, therefore, that melancholia has no relation to emotion, or even (to take the opposite view) that there is no difference between mourning and melancholia, and that mourning is already the impossibility of mourning, and is already melancholic in its essence. The point is rather to recognize the distinctive position of the subject in each case and the intricacy of the morphology Freud points to—a matter that requires both philosophical and clinical precision. Indeed, if Freud seems at first glance to use a looser vocabulary, without demanding a division between affect and emotion, as though "grief" and "guilt" were both at the same level, such that mourning and melancholia were both "emotional states," a closer look complicates the matter. When Freud notes that the ego is distinctively split in melancholia, he observes not only that *the ego feels guilt* (and that we are indeed dealing with an emotional register in some degree), but also that *some other agency takes satisfaction* in punishing the ego, depriving it of any access to life—as if the melancholic were buried in a tomb. Freud's elaboration of this point suggests that we are faced here again with an important difference, such that, while the ego is mortified with *a feeling* of guilt, this other agency appears under the heading of "satisfaction," which is to say, as a *discharge of energy*, the punishing discharge of the superego, which—from another scene or another place—takes its own satisfaction in the ego's suffering. This is what Freud means by claiming that there is a difference between the pleasure and pain of the ego, and the sexual satis- faction of the drive. Here again, therefore, the drive entails a particular mode of enjoyment (*jouissance*), an affective discharge that lies outside the sphere of the ego, which for its part is taken up with the "emotions" of guilt or self-castigation. This dimension of obscure and punishing *jouis- sance*, in which the position of the subject is compromised, is what distin- guishes the "guilt" of the melancholic from the "grief" of the subject who mourns. *Trauer*, or "grief," as the emotion that characterizes mourning, is thus the alternative to the affective distribution of melancholia, with its paralyzing force, which we sometimes call "guilt" or "self-hatred," but which comes closer to the satisfaction of the drive.

If I begin by suggesting that the difference between mourning and mel- ancholia can be understood more clearly if we distinguish between emo- tion and affect, then, and if I suggest that the charge of *jouissance* that Freud sees in the melancholic's self-reproach must be understood as an affect and distinguished from the emotions of love and hate that character- ize the mourner's relation to the lost object, this is partly because it raises a clinical question: How do we pass from melancholia to mourning? How is the *jouissance* of the symptom of self-reproach, in which the subject's own voice is lost, to be replaced by a genuine emotion of mourning? What allows the painful satisfaction that appears in the subject's self-incrimina- tion and all its affective discharge to be transformed into a symbolic elabo- ration wherein the object can finally be lost, detached from the tomb of the ego and allowed to pass away?[9] How does one give up the *jouissance* of self-hatred and the punishing satisfaction of the drive, and pass to the level at which the object can really be lost so that the voice of the subject can return? In Lacan's terms we can ask how *jouissance* condescends to desire: "*jouissance*," he writes in a famous formula, "must be refused, so that it can be reached on the inverted ladder of the Law of desire" (E, 324). How is this transformation possible?

From the earliest burial mounds to the most elaborate ceremonies, mourning has always confronted the task of negotiating the border between the symbolic and the real, finding a symbolic containment for the void, which is also the passage to the future. These questions lie at the heart of Brennan's work, insofar as she is deeply concerned with the transformation of affect, especially as it circulates within the body politic. As Brennan showed us again and again, the destinies or "vicissitudes" ("destiny," *Schicksal*, is the term Freud uses for the title of his paper, "Triebe und Triebschicksale," "The Drives and Their Destinies") of our affective life are diverse and can lead either to debilitating exhaustion and passivity or to forms of vital and productive creation in which our desires are expressed and mobilized. But how are we to grasp this difference clearly? This is where clinical and philosophical interests overlap.

Brennan shows us how affect that cannot be tolerated within the economy of the modern ego—everything that the imaginary ideal fails to contain—does not simply disappear, but is transmitted to others, who become its carriers, and she argues that this burden is in turn passed down historically even to those who did not experience the original events. One thinks here of traumatic memory, which allows the events of the Holocaust, or slavery, or genocide, to be lived even by those who had no direct experience of them. In this context, it becomes difficult to speak of "the subject" in an abstract way, not only because the subject is no longer simply a "personal" entity, but also because this differential inheritance within social life makes the generalized concept of "the subject" conspicuously inadequate. This is why a more precise geography, such as the one I have outlined between mourning and melancholy, in which differences appear as having genuine significance, takes on an ethical as well as a clinical significance.

The reference to trauma introduces yet another difficulty, moreover, for, by raising the question of "events" that were never experienced as such, but that nevertheless become part of the subject's existence and continue to have effects, the concept of trauma obliges us to speak of "unprocessed" or even "unsymbolized" experience, which can only lead to the enigma of an experience that is never experienced, never given an adequate place in the order of historical memory. Such is the status of the "traumatic event" in current discourses which argue that the distinctive feature of trauma—what separates it from ordinary experience—is precisely that it occurs with a shock or suddenness that prevents it from entering the

ordinary classificatory schemas of mental life, with the result that the traumatic event is confined to a sort of limbo, imprinted upon the subject
without becoming part of the subject's "experience" and thus unable to
find its place in a memorable narrative.[10] If the trauma returns in flash-
backs and nightmares, if it reappears out of the past like a ghost, this is
because the "event" of the trauma never took place, in the sense that it
never came to be properly inscribed in any symbolic chain. But this does
not mean it simply disappeared. On the contrary, forgotten but not forgotten, it remains, and is even transmitted, but it is not handed down in
the manner of ordinary historical memory. Indeed, for some thinkers, the
"event" of trauma, because it does not have a discursive form, can only be
betrayed by efforts of narration and can only be truly witnessed as a break
in language itself. In fact, the clinical question concerning the possibility
of *transforming* traumatic events, and thus having an effect upon them,
depends precisely on the degree to which the limitations of ordinary narrative knowledge are acknowledged. Psychoanalysis, Lacan said, is a way
of working on the real with symbolic means, but this does not mean that
one can ignore the distinctive character of the real itself. Something similar emerges in trauma theory. Speaking of Paul de Man, for example,
Cathy Caruth notes that the trauma has the status of a "disruption" in
language, a moment one might call "performative" (meaning that instead
of saying something, it acts): "Philosophy must, and yet cannot, fully integrate a dimension of language that not only shows, or represents, but acts.
Designating this moment as 'fatal,' de Man associates it with death" (Caruth 1996, 87).[11]

At stake in this discussion, therefore, is another version of what we have
introduced through the distinction between mourning and melancholy,
namely, the limits of the symbolic order and the need for a clearer account
of those limits—which Lacan takes up especially in terms of the real and
jouissance. The need for a more satisfactory account of this limit is in fact
a principle reason for Brennan's interest in Lacan:

> Derrida's critique of anti-foundationalism is a critique of a self-presencing sub-
> ject. I have called the fantasy foundational because I am in full agreement with
> this critique, as far as it goes. . . . By Derrida's account the subject is born into
> a play of signification, and does not found it. Against the idea of the founda-
> tional present subject is the play of difference. But the foundational fantasy, as
> I will describe it, requires a different kind of foundation. It requires a founda-
> tion before the foundation, a foundation which is conceived in non-subjective
> terms.[12]

Brennan refers to Spinoza here and to a certain sort of naturalism, which she calls "matter" and "flesh." The terms are not entirely worked out in this book, as she herself points out, but the thrust of the argument is to explore an alternative to what she sees (perhaps unfairly) as deficient in Derrida, Foucault, and other proponents of the "linguistic turn." Remarkably, and no doubt because of her immersion in Freud, she does not join the ranks of those who confuse Lacan with a purely "linguistic" theory (whatever that might be). Rather, she sees Lacan and Freud as offering a way to think the limit of representation:

> Derrida's position, like Foucault's, stops short after uncovering the basis of the subject's illusions about itself. It does not go on to postulate an alternative source of meaning. I will challenge this by postulating a three-stage rather than a two-stage process. That is to say, in the (Derridean) two-stage process, the foundational present subject of meaning is composed of a play of difference in which there is no meaning or inherent conation [a term she takes from Spinoza]. . . . In the three-step process, which conceives a foundation before the subjective foundation, the subject's construction of its illusory priority is both an active appropriation and a theft . . . the subject invests itself with the properties that animate the generative logical chain of nature.[13]

If, however, we follow the path of trauma theory, or indeed that of psychoanalysis (which is not to say these are the same, since in fact there are significant divergences), and if we follow Brennan's own path with respect to her interest in the historical transmission of "forgotten" or "unrepresented" events that nevertheless leave their marks on human experience at the level of affective existence, it is not clear that she needs the reference to a "foundation before the foundation," or even that this reference makes her argument. The decisive feature of affect, as she herself explains it, is that it always circulates, for better and for worse (that is, sometimes in the service of vitality and sometimes as the mark of forgotten conflict) through discursive and institutional networks of power and representation. Affect itself is thus a phenomenon that does not appear in nature. It belongs to the human being as a being for whom "the time is out of joint." In this, Brennan would have agreed with Foucault and Derrida. This does not mean that we should ignore the differences between the destitute and the privileged, any more than we should pretend that mourning and melancholia are both emotions at the same level when fact they entail a significant difference with respect to the possibilities of subjective life.

This is where Lacan, and in particular the distinction between affect and emotion, would have pushed her formulations further. The real in Lacan is not a natural, prediscursive foundation, which the symbolic could either approximate or betray. Correlatively, affect is not a biological energy that, if it is not symbolically contained, overflows onto its unfortunate recipients. The real is, rather, an effect of symbolization, and thus an abyss in the field of meaning, a product of the Other, in Lacan's language; consequently, it does not have the status of a natural entity (as Brennan wished in some of her more speculative and idealistic moments), but is rather a void introduced into being by the operation of representation. Like the "traumatic event," it cannot be confused with what one might imagine "actually happened," since its traumatic status depends upon the return, after the fact, of an event whose peculiar character consists in the fact that it never simply "took place." All the temporal problems of memory, historical time, and the organizing chains of signification must be primordial to the very possibility of trauma, which cannot be grasped by any reference to a pre-linguistic domain.[14]

Brennan's work explores the transmission of affect in considerable detail, and she develops the theme of affective mobility at the level of both subjective and political life. In relation to what she called "femininity," for instance, she describes a psychic position that could be assumed by anyone, but that was characterized by the assumption, on the part of a given subject, of all the excess energy that the "normal" and "masculine" ego could not contain within itself. "Affect" here was not a private or personal matter, but was understood largely as a silent or barely articulated experience of exhaustion or incapacity that was distributed unevenly in the social sphere. But affect in her work could also include experiences of exhilaration and vitality, and she tied this alternative between life and death to political movements, which have the capacity either to function in powerful historical ways, or to lose their energy and force. And if she herself did not distinguish between affect and emotion, or rely to any great extent on a Lacanian framework—open though she clearly was to Lacan's thinking—we might venture to suggest that such a distinction between affect and emotion, together with a sharper account of what Lacan develops under the category of *jouissance*, might cast some light on precisely these alternative destinies, and thereby contribute to her own intellectual itinerary, and clarify some points that remain obscure in her work.

IV

Let me therefore, in the little time I have left, try to link these remarks a bit more closely to Brennan's work on femininity, as it appears in Freud's work, which *The Interpretation of the Flesh* mapped out so carefully. In his early work on hysteria, we know that Freud regarded the symptom not as an organic disease, but as a somatized form of memory, a peculiar memory, then, insofar as it was not remembered by the conscious mind but inscribed at the level of the flesh. When he writes that "hysterics suffer mainly from reminiscences," then, Freud is speaking of a bodily symptom, and not of reminiscence in the ordinary sense, since the mind forgets what the symptom remembers. There is thus a disjunction between "consciousness" and "the body," even if the body is clearly not a natural phenomenon but is fully implicated in the functions of representation. We also know that in his attempt to explain the dissolution of the symptom under hypnosis, and even later under psychoanalysis proper, Freud observes that it is not sufficient for the patient to recall the repressed memory, or simply to symbolize what had fallen outside the field of representation and landed in the body as a result. In order for the symptom to be dissolved, the repressed memory must be recalled, along with the affective charge that was attached to the initial traumatic event. Memory without affect is insufficient, he says. In Lacanian terms, we could say that the *jouissance* of the symptom will not be reached by symbolization alone. What is required is, rather, that speech and memory and the order of representation be mobilized in such a way as to have an effect on the affective charge that was attached to the original traumatic experience:

> For we found, to our great surprise at first, that each individual hysterical symptom immediately and permanently disappeared when we had succeeded in bringing clearly to light the memory of the event by which it was provoked *and in arousing its accompanying affect*, and when the patient had described that event in the greatest possible detail *and had put the affect into words*. Recollection without affect almost invariably produces no result. ("On the Psychical Mechanism of Hysterical Phenomena," SE, 2:6, my emphasis)

In Lacanian terms, we can say that the symbolic order is not the whole truth. Despite his purportedly linguistic and structuralist orientation, it is clear that Lacan never regarded the symbolic order as a sufficient theoretical domain—not because there is also a question of the imaginary, as is so often said, but rather because psychoanalysis is a way of working on the real with symbolic means. Symbolization in itself is not a sufficient agenda for Lacan, just as, for Freud the memory or discourse without affect is insufficient to produce a shift at the level of the symptom. By the same token, however, we can say that there is no access to the pure affective charge of the trauma *without* representation, and that the real of the symptom, as it is understood in psychoanalysis, can only be approached through the detour of the symbolic order.

This relation between the symbolic and the real of *jouissance* was the core of Freud's work on the hysterical symptom, and it is precisely this relation that led Brennan back to the problem of affect and energy in Freud—not as an *alternative* to the excessively linguistic or purportedly structuralist formulations of Lacan, but much rather as an effort to unfold and conceptualize the *relationship* between the symbolic order and "energy," or "emotion" and "affect," together with what Freud developed under the heading of the "drive," which appears on the border of language. Although *affect* and *emotion* are often used interchangeably, it should be clear that all these terms demand a more careful exposition. Psychoanalysis is a means of working on the real with symbolic means, and this was already clear from Freud's early accounts of traumatic memory and the hysterical symptom, even if Freud did not use Lacan's vocabulary. The same distinction reappears later in Freud's work. In his article "Repression," where we might expect Freud to place the strongest possible emphasis on the symbolic order with reference to the familiar formations of the unconscious—the lapsus, the dream, free association, and all the verbalized forms of negation and denial that Freud presents as the surest sign that something unconscious is appearing in speech under the disguise of censorship or a repudiation by the ego ("You'll think it's my mother in the dream," Freud says, "but it's not my mother")—even here, in the midst of this account of the symbolic nature of unconscious manifestations, Freud is far more careful and precise: "In our discussion so far," he writes, "we have dealt with the repression of an instinctual representative, and by the latter we have understood an idea or group of ideas which is cathected with a definite quota of psychical energy (libido or interest) coming from an instinct" ("Repression," SE, 14:152). At this point in Freud's discussion, we seem to be concerned with a division, *within the field of representation*, between those highly cathected ideas or signifiers or "instinctual representatives" that are repressed and those that are not repressed (conscious and unconscious "ideas" or signifiers, one might say). But Freud now adds that "some other element" has to be accounted for:

> Clinical observation now obliges us to divide up what we have hitherto regarded as a single entity; for it shows us that besides the idea, some other element has to be taken into account, and that this element undergoes vicissitudes of repression which may be quite different from those undergone by the idea. For this other element of the psychical representative the term *quota of affect* has generally been adopted. It corresponds to the instinct insofar as the latter has become detached from the idea and finds expression, proportionate to its quantity, in processes which are sensed as affects. From this point on, we shall have to follow up separately what, as the result of repression, becomes of the *idea*, and what becomes of the *instinctual energy* linked to it. (Ibid.)

Thus, besides the ideas that are "cathected with a definite quota of psychical energy" and either mobilized by consciousness or repressed, we must now confront a "quota of affect," an element that is "detached from the idea," and given a different destiny. ("This element," Freud says, "undergoes vicissitudes of repression which may be quite different from those undergone by the idea.")[15]

Now, this new division between the field of representation and the "quota of affect" is not as simple as it might seem. We cannot simply speak of a difference between the "idea" and "energy," or the "signifier" and the "drive," as if it were a matter of separating the "psychic" domain of representation from the domain of "bodily" experience or "affective" energy. For one thing, it is clear from Freud's formulation that the "psychic" domain of representation already entails a certain appeal to "energy" or "libido," and Freud thus speaks of "an idea or group of ideas which is cathected with a definite quota of psychical energy (libido or interest) coming from an instinct"; for another thing, this "new element," while it is distinct from the "idea" or signifier, cannot be construed as a bodily experience that would be altogether unrelated to the sphere of representation. Accordingly, Freud writes that "some other element *representing the instinct* has to be taken into account," and he goes on to offer the following definition: "For this other element *of the psychical representative* the term *quota of affect* has generally been adopted" (ibid., my emphasis). Thus, on the side of representation, there is energy, and on the side of affect, there is representation.[16]

Nevertheless, if this development in Freud's work is serious, we cannot simply obliterate the distinction he seeks to make (any more than we should obliterate the distinction between mourning and melancholia, or indeed between emotion and affect). This much, at least, is clear: instead of a simple division between the "psychic" sphere of representation or ideas and the "bodily" sphere of immediate presence and natural energy, we have a more complex and tangled relation, but one in which it is still possible to differentiate—and as Freud says, "to follow up separately"— what he calls, in a tentative and no doubt problematic way, the "idea" and this "other element" which has become detached from the idea and appears as a "quota of affect" that follows a different path and is subject to different vicissitudes. Given this peculiar relationship of intertwining, in which a difference emerges despite the fact that instinctual energy and representation appear on both sides, one might say that Freud, with this distinction, seeks to isolate, not an "outside" to representation, a domain of natural immediacy or affect or emotion that no representation would touch (e.g., the familiar notion of "instinct"), but rather a point *within* the domain of representation that remains essentially foreign, excluded, and impossible to present—"detached," as Freud says, from the idea or representation. Such is the relation between the symbolic and the real—the latter being understood not as a prelinguistic reality or as an affective core that would somehow precede representation, but rather as an effect of the symbolic order that is nevertheless not reducible to a symbolic phenomenon. In Lacanian terms, we are concerned here with the difference between the Other and the object a, and it is above all the theory of the drive that obliges us to acknowledge this distinction.

It is remarkable that Brennan seized on this issue at a time when everyone else was denouncing the purportedly linguistic excesses of Lacanian theory, but it is even more striking that she was able to grasp this issue of energy, drive, and affect as a key to the question of femininity at a time when most Anglo-American interpreters of Lacan were focusing on the imaginary and addressing the question of femininity in terms of the supposed confinement of women to the imaginary order, such that entry into the symbolic order was assumed to be a male or masculine privilege. Such a view (the more familiar one) allowed Lacanian theory to be quickly absorbed by the discourse of social construction, in which femininity and masculinity were seen to be structured by symbolic conventions rather than by any natural foundation. In this account, the question of femininity could readily be inserted into the discourse of gender, organized by what came to be called the "cultural imaginary," and made compatible with other forms of social theory. Femininity could thus be grasped in terms of imaginary and symbolic identifications, but in the process, psychoanalysis itself underwent a profound distortion: the question of affect was eliminated, the *jouissance* of the symptom could not be addressed, the clinical specificity of psychoanalysis disappeared altogether, and the question of femininity came be formulated in imaginary terms, such that femininity was reduced to a relation to the mother that the symbolic "law" of culture somehow obliged the masculine subject to relinquish or transcend, and indeed to denigrate and renounce, while the feminine subject remained confined, in this account, to the prison of the imaginary order. The very absorption of psychoanalysis into the discourse of social construction allowed psychoanalytic feminism to be integrated into more familiar and canonical forms of knowledge, but the question of femininity as Freud had formulated it simply disappeared. This is what Brennan proposed in *The Interpretation of the Flesh*. As she wrote in her chapter "The Division of Attention," "the minute the real riddle of femininity is approached, the debates digress."[17] "This digression can take the form of invective against the *Penisneid* of Freud's critics; or polemic against Freud's patriarchal bias," but in either case, Brennan writes, "the logical direction of the enquiry is diverted."[18]

Her brave and quirky independence of mind and what one might even call her lack of piety allowed her to propose a connection that no one else at the time had really articulated: "It is in relation to repression that Freud formulated his hydraulic metapsychology," she writes. "This hydraulic physics may seem to be a long way from . . . the riddle of femininity, but this book's argument should show that the distance between the two is not as great as it first appears."[19] If we follow this connection, it becomes clear that femininity, in Brennan's account, can no longer be approached as a gender role, or as a form of social identity in the usual sense, because these forms of identity are too closely bound up with the individual subject as a unit—too bound up, one might say, with the imaginary ego, like the very theories of femininity that Brennan tried to challenge. It is this distinction between femininity in the psychoanalytic sense, and its misleading equivalents in social theories of gender, that Brennan sought to maintain when she wrote that "Womanhood, or the feminine (whatever that is), is not identical with femininity in Freud's sense."[20] For Brennan, femininity is not a form of social identity, either imaginary or symbolic, but is closer to a moment, a possible modality of energy, a transformation of affect that emerges in the relation between subjects. This is why femininity can be tied to the problem of affect, energy, and the transmissibility of emotion.

"We should investigate the assumption that individuals are the sole and self-contained points of origin for their emotions," she writes; and we should recognize that "emotions can cross the boundaries between individual persons."[21] If, in the course of a conversation, "the hysteric assumes the rational mantle," she observes, "the dramatic and irrational emotions sometimes pass over to the previously rational interlocutor."[22] "Emotions or affects can be reversed," she writes, and this is why femininity cannot be understood as a form of identity that attaches to certain culturally defined gender roles in any sociological or generalized way, much less as anything that could be attached to biological sex, but should rather be approached as transformation of energy, a disposition or possibility or modality in the relation to the other that can be assumed or actualized by any subject at a particular moment. "Femininity was a riddle," Brennan says, "because Freud could not explain why certain drives and affects were turned against the subject in a disabling way." "Unlike many feminists," she writes, "I have no quarrel with Freud's belief that a disabling femininity exists. Where I depart from Freud is in this: he worked with a model of a human being that was energetically self-contained."[23] This is a remarkable thesis, or intuition, and it is all the more remarkable that she could say in 1992, that "the riddle of femininity will be clarified after the matter of the drives is discussed"—remarkable, because the question of the drive is still almost never discussed, even when energy and affect are mentioned, as they are increasingly today.[24]

Indeed, if the question of the drive tends to be avoided even when energy and affect are addressed, this is perhaps another manifestation of the diversion or digression in which psychoanalysis is avoided in favor of more familiar forms of knowledge. Brennan's remark that "the riddle of femininity will be clarified after the matter of the drives is discussed" thus stands before us still, as a challenge and a provocation.

CHAPTER 4

Telling Tales of Love: Philosophy, Literature, and Psychoanalysis

The water in which Narcissus sees what he shouldn't is not a mirror, capable of producing a distinct and definite image. What he sees is the invisible in the visible . . . a representation without presence . . . the nameless one whom only the name he does not have could hold at a distance. It is madness he sees, and death.

—BLANCHOT, *The Writing of the Disaster*

Credule, quid frustra simulacra fugacia captas?
  Quod petis est nusquam.

Foolish boy, Why do you seek a fleeting image in vain?
What you desire is nowhere.

—OVID, *Metamorphoses*

Telling Tales: Of Philosophy and Literature

Can we believe that narcissism has a history? Can we speak of an early form of narcissism, regulated by the ideals of Athenian democracy or the virtues of the Platonic city and later transformed by the subtle revisions of Plotinus and the advent of Christian doctrine? Can we believe that there is, alongside the history of madness, "a new insanity," *novitasque furoris* (TL, 117), a new insanity of narcissism, born in the first centuries of the Christian era and still living today, in a modified but essentially Plotinian form?[1]

This is indeed what Kristeva suggests in *Histoires d'amour* (Tales of Love): "Platonic dialogism," she writes, "is transformed, with Plotinus, into a monologue that must indeed be called speculative" (TL, 109). Neo-Platonism thus appears as the force capable of "setting into motion the internalization of reflection in order to transform Platonic ideality into speculative internality" (TL, 115). Plotinus would be located "as if at the start of a new era, the Christian era that led us to assume our humanity through the imposing suffering of Christ" (TL, 115). In the history of philosophical narcissism, Plotinus would thus inaugurate a decisive chap-ter—a new formation of the soul's interiority whose legacy we still retain today.

Alongside this philosophical trajectory, close by and yet distinct, in an-other neighborhood of thought or language, the same story would be echoed in the halls of literature. "Only in the beginning of the Christian era," Kristeva writes, "did the fable of Narcissus enter the domain of liter-ature. We owe its first *complete* variant to Ovid (43 B.C.–A.D. 16)" (TL, 103). Let me stress these dates, and the idea of a datability of the proper name that accompanies this account. The proper name of *Ovid*, the prop-erly "Ovidian" formulation of the myth, and indeed the very name of *Narcissus* as well, would thereby be situated *in time*, in a time that would already be given in the world and would not itself depend on the advent of the name, understood as the origin of time.[2] "Narcissism" here would not entail a psychic event whose character would bear on the very advent of temporality, but would simply fall within the already given time of a chronological succession. All this is quietly supposed by the opening ges-ture of Kristeva's account: the "first *complete* variant" of Narcissus in its literary form ("the fable of Narcissus") appeared with the work of one who is named "Ovid (43 B.C.–A.D. 16)."

The history of literature would thus echo the history of philosophy, or rather, would serve as the origin that philosophy itself would echo: as Kris-teva recalls, Ovid precedes Plotinus, anticipating his thought and provid-ing in advance the mirror in which Plotinus would be able to reflect (would come to see himself). As Kristeva puts it at the conclusion of her account of Ovid's myth, "the *reflection* of which Narcissus became enamored and which led him to his death *became* [my emphasis] the fundamental topos of a thought that parted with ancient philosophy to nourish speculative thinking" (TL, 105). This new thought would include both the Gnostics, who "viewed the perceptible world as the result of a fault," and "Plotinus

(A.D. 205–70)"—we again mark these dates, which resemble in their brevity the austere engraving on a headstone—for whom, in contrast to the Gnostics, "the *primary reflection* that created the cosmos is a necessary process" (TL, 105–6).

Thus, even if Plotinus will ultimately turn away from the world, like the Gnostics (and in accordance with a certain Platonism), even if, as he says in the *Enneads*, "we must close the eyes of the body, to open another vision," it remains the case that the perceptual world is not, for him, simply error and fallenness, since "form alone can penetrate into the soul through the eyes" (TL, 110).[3] The eyes of the soul cannot open, according to Plotinus, without the material ground of perception—"no more than reflection," Plotinus says, "can exist without a mirror or a similar surface" (TL, 391 n. 3). The new formation of speculative interiority inaugurated by Plotinus—turned inward toward the psyche, rather than upward toward the ideas—would thus be distinguished from Gnosticism insofar as it acknowledges a moment of absolute dependence on "form," which is not immediately ideal, but retains a sensory dimension, what Kristeva will go on to call an "objectal" dimension, an exteriority that will "penetrate . . . through the eyes" (TL, 110). Nevertheless, this momentary grounding of reflection in material exteriority does not fail to take a narcissistic turn, when Plotinus insists, in a gesture marked by melancholy and anguish, on the *idealization* of the very process of reflection—what Kristeva calls the "luminous, reflective closure of psychic, autoerotic space under the constituent eye of the One" (TL, 117). Thus, even Plotinus "did not seek an object to halt his anguish. He lashed himself down to the archetype or rather to the source of objecthood—image, reflection, representation, speculation . . . unifying them within the inner space of the Self" (TL, 117). And following in the steps of Narcissus, who likewise "is not located in the objectal or sexual dimension," so Plotinus will also find that "insanity comes from the absence of the object, which is, in the final analysis, the sexual object" (TL, 116).

In this account, or according to this story, literature would come before philosophy, providing the origin that philosophy would come to divide in half, giving us, on the one hand, an account of the perceptible world as fallen, shadowy and erroneous—a world of sense perception that will eventually be subjected to by Descartes's methodical doubt—and, on the other hand, a Plotinian account in which reflection, both sensory and psychic, is not simply error and fallenness, but rather the condition for the possibility of creation, as the imagination will be for Kant and Heidegger.

It is this genealogy and this double trajectory (of the object and its absence) that the translator of *Tales of Love* emphasizes at the beginning of his translation, while inscribing *Tales of Love* within a history of Kristeva's work: "The sociological and cultural investigation of *Powers of Horror* is replaced with a philosophical and a theological one, which is conducted along two paths. One survey leads from Plato and the Bible through Ovid and Plotinus to Dante, Valéry, and Gide; the other goes by way of Paul, Bernard de Clairvaux, and Aquinas, to Mozart's *Don Giovanni* and Shakespeare's *Romeo and Juliet*" (TL, vii). For the translator, Kristeva's trajectory thus passes from the sociological and cultural domain (*Powers of Horror*) to the philosophical and theological domain, each of these traditions being mapped in terms of its attachment to—or abandonment of—the object.

In the chapter entitled "Narcissism: A New Insanity," philosophy and literature would thus be intertwined in an intimate trajectory that preserves the identity of each, while revealing their common destiny. We can therefore believe, and even narrate for ourselves, the history of philosophy and literature, which is also our own history. Such is the initial thesis linking Ovid and Plotinus in a chronological chain that will eventually bind us in turn and lead to the present day: the "tragic, death-bringing solitude of Narcissus" is a new historical formation, "on which will be founded a man very different from the political and erotic animal of the ancient world" (TL, 118–19). And this new formation is a legacy that will be inherited, according to Kristeva, for "the Christly passion and the arts of all Churches have come to root into . . . that psychic space of love that the Narcissan myth and the neo-Platonic logos had actually just completed" (TL, 117).

The Place of Psychoanalysis

There would thus be a history of narcissism. And yet, we should perhaps reflect for a moment on the curious position that psychoanalysis occupies within this history—on the peculiar absence of psychoanalysis, or perhaps its omnipresence, in the chronicle and calendar of narcissism. Between literature and philosophy, various trajectories and traditions would be elaborated and transformed, as Kristeva passes from the "sociological and cultural investigations" of her earlier work to the "philosophical and theological" interests of the present volume. But in this history that passes

through philosophy and literature, psychoanalysis would either be ignored, would be present *at all stages of the narrative*, as if it did not submit
to chronological time, as if narcissism did not need to wait for Freud to
invent it, but were already waiting in the wings, or indeed fully present
onstage, in the texts of Ovid and Plotinus, even in the Platonic city, in the
form of an *old insanity* that this "new insanity" would presumably displace.
(A short parenthesis on reading, then: *Novitas*, the "new" in the title of
Kristeva's chapter "Narcissus: The New Insanity," would thus repeat the
question that has already been posed by the datability of the proper name.
More precisely—since this is really our question—the "new" in Kristeva's
chapter would be a quotation that conceals what it quotes: presenting itself
as the assertion of a distinctive historical emergence, this "new" insanity
would document itself by quoting an Ovidian phrase that, for its part,
would seem to acknowledge a more ancient and mythical inheritance, a
"new" insanity that merely echoes and repeats the "old" insanity of the
Platonic city. Ovid's *novitasque* would thus appear to remember what Kristeva's "new insanity" is tempted to forget.) Psychoanalysis would either
have no place in the narrative or would be *intertwined* from the very beginning with these other domains, in which case it is difficult to see what
separates psychoanalysis from literature and philosophy, two disciplines or
domains that would at least seem to be provisionally distinguished—
capable of echoing or resonating with each other, but nevertheless not
identical with one another. Psychoanalysis would either be left out of account, or it would be *the medium* in which the entire genealogy takes place,
the conceptual frame that allows us to grasp what is *really* happening in
the history of subjectivity, behind the stories that philosophy and literature
would tell about themselves. And since psychoanalysis is never simply ignored in Kristeva's work, we can only conclude that it serves as the general
medium in which her account takes place. Not only her "sociological and
cultural" work, but also her "philosophical and theological" analyses
would take place against the background of psychoanalytic theory, which
elucidates and clarifies a trajectory of the subject that is usually lost in the
standard histories of philosophy and literature. Psychoanalysis thus allows
us to recover what is forgotten, or to remember what is concealed by the
usual histories of literature and philosophy, insofar as it listens neither to
the story of the gradual emergence of truth and reason nor to the history
of the development of artistic forms, but to the subject who is speaking in
philosophy and art, and whose destiny unfolds within those disciplines.

The difficulty that arises is therefore obvious: unlike all these other domains whose histories can be written, psychoanalysis would be the medium or ground of the narrative, the conceptual background or reflecting surface in which these other discourses would be brought to recognize themselves. Through the medium (and theater) of psychoanalysis, we would be able to see and recognize for the first time the truth that is hidden in the history of literature and philosophy. But psychoanalysis itself would not appear *within* the story: it would not be given in an image or a narrative, but would rather be like the watery pool which suspends before us on its delicate surface the image we are invited to contemplate, the image of philosophy or literature. The ungraspable liquidity of psychoanalysis, its watery invisibility and omnipresence, would thus be *the element* in which this history is formed, like air and earth and fire, those other mythical elements. Psychoanalysis would be like water, like Cephissus and Liriope, the father and mother of Narcissus, the first a god of the river, the second a water nymph, who, anticipating Narcissus and laying out his destiny in advance, is herself transformed into a lily, "that other flower of moist areas," Kristeva says, "the funeral narcissus" (TL, 103).

Thus, between literature and philosophy, on the one hand, and psychoanalysis, on the other, between that which enters into history and that which accompanies history without itself being inscribed in the calendar of time, a question would emerge—a question that not only concerns Kristeva's text, but ultimately bears on narcissism itself, insofar as one must eventually ask whether the event of narcissism is in fact a historical event or whether, like psychoanalysis in this text, it flows alongside the entire course of historical time, without belonging to a particular moment or a given temporal instant.

Can we believe, therefore, that we are really dealing with a history of narcissism in *Tales of Love*, as it might seem at first glance? Can we believe, moreover, that there is in fact a history of narcissism? Is this text in fact a history, and does the phenomenon of narcissism enter into history? And what would it mean to believe or doubt, that is, to enter into a debate in which doubt and belief, certainty and skepticism, are the organizing virtues? Is not the entire apparatus of doubt and belief, documentary evidence and theoretical vigilance, already part of the narcissistic story, in which recognition and misrecognition, seeing and believing, play their deadly game, mixing the imaginary and the real at the heart of the constitution of the subject? To doubt the story that is being told by Kristeva would already be to enter the arena of narcissism—of representation, evidence, and suspended belief. At the same time, however, if we were not to doubt, if we were simply to believe, taking Kristeva's history for granted, an entire network of questions and difficulties would have to be set aside.

The Catastrophe of Narcissism

In fact, this history of narcissism already puts in place a temporal structure that narcissism itself should not allow us to believe. The time of narcissism is the time of a disaster, the time of an event whose traumatic character repeats itself at every moment, beyond the recovery of historical memory.[4] In its most basic structure, the event of narcissism therefore resembles a trauma, an event that should not be too quickly inserted into the chronicle of ordinary time. The moment of narcissism recalls the experience of war and other traumas that Freud discusses in *Beyond the Pleasure Principle*, where he stresses the peculiar temporality of the traumatic event—not simply the fact that it repeats, refusing to pass away and returning in dreams or nightmares that bring the subject back to the experience of trauma, in apparent violation of the principle of pleasure, but also the fact—far more enigmatic—that the trauma repeats because it was never experienced in the first place, never symbolized and made present as such to the subject. We must return here to the date and the datability of the event—the date of the "event" of narcissism. The experiences of war and other traumas do not belong to past time. They continue to intrude upon the present, blocking the experience of the here and now, and asserting themselves in place of immediate experience—as if blinding the subject and interrupting vision with a kind of memory that does not appear as "memory," or as a recollection of the past, but rather *returns*, presenting itself in place of the present, so that the subject's own experience is lost. The flashback, the nightmare, the return of traumatic memory, are distinct from historical memory, insofar as they concern an event that has not been integrated into historical time, ordered by a relation to the past and the future. Freud thus tells us that in traumatic events—if they can be called "events"—the past is *repeated instead of being remembered*. And if the trauma repeats in this way, Freud says, it is because the traumatic event was never experienced as such, never made present in relation to a future and a past, never given a place in any symbolic chain or any network of protentions and retentions. What repeats is therefore something that somehow never "took place," a past that was never "present," which does not mean that it is merely nothing, a figment of the imagination or a purely mythical event, but rather that it happens without happening, as death happens for Heidegger, arriving without arriving, or like the murder of the father, the traumatic event that is recounted in the story of the primal horde in *Totem and Taboo*, an event that occurred, as Freud tells us, before history as such, before the beginning of historical time, in a mythical moment that explains how time in fact began.[5]

As the very structure of the "mirror stage" suggests, the traumatic event—the very advent of the ego—takes place before the subject is able to bear witness, before the "I" can utter any yes or no, and because it stands at the origin in this way, "before" the subject, we can only conclude that the trauma was never present to the subject as such, and *this* is why it cannot pass away or belong to the past, as a present that once was. Because it does not belong to the past, moreover, the traumatic event is constantly expected to return from the future, like a catastrophe that is about to occur—a catastrophe (like object-loss in Kristeva's text) that must be avoided at all cost, avoided like madness itself, which, in Kristeva's account, already happened with Ovid and Plotinus and yet must be avoided in the present age, where it emerges like an impending catastrophe, a "new malady" that may well be the defining catastrophe of our time, a narcissism that, although it was invented by Ovid and Plotinus, is only on the verge of arrival. As Blanchot says, "We are on the edge of disaster without being able to situate it in the future: it is rather always already past, and yet we are on the edge or under the threat, all formulations which would imply the future—that which is to come—if the disaster were not that which does not come, that which has put a stop to every arrival."[6]

Is there a history of narcissism, then, and can we really believe that the name *Narcissus* is datable in the way that Kristeva at least seems to suggest? Can we give Narcissus a date of birth in the works of Ovid and read narcissism's old age (its repetition or its end) in the contemporary world? This is a two-fold question, bearing on our knowledge of the past (or, more fundamentally, on our approach to it), and also on ourselves. Is Kristeva indeed willing, as she herself says, "to grant Narcissus such a crucial part in the history of western subjectivity" (TL, 115)? Should we therefore stress, as Kristeva does, "the originality of the narcissistic figure and the very particular place it occupies, in the history of Western subjectivity" (TL, 105)? Should we, moreover, *see ourselves* as the heirs of this particular

Western formation? Is the "new insanity" of her title intended to designate a historical invention, one that we ourselves would inherit today? Is there a transmission and inheritance of narcissism, and can we give a history of this narcissism, *une histoire*, as Kristeva suggests in *Histories d'amour*?

Or are we only telling tales when we tell tales of love? Is the narrative therefore a fiction, a myth, a web of words designed, not simply to describe or document, but rather to contain and make more tolerable a narcissistic wound that accompanies the subject through all the various historical formations that mark its symbolic life?[7] Can we put narcissism on the calendar, as we would at least seem to be able to do with philosophy and literature, or is narcissism rather—along with psychoanalysis itself—the kind of watery event or possibility that haunts the time of the narrative at every stage of its development?

In this view, the trauma of narcissism cannot be regarded as a historical event, an event in the history of thought or literature, with a beginning, a middle, and perhaps an end. Though capable of various transformations, of being cast in various versions or metamorphoses—with Ovid and Plotinus for example—narcissism itself would not have a historical birth or death. Instead, the event and the disaster of narcissism would repeat compulsively, like an original trauma that every narrative and every philosophy would bear within themselves, in a more or less visible way. The symbolic and cognitive presentation of this trauma—the philosophical and linguistic forms that appear to master and represent it (including Kristeva's historical rendering)—are certainly open to remarkable variation, but narcissism itself is not reducible to the images and words that offer to contain it. In this view, narcissism is not so much a "new insanity" as the insanity of a trauma that can only repeat itself. Plotinus would therefore not be (the father) at the origin (of a new insanity), but would only rework and transform the insanity of a more ancient Platonism that he cannot overcome or surpass—as if, true to the name of "neo-Platonism," he were telling a tale that was passed to him from his ancestors, from those who taught him to speak, to take up their story, a story that he repeats, but also figures as his own, through a language that makes it new. In Ovid, likewise, the *novitasque* that is repeated in Kristeva's title "Narcissus: A New Insanity" can no longer mean "new" in a historical sense, but rather is something that repeats itself anew with every generation. This would indeed be the "other" story told behind the narrative that we apparently find in *Tales of Love*: for as Kristeva in fact notes, the entire drama of shadow, sight, and reflection in Plotinus is constructed with "Platonic instruments" (TL, 108). The "new" insanity is thus, at bottom, the transformation, and even the repetition, of a difficulty that was not invented ex nihilo by Plotinus or Ovid, but was rather inherited from an earlier time. Thus, contrary to first appearances, narcissism itself is not a historical phenomenon—the invention of a particular moment, or the contingent product of a particular philosophical or literary outlook—but rather an event that compulsively repeats itself as it passes from generation to generation.

For Ovid, too, it is transparently clear that the story of Narcissus is already very old, its precise unfolding being closely tied to a series of similar stories. Kristeva herself explicitly points this out. "Much emphasis," she writes, "has been placed on the morbid, narcotic, chthonian meaning of this legend," the "subterranean torpor" that "links the fable to the vegetative intoxication of Dionysus" (TL, 105). In fact, just as "Narcissus dies after he has seen himself," so also "Pentheus dies for having seen the mysteries of Dionysus" (ibid.). In a parenthesis, Kristeva notes that the painter Poussin will later recall this connection "in his *Birth of Bacchus*, which pairs the two myths and the two heroes" (ibid.). Ovid's Narcissus is therefore not the first to see what he should not and to be punished for a kind of idolatry, a fascinated vision that sees what is not really there—an image that is neither another nor himself, but an illusion or mystery that blinds him, cutting him off from the other and finally bringing about his death. These details about Dionysus and Poussin are not simply ancillary information, the sort of casual historical references that are supposed to characterize (the genre of) scholarly knowledge, a layering of incidental facts and information which have no real bearing on the philosophical argument of the text. On the contrary, they register the difficulty of the historical localization that Kristeva at first seems to have in mind.

The story was therefore not invented by Ovid, and its historical origin cannot be so quickly secured. As Blanchot points out in *The Writing of the Disaster* and as Kristeva herself acknowledges, but without pursuing its consequences, there is already by the time of Ovid a well-established tradition of fables around Narcissus, in relation to which Ovid is in fact a notorious innovator and a quite self-conscious revisionist. As always in the *Metamorphoses*, the story being told is already an ancient one, and Ovid (like the Greek tragedians) is a latecomer, a commentator and a receiver, whose task is to hear and understand anew what has already been said in a mythological past. "Mythologists do not fail to indicate," Blanchot writes, "that Ovid—an intelligent, civilized poet, upon whose version of the myth

the concept of narcissism is modeled (as though his narrative developments indeed contained psychoanalytic knowledge)—modifies the myth in
order to expand it and make it more accessible."[8] What is more, the explicit attention Ovid pays to the reception and repetition of antiquity is
accentuated in a more general and systematic way by the imbrication and
layering of tales that we find in the *Metamorphoses* as a whole, every story
introduced by another story, as if each tale were not really a new invention,
but a commentary on another tale, the allegory or echo of the previous
story, the whole series being linked in a symbolic chain—or intertwined
like snakes.

So it is with the story of Narcissus and Echo, which Ovid introduces
by recounting to us how it was that the prophet Tiresias, who can see the
future, was blinded by Juno as punishment for having spoken against her.
We recall very well how this came to pass: one day, Jupiter—who was
drunk at the time and feeling pretty good, forgetting his cares and his
anxiety ("diffusum nectare, curas / Seposuisse gravis vacuaque agitasse re-
missos"; lines 318–19)—turned to Juno and said, "I'll bet that you women
have more pleasure in love than we men." Juno disagreed (as often happened with these two), and in order to settle the dispute—each insisting
upon the other's greater pleasure, without knowing in fact or by experience—they turned to Tiresias, for he alone knew what love was like for
both the man and the woman. One day, he had come upon two snakes
intertwined in the woods, writhing together, and taking his stick, he pulled
them apart and was instantly transformed into a woman.[9] He thus lived as
a woman for seven years, until one day he saw those snakes again, insinuat-
ing with each other, and thinking that the same cause might produce the
same effect (or the reversal of that effect), he once more forced them apart,
after which, he again became a man ("taking on again," as Ovid says, "the
form and the image of his earlier self," "forma prior rediit genetivaque
venit imago"; line 331). And so, when Tiresias, having been appointed as
judge, took the side of Jupiter, Juno punished him with blindness. "Iudicis
aeterna damnavit lumina nocte"; line 335), Ovid says, "she damned his
vision to eternal night, condemning the eyes of Justice to be blind." Like
the story of Echo and Narcissus, and indeed like the story of justice that
Oedipus brings upon himself, this too is a story in which blindness and
sexual difference are brought together, and a story of punishment as well.

Thus, like the work of Plotinus, which fashions itself with Platonic instruments, so also the myth of Narcissus is not new with Ovid, but is
rather inherited and repeated: the time of Ovid's "new" insanity is thus

less easy to grasp than one might think, and it is not clear that this time will be datable in the way that one might date the signing of a treaty, a scientific discovery, or some other "historical" event. Nor is this difficulty restricted to the tale that Ovid tells about Narcissus. On the contrary, it extends to narcissism itself, for the "event" of narcissism—if one can speak of an "event" of narcissism, when it is really a question of something that never occurs, and at the same time never passes away, something that is impossible, a self-apprehension of the ego that is not a self-apprehension, a "splitting" that brings death at the very moment it brings the subject into being—already introduces a break with historical time and its sequence of localizable occurrences. Thus, while we have suggested that, for Kristeva, a provisional line might be drawn between philosophy and literature, on the one hand (insofar as their histories can be written), and psychoanalysis, on the other hand (in its watery omnipresence), the historical datability of philosophy and literature is no longer so clearly secured.

At the same time, however, this is not to say that narcissism *simply* has no history, for, as Kristeva observes, the "instruments" inherited from Plato are "dramatized, humanized, and eroticized by Narcissus," in a transformation that can be marked, only to be transformed or translated again, to "become with Plotinus *logical elements* of the elaboration, beyond narcissistic madness, of that Western consciousness of self" (TL, 108, my emphasis). Nevertheless, if narcissism repeats itself compulsively, like a destiny or fate that every narrative and every philosophy would bear within it in a more or less visible way, this means that we cannot confuse the symbolic and imaginary presentation of this trauma with the enigmatic structure that essentially comprises it. And if narcissism points us toward this constitutive "event," the thinking that aims at narcissism itself would have to consist, not so much in the documentary narrative that Kristeva appears to present, but in a task of thinking, whose effort would be to remember—to repeat, remember, and work through—a trauma that has always already claimed it in advance. It would therefore be a mistake to believe that we are concerned simply with the invention of a new world, casting off (or doubting) everything that has gone before and starting from a new ground of certainty; indeed, given these temporal difficulties and the fact that the true structure of the trauma would not consist in a localized chronological "event" that one might (secondarily) remember or forget, one can only conclude that the trauma itself is *in* the memory, in the structure of remembering and repeating, and nowhere else. As Plotinus says, explaining the origin of his own "new" invention, "the reunification of the soul within the ever-present unity of intellect": "Human souls rush down here because they have gazed at their images as in the mirror of Dionysus" (TL, 107)—a passage Kristeva marks as "another mythical reference . . . in Plotinus." The "new" insanity of Plotinus is thus not to be confined to a historical moment, but is itself the memory, the echo, of a Dionysian myth, and Kristeva herself repeatedly stresses these "reflections" of archaic and mythical doctrine within Plotinian thought. Thus, commenting on the text of Plotinus, she writes: "Let us recall that, according to one version of the myth, Dionysus as a child allows himself to be seduced by Hera by means of a mirror, before undergoing the ordeal of the Titans, who cut him up into pieces that are then put together again by Athena and Zeus" (TL, 107).

Of Narcissism Itself

Is there, then, a history of narcissism, with an origin in Plotinus or Ovid, and an end or culmination in modernity? Or is it rather a matter of telling tales, when we speak of the formation of the subject? And if *the literary and philosophical exposition of narcissism* in fact reveals a structure that cannot be historically confined to a particular moment, what would this mean for *narcissism itself*, as it is understood, not in literature or philosophy, but in the domain (and genre) of psychoanalysis—if one can pretend to suppose, after what we have just seen, that this psychoanalytic domain is "no longer" the domain of philosophy or indeed of literature, but a distinct and strictly separable genre?

In order to do justice to this question, we would have to ask not only about Kristeva's text, and the peculiar tension that marks it—narrating the history of subjectivity while taking back a certain number of formulations, as we have tried to show, with observations that acknowledge an archaic repetition. We would also have to ask about narcissism itself, about the story or history of narcissism as it appears in certain versions of psychoanalysis, where we are told about the moment of the "mirror stage," which replaces a moment of bodily incoherence with a new unity, only to be again transformed (or metamorphosed) by the order of language. Does Freud himself (like Lacan, who only repeats what Freud has shown us) not speak of a "primary narcissism" and of its later transformation, through the Oedipal conflict, into something like "secondary narcissism"? Does he not also speak of a period *before* narcissism, before the Lacanian "mirror stage," in which the subject's body is not yet coherent—a stage before the constitution of the body? The essay "On Narcissism" is perfectly clear on this point: "We are bound to suppose," Freud writes, "that a unity comparable to the ego cannot exist in the individual from the start; the ego has to be developed. The auto-erotic instincts, however, are there from the very first; so there must be something added to auto-eroticism—a new psychical action—in order to bring about narcissism" (SE, 14:77). Narcissism is thus not present at the beginning. A new psychical action is necessary to bring about narcissism. That "new psychical action" is, of course, the "mirror stage," the "moment" (but in what kind of time?) when the child passes from bodily fragmentation to imaginary completeness, the inaugural moment in which the body is "given" by being transformed from a disorganized assemblage of bodily zones, each of which is capable of a certain pleasure, which Freud calls autoerotic, to another organization, in which the pleasure of the ego will become possible. Thus, as Lacan says, "we have only to understand the mirror stage as an identification, in the full sense that psychoanalysis gives to that term: namely, the transformation that takes place in the subject when he assumes an image" (E, 2). As we know, this initial "form" (with its captivating beauty, as the cognate *formosa* suggests) of the imaginary ego will later be subjected to yet another transformation with the advent of language, which will allow the subject to identify with signifiers—a possibility harbored by the name, which will carry the subject beyond the realm of the image, toward something resembling the "other"—an alterity that, while it at first falls prey to the image (appearing only as an alter ego), can finally emerge as an "other" for the "subject." Lacan acknowledges this later transformation when he writes that the mirror stage reveals to us the I "in its primordial form, before it is objectified in the dialectic of identification with the other, and before language restores to it, in the universal, its function as subject" (E, 2). In psychoanalysis, too, there would thus be a history of narcissism—if not the history it acquires in Kristeva's text, then the series of stages that narcissism itself undergoes, according to psychoanalysis.

And yet, here too the matter is not so clear. Does Lacan not famously acknowledge that the moment of the mirror stage amounts to "the assumption of . . . an alienating identity, which will mark with its rigid structure the subject's entire mental development" (E, 4)? In this view, the fundamental feature of narcissism would lie in its *constitutive* character, in the fact that narcissism entails an initial formation of the ego—a first, traumatic rupture with natural existence—whose later redeployments and translations will never overcome that constitutive foundation. In "On Narcissism," Freud likewise observes that the origin of the ego has a formative and structural character that no revision and no retroactive reworking will be able to forget (not only because of its constitutive character, but also because, as we have suggested, the inaugural "event" of narcissism cannot, properly speaking, be remembered). Narcissism will therefore never pass away, like an event that acquires a date or a moment that eventually belongs to the past. Speaking of the projective identification that supposedly marks a stage in the "maturation" of the subject—what Lacan speaks of as the displacement of the first, bodily ego into a transitive identification with the alter ego—Freud writes that the subject now projects into the future another possible identity, an "ideal ego" toward which the present ego can aim. This will be a new formation in which the initial self-absorption of the child is supposedly transcended, cast off and left behind, as a moment that now belongs to the past. And yet, no sooner has Freud deposited this notion into his text than he finds it necessary to explain that the process is not so linear:

> This ideal ego is now the target of the self-love which was enjoyed in childhood by the actual ego. The subject's narcissism makes its appearance displaced onto this new ideal ego, which, like the infantile ego, finds itself possessed of everything that is of value. [*Diesem Idealich gilt nun die Selbstliebe, welche in der Kindheit das wirkliche Ich genoss. Der Narzissmus erscheint auf dieses neue ideale Ich vershoben, welches sich wie das infantile im Besitz aller wertvollen Vollkommenheiten befindet*]. (SE, 14:94)

Thus, contrary to first appearances, "primal" or "primary narcissism" is not a stage that is eventually given up. Indeed, as Freud adds in his laconic way, depositing the most obscure theoretical difficulties into a prose that is altogether misleading in its urbanity: "As always where the libido is concerned, man has here again shown himself incapable of giving up a satisfaction he had once enjoyed" (ibid.). We cannot stop here, however, for the matter is still more complicated: it is insufficient to say that the primordial narcissism of the child ("the self-love which was enjoyed in childhood by the actual ego") remains present in its future transformation, in the form of the ideal ego, which now attracts the self-love of the subject, for the peculiar fact is that the origin itself, the very moment of the emergence of narcissism (the "satisfaction he had once enjoyed"), does not appear to lie at the beginning, but would seem to emerge for the first time

only through this "later" form. This is indeed the sense of Freud's meticu-
lous phrasing, in which "narcissism *makes its appearance displaced*" (my emphasis). It is thus as if narcissism had to take place twice—through a certain
repetition—in order to appear at all. Narcissism itself—not merely a later
form or stage of narcissism, but the very thing itself: *Der Narzissmus*—
would "first" show up and make its entrance (*erscheint*) only on the basis
of this "new" form ("auf dieses neue ideale Ich vershoben"). What Freud
is saying here is that it is only on the basis of the "ideal ego" that the
psychic economy is able (or we might say "condemned"), nostalgically, to
produce for itself a backward glance, a new temporal arrangement, that
will allow this ego to speak to itself of a "former time," to represent for
itself a mythical past that the childish ego once (as in "once upon a time")
enjoyed. This is what it means, and this is the peculiar structure under
consideration, when Freud writes that narcissism is *first born* (or "makes
its appearance") the moment the ideal ego "now" receives (the auto-
affection of) a self-love which is *construed as* the recapturing of a "lost
enjoyment," a mythical satisfaction that is now attributed to an archaic
time called "childhood" "Diesem Idealich gilt nun die Selbstliebe, welche
in der Kindheit das wirkliche Ich genoss."

In fact, as the passage continues, the two moments of the ego we have
just articulated in their peculiar temporality are further elaborated, and we
find yet another moment, so that Freud's account would complete the
same three moments already isolated by Lacan—the ego in its primordial
form, the ego in its relation to the alter ego (identification with the other),
and what Lacan calls the "restoration" (another word whose temporal dimension would lead us into difficulties) of the "subject" in the dimension
of the "universal." Precisely these moments appear in the Freudian text,
in the very passage we have just cited, where Freud speaks (as we have
seen) of the "ego"—what he calls the "actual ego," *das wirkliche Ich*—the
"ideal ego," and finally (as the passage continues) the "ego ideal," the
last of which (corresponding to Lacan's "symbolic identification") opens
a future in language that seems at first glance to amount to the only way
out of narcissism. The passage from the ideal ego to the ego ideal (in
Freud's language) would thus represent the passage into the universal, the
order of symbolic mediation, which gives life to the statue that would
otherwise be petrified by the Medusa effect of the imago.[10] In short, with
the arrival of the ego ideal, projected into the future through the symbolic
apparatus (like a little spool of thread with its phonemic attachment), the
image that was given in the mirror will no longer be sufficient, and the

subject will desire something more, something else, an identity that might capture the recognition of others. Imaginary narcissism would thus be normalized and moderated by language and exchange, and by the mechanism of a newly social identification (the notorious "identification with signifiers"). *It is thus as if speech itself were the consequence and by-product of narcissism,* less a rational tool of communication between already existing "subjects" than a fantastic and desperate invention spewed forth by the human animal in an attempt to fashion an exit, or at least to heal the wound, of the narcissism that brought him into being. Again, this chronological mapping of stages is clearly irreducible to any historical sequence, for Freud notes that even with the ego ideal, the child

> is not willing to forgo the narcissistic perfection of his childhood; and when, as he grows up, he is disturbed by the admonitions of childhood and by the awakening of his own critical judgment, so that *he can longer retain* that perfection, *he seeks to recover it* in the new form of an ego ideal. *What he projects before him as his ideal is the substitute for the lost narcissism of his childhood,* in which he was his own ideal. (SE, 14:94, my emphasis)

Infantile narcissism is therefore not actually *transcended* by means of social identification: on the contrary, it is *projected* into the future, so that it can be "found again," recaptured and preserved. Freud thereby suggests that the very formation of "conscience," the awakening of "critical judgment" that comes with the incorporation of the admonitions of others (an internalization of the law) and leads us to give up our infantile demands, is at the same time a repetition of the narcissism it promised to transcend. At every stage, it seems, the transformation of narcissism is less a sequence of discrete historical stages than a process of repetition and reiteration, all of which is set in motion by the "originally" narcissistic constitution of the subject.

Sacrifice, Responsibility

We have tried to mark a tension in Kristeva's book, a peculiar vacillation between history and repetition, between the history that at least *seems* to characterize philosophy and literature in this text, and the watery omnipresence of psychoanalysis, that does not enter into history, but accompanies its entire unfolding. This tension is apparent in Kristeva's title, in the very word *histoires*, which shuttles between "story" and "history." But the difficulty has not been restricted to the tale Kristeva tells about Narcissus. On the contrary, it extends to narcissism itself, in the sense that the "event" of narcissism (if one can speak of an "event" when it is really a question of something that never occurs) gives rise to a "past" that only emerges "later," as a lost origin—one that the subject, moreover, projects into the future, in order to "recover" and possess this time that never was. Like the moment of the glance that fixes Narcissus before the watery pool, so narcissism is also an event that is impossible, a self-apprehension of the ego that is not "self"-apprehension, but rather the figuring forth of an "identity" that is not the subject ("He did not know what he was seeing," Ovid's narrator tells us portentously; line 430), an identity that brings petrification and death in the very moment when it brings the ego into being—only to promise, by means of this lure, an escape, another way forward, the possibility of attaining one day an existence that will recapture an original plenitude, a past that never was, or never was until the promise cast it forth, in the form of this absolute past.

The catastrophic character of the Ovidian story makes his version less sanguine, perhaps, than Kristeva's, or indeed than the tale told by psychoanalysis, which holds out the promise of an end to narcissism, or—if not an end—then a future for narcissism in which love is not altogether impossible. It is perhaps this promise that Derrida is willing, for a moment, to read in the sacrifice of Isaac, a story that shows us an Abraham whose decision (if it can even be called a "decision," any more than the look of Narcissus can be said to be the act of a subject) to accept this absolute loss paradoxically gives rise to a future, a "still-more-time," a possibility in which, despite (and because of) sacrifice and death, *time remains*:

> The instant in which the sacrifice is as it were consummated, for only an instant, a *no-time-lapse* . . . this is the impossible to grasp instant of absolute imminence in which Abraham can no longer go back on his decision, nor even suspend it. *In this instant*, therefore, in the imminence that doesn't even separate the decision from the act, God returns his son to him and decides by a sovereign decision, by an absolute gift, to reinscribe sacrifice within an economy by means of what henceforth comes to resemble a reward.[11]

This "sacrificial" instant is the time of the narcissistic wound, the time of the subject, which does not begin in identity with itself, but passes in an instant (the blink of an eye) from being "nothing" to being "something else," from incoherence to alienation. The *moment of representation* is the moment of a subject who is not a subject before he sees himself and who is already lost the moment reflection begins—a subject who is nothing before the image gives him to himself and who is already something else as soon as the image arrives. The time of the subject is thus an impossible time, the time of an instant of transition (*Untergang, metabole*), a moment that gives and takes away, in a movement of constitution that is equally the destitution of the subject.

It is also the time of the voice of Echo, who calls to Narcissus and is never heard, who calls in words of love that are at the same time not her words, not the words of any subject, but only the borrowed words of the other, twisted and cut short in a mechanical reverberation, an echo that only repeats the desire of Narcissus—who in fact *has* no desire and *expresses* no desire—an echo that returns his words in an inverted form, which he is unable to hear. The voice of Echo thus repeats this impossible time, echoing a desire that does not (or not yet) exist, and returning it as an expression of "love" in which no voice of any subject is present. And yet, in an ethical gesture that could be inflicted only by psychoanalysis (as Ovid tells us in advance), *this* is what Narcissus is called on to "recognize." In fact, it is precisely for failing in response to this perverse and impossible call that he is punished by the gods and condemned to his mythical fate. The time of the voice is thus like the time of the gaze of Narcissus himself, who, looking into the pool, does not see or recognize himself ("Quid videat, nescit," Ovid's narrator says; line 430), but rather falls in love with an image, the simulacrum he mistakes for another—another to whom he then speaks, saying, "I can almost touch you; only the smallest distance stands in the way of love. Why do you deceive me, disappearing when I reach for you? [*Posse putes tangi; minimum est quod amantibus obstat. / Quisquis es, hucexi; quid me, puer unice, fallis? / Quove petitus abis?*; lines 453–55]." What stands in the way of love is this image, an image that is neither of another nor of himself, an image that kills him and that represents nothing—neither Narcissus nor the other—but rather hovers on the surface of a fragile pool, giving Narcissus to himself for the first time, but in a form that petrifies and brings death. The time of this representation that gives the subject would be a suspended time, an instant suspended between a subject who is not yet given and a subject who comes into being in an instant that brings his disappearance.[12] Between the traumatic advent of the subject and his disaster, there would be no time at all, as if origin and end were given in a strange simultaneity.

How, then, can we say that Narcissus is responsible for his failure to respond to the other? If the Ovidian myth is indeed an allegory of narcissism in the psychoanalytic sense (if the fable speaks to us, in Blanchot's words, "as if it already contained psychoanalytic knowledge"), how can we say that Narcissus has failed to recognize the other, to respond to the call of the other, or that he is in some way responsible, when there is no subject there before he arrives at the pool, where he sees himself for the first time? How can we speak of Narcissus as already claimed by the other, already responsible, before the subject has even arrived on the scene? And still more sharply, how can we say that, in addition to being responsible in advance, responsible before he can "take responsibility," before he can subjectivize and internalize this relation to the other, he is also *guilty* for failing to respond, and even *due to be punished* as a result?

This is indeed the harsh law that the Ovidian myth proposes, in a story that unfolds in two stages, which have been admirably detailed by Claire Nouvet: one (the first) in which he fails to respond to Echo, and another (which comes second) in which he is given to himself in a first reflection. In the logic of the myth, which clearly defies the linear time of narrative, Narcissus is already guilty in the first scene, before coming into being as a subject, before his "constitution in the mirror stage" of the second scene; and the second scene, which one might wish to read simply as the moment in which the subject is constituted, must in fact be understood as a punishment for an earlier, archaic or prehistoric crime. It is his crime in the first scene that destines him for punishment in the second—his encounter before the watery pool being explicitly presented as a *punishment* for his failure to respond (according to a logic that enchains the destiny of Narcissus in a story that has already taken place with Echo, who for her part could not be heard as another, having been deprived of her voice for earlier crimes against the goddess Juno). The very advent of the subject, narcissism itself, in its "inaugural" moment and prototypical staging—a single figure suspended above the watery abyss—would thus have to be read, not merely as an inaugural moment, a beginning or constitution, but as a punishment, an extended moment or "stage," which therefore only takes place against the background of this divine Other, this Law that "already" destines the subject for exile and death, as a punishment for "earlier" crimes. This is the archaic justice of the myth, the harsh law that holds Narcissus responsible for an event—a relation or nonrelation—that occurred before any reflection took place, outside historical time, in a primordial or mythical moment before the advent of the subject, in a past that was never present and that Narcissus will never remember. The moment of the look that is staged by Ovid, and by psychoanalysis as well, must be read against the background of this law. Indeed, the very look itself would capture the essence of this law. As Derrida says: "This look that cannot be exchanged is what situates originary culpability and original sin; it is the essence of responsibility."[13] Hovering for a moment before the pool, *Narcissus cannot remember* the "earlier time" that brought him to this place of origin and end. And yet, as we must also acknowledge, *his experience will also testify to this immemorial past*, as the second scene bears witness, after the fact, to the earlier scene.

This adds a final element to the operation of the law, allowing us to see the punishment of Narcissus somewhat more clearly. The law of the gods may punish us for crimes we cannot remember, which took place before there was time for reflection; but the gods—however frivolous they may be, and however captivated by their own affairs—do not merely use us for their sport. Thus, while Narcissus will never remember the crime for which he has been punished, we must also acknowledge that he knows of his crime after the fact, and knows *because he is brought to justice* for his role in this archaic and immemorial event. In the logic of the myth: his punishment comes not as arbitrary brutality, but as evidence, indeed, as a memorial, that something has taken place. If Narcissus is punished for a crime that took place "before the subject," then, and brought to a watery end, this punishment also gives, in the sense that it alone shows this relation to the other, an immemorial relation which—without this law and this punishment—would disappear without a trace. Thus, for an instant, and after the fact, Narcissus will recall this immemorial responsibility for us, *precisely because he is punished*. It is this divine law, this disastrous advent that gives and takes away, this "event" that occurs outside historical time, that the structure of narcissism confronts, and that then reiterates at every stage, in a logic of repetition that will always be forgotten by narrative, which, for its part, at least offers, for awhile, a little refuge.

CHAPTER 5

The *Place* of Memory in Psychoanalysis

Let us not forget psychoanalysis. The forgetting of psychoanalysis could not be one forgetting among others and cannot fail to produce symptoms.

—DERRIDA, "Let Us Not Forget"

First, then, we must comprehend what sort of things are objects of memory; for mistakes are frequent on this point.

—ARISTOTLE, "Of Memory and Recollection"

I have carefully avoided any contact with philosophy.

—FREUD, "An Autobiographical Study" (20:59)

The thread of memory can guide us through the labyrinth of Lacan's categories, the imaginary, symbolic, and real—but not without difficulties, which we may as well confront in order to clarify a few technical details along the way, above all the twist that leads from the "Rome Discourse" to *Seminar XI*, from the Other to the object, along the path of the transference.

The Silence of the Gestalt

A first approach to memory might be sought in the imaginary: setting out from the image or sensory impression, one might be led to conceive of memory as the faculty that recollects an image or perception after it has passed away. Following this line of thought, both perception and memory (phenomena of "consciousness"?) would belong to the imaginary, the former taking in an image or impression in the immediacy of the present, the latter recalling it after the fact, the difference between the two residing in a temporal factor. A link is thereby established, not only between the image and time, but also between the body and the mind, the sensory apparatus and the mental faculties.

There are good historical precedents for such an analysis. As Aristotle says in his treatise on memory, "only those living beings who are conscious of time can be said to remember" (449b28–30). Which living beings, one might ask, are "conscious of time"? Are we to place memory somewhere along a hierarchy of living beings, a natural order in which time might also be located? "Time" here refers particularly to *past* time, for Aristotle points out that one does not, properly speaking, "remember" the present or the future. In this way, a series of distinctions is quickly established between the three ecstasies of time, each with its respective faculty (of body or mind?): "*sensation* refers to what is present, *expectation* to what is future, and *memory* to what is past" (449b27–28, my emphasis). Through memory, then, the past and present would be connected, in that a sensation, once it has passed away, can be recalled in the mind. As for the future: "It is impossible," Aristotle remarks, "to remember the future, which is *an object of conjecture or expectation*" (449b10–11). The science of memory would thus be confined to the past and the present (like our discipline of history, that reconstruction in the present of what once was). And yet Aristotle adds parenthetically: "(there might even be a *science of expectation* as some say there is of divination)" (449b12, my emphasis). A curious remark for the philosopher dedicated to "science" (especially biology), Aristotle's observation recalls Lacan's statement in the "Rome Discourse" that psychoanalysis is part of a "movement that is now establishing a new order of the sciences" (E, 72), the principal feature of which is the distinction it makes between "exact sciences," natural sciences modeled on the experiment and bound to clock-time, and what Lacan calls "conjectural sciences," which confront "the intersubjective time that structures human action" (E, 73–75; see also SXI, 43).[1] As an action or praxis that bears on human time, then, psychoanalytic memory cannot ignore the dimension of the future: "The point is that for Freud it is not a question of biological memory, nor of its intuitionist mystification . . . but a question of recollection, that is, of history, balancing the scales, in which conjectures about the past are balanced against promises of the future" (E, 48). Thus, although memory, strictly speaking, joins the present and the past, the question of the future cannot be left aside, since memory entails a reflection on the structure of time, and even poses problems for the term "science" by linking it to "divination" (Aristotle) and "conjecture" (Lacan).

Ten years later, Lacan opens *Seminar XI* by returning to this question: rather than simply claiming that psychoanalysis, buttressed by the new techniques of formalization provided by Lévi-Strauss and Saussure, has now become a science, rather than beginning with the measure already given as to what constitutes a science, and then asking whether psychoanalysis has attained this status, Lacan begins with a question about the status of psychoanalysis, positioning it in relation to the two poles of science and religion: "psychoanalysis . . . may actually enlighten us as to what we should understand by science, and even by religion" (SXI, 7). We have here a first indication of our direction: whereas in the "Rome Discourse" the "return to Freud" tended to unfold as an effort of formalization guided by the regularities of the symbolic order—the autonomous, objective field of the "Law"—now it is a matter of introducing something beyond the limits of formalization, an "element" that falls outside the systemic operation of the law and marks an impossibility of closure, an "object" that is missing, which Lacan addresses in terms of radical particularity, something that concerns the transference, and may be formulated in terms of *desire*. Unlike the structuralist projects of linguistics and anthropology, which still provide the major point of orientation for our reading of Lacan and which succeed in establishing themselves as sciences only by bracketing the problem of the subject and focusing on the a priori laws governing language or exchange, psychoanalysis returns to the question of the relation between the subject and the law. For the "science" of psychoanalysis, if it is a science, this means that it cannot be a question of attaining a truth that would be universalizable, repeatable by anyone; it does not seek a proper degree of objectification by eliminating desire: "What must there be in the analyst's desire for it to operate in a correct way? Can this question be left outside the limits of our field, as it is in effect in the sciences?" (SXI, 9). We have quickly passed from the image through the symbolic toward the element of lack that comes to be designated as the object a, the fragment of the real. With this trajectory in mind, let us take up the thread of our argument again.

For Aristotle, memory links perception to time, but it also entails a connection between the body and the mind: in fact, memory has two aspects, bearing on mental content (*hypolepsis*) as well as perception (*aisthesis*)—"in the former case remembering that one *learned or thought* a thing, and in the latter that one *heard or saw or perceived* it in some way" (449b19–23, my emphasis).[2] Despite this link binding memory to "thought" as well as "perception," Aristotle does not ascribe it uniquely or essentially to the rational animal: "memory," he writes, "is found not only in man and beings which are capable of opinion and thought, but also in some other animals" (450a15). As a result, memory "would seem to belong incidentally to the thinking faculty, but essentially to the primary sense-faculty" (450a13–15). Not an exclusive feature of the rational soul, memory would be aligned with the faculties of sense, incidentally bearing on ideas as well. As Aristotle says in "On Sense and Sensible Objects," "the most important characteristics of animals . . . are clearly those which belong to both soul and body, such as sensation, memory, passion, desire, and appetite generally, and in addition to these pleasure and pain, for these belong to almost all living creatures" (436a7–11). Aristotle would thus appear to locate memory in nature, initiating a discourse that leads to the contemporary idea that, whereas some animals are simply trapped in the immediate present of stimulus and response, bound by the inflexible mandate of "instinct," higher organisms ("almost all living creatures") are able to remember, and can therefore—this will be decisive—*learn from experience* and *adapt to reality* (like the raccoon, "taught by a judicious conditioning of his reflexes to go to his feeding trough when he is presented with a card on which his menu is listed," in Jules Masserman's experiment, discussed by Lacan in the "Rome Discourse"; E, 62). From this imaginary point of departure, from memory understood as a "cognitive" event that has its origin in a "real" perceptual experience, we are soon led to the language of adaptation, reality, and learning that is supposed to characterize more advanced organisms. Despite this contemporary psychological model, one wonders whether Aristotle's thought was ever so natural, or so sanguine about adaptation to "reality." We know this question was central to Freud, who found human memory to be conspicuously maladaptive.

Memory poses a question of time, then, but also a question of place. In what part of the organism-soul does memory reside? If "sensation" is of the body and "expectation" is of the mind, does "memory" somehow provide a link between the two, binding the raw experience of the organism to the distant and peculiar legislations of the will? Does memory shuttle back and forth, uniting the three aspects of time, weaving a fabric of the past and present, and perhaps even of the future, the "conjecture" of the soul, its hope and yearning? Does memory, in fabricating time, also weave a unity for the organism-soul, joining the passing experience of the body to the retentive knowledge of the mind, as well as to what Aristotle calls "appetite," "passion," and "desire"? Where shall we *locate* this faculty that is said to "belong to both soul and body"? What is its *place*? We know this question was central to Freud, who refused to locate the unconscious anatomically. In spite of these difficulties, our point of departure locating memory in the image, would seem to be confirmed when Aristotle remarks that, since memory is not exactly the perception itself, since it concerns *something that is absent* (*apontos*) and must be revived in the mind, "it is obvious, then, that memory belongs to that part of the soul to which imagination belongs" (450a23–24).

Wordsworth, recalling Aristotle, notes that the poet, who is by definition endowed with a lively imagination, does not simply "imagine" in the sense of "making things up." It would be more accurate, Wordsworth observes, to say that those possessed with imagination are "affected more than other men by *absent things as if they were present*."[3] It is as if the imagination, far from being the free and spontaneous faculty of creation for which it is often mistaken, were essentially bound to recollection. Hence Aristotle's remarkable claim: "All things which are imaginable are essentially objects of memory" (450a23).[4] In the first book of his magnum opus, *The Prelude*, Wordsworth gives us an initial sign of the awakening of the child's poetic faculty in the episode of the stolen boat: after seeing a "huge Cliff" suddenly rise up on the horizon as his guilty craft moves across the water, the narrator turns homeward "with grave /And serious thoughts," the image working still upon his mind. "After I had seen / That spectacle, for many days, my brain /Work'd with a dim and undetermined sense / Of unknown modes of being":

> in my thoughts

> There was a darkness, call it solitude,
> Or blank desertion, no familiar shapes
> Of hourly objects, images of trees,
> Of sea or sky, no colors of green fields;
> But huge and mighty Forms that do not live
> Like living men moved slowly through my mind
> By day and were the trouble of my dreams.[5]

In addition to being overwhelmed by this impression that does not pass away, captured by a bodily perception that remains "in [his] thoughts" after the fact; in addition, moreover, to the peculiar work of "negation" exercised, not by the image, which simply presents what is there, but by the memory, which intrudes upon what is immediately present, canceling the "familiar shapes" of nature, inducing a "blank desertion" that negates perception ("no shapes," "no colors"); in addition to these, we find a sublime *fecundity* in memory, for it not only establishes a continuity between the past experience of the body and its retention in the mind, but also has a generative force, propelling the subject into a future inhabited by *figures that never were*, a world beyond perception, composed of "Forms that do not live / Like living men." "Mighty Forms," such as guilt, perhaps, which are not, strictly speaking, "remembered" and do not strictly derive from the image or its recollection, guilt being an "affect" that, however "experiential" and "bodily," cannot be said to derive from perception or from a recollection of the past, but is rather a *surplus* generated in the course of memory. As if it were a matter of "conjecture" or "divination."

As with Aristotle, so with Wordsworth, all of these elements would seem to unfold on the basis of the image and its recollection. History itself, the peculiar rupture that separates humanity from the pure presence of the natural world and plunges us into another time, a world of "Forms," might thus be construed in terms of immediate experience and its recollection after the fact, both of these being imaginary in Lacan's sense. In "the tradition" (as we are taught to remember it), everything happens as if the signifier could go without saying, as if the silent work of memory could generate all the elements of what we call "subjective life." The signifier would thus be a mere appendage, a tool in the hands of the most clever monkey, helpful for "communicating," no doubt, but in no way constitutive of the life it serves.

Indeed, Lacan suggests in "The Mirror Stage" that an image or *Gestalt* provides the very foundation of the ego, its *Urbild*, a first minimal "form" that affords the mind a unified presentation of the body, an initial point of identification that also brings with it a temporal factor: the mirror stage "is experienced as a temporal dialectic that decisively projects the subject into history" (E, 4). Here too, the unity of the organism-soul and the gathering of time within its horizon would seem to be accomplished at the level of the image, in accordance with "the tradition." We might add that this imaginary incarnation is also the institution of narcissism, which is perhaps nothing other than an insistence upon the past, a commitment to an identity that *tends to repeat itself*. The subject, whose very origin is given only through the speculative movement of conjecture that we call "anticipation," a prospective identification with an external unity that it does not actually possess, is thereby *thrown* into the drama of ex-sistence, "a drama whose internal thrust is precipitated from insufficiency to anticipation" and leads to "the armor of an alienating identity, which will mark with its rigid structure the subject's entire mental development" (E, 4). Thus, behind the image and its recollection, and behind the temporal structure of anticipation that provides the "body" with its peculiar unity, we would also seem to find repetition, all of this generated through the imaginary. Everything happens as if language were exterior to memory, a means of articulating or representing what is recalled, perhaps, but in no way intrinsic to recollection itself. For Aristotle, Wordsworth, and Lacan, the signifier would not thus be essential for the sort of consciousness we call "memory." In short, setting out from the image and its recollection, we might weave the entire tapestry of life—memory and embodiment, learning and adaptation, the plague of guilt and the rapture of narcissism, history, time itself, and even the tendency to repeat—all of these derived from the imaginary, that first formation of the unitary ego that persists through all change, unable to forget, and seeking throughout the course of its history to gather itself together, to recollect itself.

Suffering from Reminiscence

And yet the memory that concerns Freud is not a conscious act that recalls the image or thought after it has passed away, but is unconscious, that is to say, *a memory that has not been remembered.* This is the meaning of Freud's early formulation according to which "hysterics suffer mainly from reminiscences" (SE, 2:7). The memory that concerns Freud here is not so much a cognitive faculty—what we might call the "ability" to remember—as the fact of a memory *outside the cognitive apparatus* of our usual psychology (which is always a psychology of "consciousness"). Freud's path starts out from this *Other* memory, this Other *place* (*ein anderer Schauplatz*, or, as Lacan puts it in *Seminar IX*, "What Freud calls . . . *die Idee einer anderer Localität*"; 56), a nonorganic memory that appears, not in the image or thought that is recollected in the mind, but in the exteriority of *discourse.* "The unconscious of the subject," Lacan says, "is the *discourse of the Other*" (E, 55, 193; SXI, 131, my emphasis).

Accordingly, the classic point of departure for locating unconscious memories is found, not in what the subject recalls, but in the symbolic "material" of the lapsus and free association. Even the body has a symbolic status here: to Freud's own astonishment, the symptom was not a phenomenon of "nature" and could not be reduced to the kind of organic illness treated by medical science, since it was a phenomenon of meaning, a "reminiscence" that, having been lost to consciousness, found itself inscribed in the flesh. Outside consciousness, the lapsus, the symptom, and free association provide symbolic material that has no apparent meaning, a spontaneous creation that appears in speech or in the body, but that is "non-sense" from the point of view of the speaker (not what I meant to say, not what I desired). Hence Lacan's definition: "The unconscious," he writes in the "Rome Discourse," "is that part of the concrete discourse . . . that is not at the disposal of the subject in re-establishing the continuity of his conscious discourse" (E, 49).

Since Lacan's work is so often "explained" by reference to Saussure, let us take another step (holding onto the thread of the symptom). It is often said that the "body"—and the symptom is of the body—is an *imaginary body* for Lacan, but this cannot be sufficient. Setting out from this theme of the imaginary body, many readers have been led to separate the imaginary and the symbolic, concluding that Lacan's work "evolves" by passing from a "mirror stage," in which the body is central, to a later preoccupation with linguistics in which everything is reduced to a play of the signifier and "reality" is lost.[6] Such a "staging" of Lacan's work is a convenient way of avoiding his thought, replacing it with a narrative divided into two contradictory periods—Kojèvian intersubjectivity eventually replaced by the formalism of Saussure, though neither of these has any bearing on the unconscious. Translated into the already digested references of the academy, Lacan's work is magically made to disappear before our very eyes, like the real itself, replaced by an imaginary narrative.[7] But it is clearly not only a matter of linguistics, of *langue* and *parole*, when Lacan distinguishes between speech and language, for in separating the ego's narrative from the linguistic material produced by the unconscious, he is concerned with the relation between the signifier and the organism, noting that "speech is driven out of the concrete discourse that orders the subject's consciousness," only to find "support . . . in the natural functions of the subject. . . . The symptom is here a signifier" Lacan adds, "a symbol written in the sand of the flesh" (E, 69; cf. 50–52).

This proposition from the "Rome Discourse" is elaborated in "The Agency of the Letter": "metaphor is the very mechanism by which the symptom, in an analytic sense, is determined . . . a symptom being a metaphor in which flesh or function is taken as a signifying element" that remains "inaccessible to the conscious subject" (E, 166). The symptom is therefore not a purely organic phenomenon, but a bodily effect *unique to the speaking being*. This is the "reminiscence" from which the hysteric suffers, without knowing why, as if history had come to an end and could only repeat itself, refusing to pass away: "there is no other way of conceiving the *indestructibility* of unconscious desire," Lacan writes, the fact that even when the ego forgets and time passes by, the unconscious remembers—as if, to recall Freud's formula, the unconscious did not know time (SE, 14:186; 5:661; 18:28). "It is in this sort of memory," Lacan writes, "that is found the chain that *insists* on reproducing itself . . . which is the chain of dead desire" (E, 167). Such is the "enigma that desire seems to pose for a 'natural philosophy'" (E, 166). Thus, in order to avoid the reduction that makes the "body" imaginary while relegating the symbolic to a purely "linguistic" phenomenon, we must consider more closely the relation between the signifier and the flesh, the status of these vital signs.

One can see here why Lacan claims that well "before Darwin . . . Hegel had provided the ultimate theory of the proper function of aggressivity in human ontology" by detaching the intersubjective structure of the desire for recognition from its biological counterpart, a model governed by survival and adaptation: "if, in the conflict of Master and Slave, it is the recognition of man by man that is involved, it is also promulgated on a radical negation of natural values" (E, 26). Given this disjunction between Darwin and Hegel (which makes "cultural evolution" an oxymoron), one would have to draw a sharp distinction between the time of *history* (a temporality of the signifier) and the time of evolution or natural *development*, a distinction that psychology, by virtue of its adherence to naturalistic models of perception and adaptation, fails to appreciate, thereby remaining pre-Hegelian. The human animal is *destined to history* precisely because it has *no natural development*: in Freudian terms, if the instinct had something like a "natural development," regulated by the stages of adolescence, reproductive maturation, and object-choice (with all the consequences of "normalization" this entails), then sexuality would remain within the order of nature and its law; but the most elementary point of Freud's discovery, which leads to his distinction between the instinct and the drive, is precisely that, whereas the instinct amounts to a sort of natural program, governed by the principles of life (self-preservation and reproduction), the sexual drive has no natural mooring, *no predestined aim and no proper object*; moreover, the drive is ultimately linked by Freud to a thoroughly nonbiological relation to death, a "death drive" that, in spite of Freud's biological terminology, is unmistakably due to the play of representation to which sexuality, in the human animal, is subject. In "The Rome Discourse," Lacan accordingly notes "the difference . . . between reference to the sup-posedly organic stages of individual development and research into the *particular* events of a subject's history" (E, 51); and again, "the anal stage is no less purely *historical* [that is to say, bound to the particularity of the subject, in his or her detachment from natural development] when it is actually experienced than when it is reconstituted in thought," and "seeing it as a mere stage in some instinctual maturation leads even the best minds straight off the track" (E, 53).

Now, the symbolic debris of the lapsus and the symptom, this realm of apparent nonsense and error, is not a matter of chance, according to Freud: emerging as a mistake or accident that interrupts speech, the dis-course of the Other is nevertheless *governed by law*. "Speak of chance," Lacan writes, "if you like," citing Freud's remark in *The Interpretation of Dreams*, but "in my experience I have observed nothing arbitrary in this field" (SXI, 45), a field that is governed by law.[8] We find here the famous "linguistic" orientation of Lacan's early text, organizing Freud's medita-tion on the lapsus, the truth that emerges in the error of the signifier, the laws of displacement and substitution that govern the apparent spontane-ity and chaos of the dream. The law here is neither that of consciousness and its intentions, nor that of the organism and its natural life, neither a law governing the constitution of "subjective" sense (a phenomenology of intentionality), nor a law given by medical science, but the law of the Other. Thus, if psychoanalysis breaks with the causality of organic medi-cine, it is also not a science of "subjectivity." As Lacan says in "The Freud-ian Thing," when it is a question of the memory carried in the lapsus, or in the reminiscence of the symptom: "The laws of recollection and symbolic recognition are, in effect, different in essence and manifestation from the laws of imaginary reminiscence" (E, 141)—in "essence," because they are foreign to the mental sphere of psychology, and in "manifestation," be-cause they appear in the alterity of the signifying chain.

Such a conception of memory will have immediate consequences for the theory of the "subject." In the "Rome Discourse," it is already evident that the subject, for Lacan, is not the active subjectivity that doubts and recollects, establishing a certain mental content ("emotion recollected in tranquility" is the phrase we remember from Wordsworth): "The subject goes well beyond what is experienced 'subjectively' by the individual, ex-actly as far as the truth he is able to attain" (E, 55). As he puts it in "The Freudian Thing," in his prosopopoeia of truth: "Whether you flee me in fraud or seek to entrap me in error, I will reach you in the mistake against which you have no refuge. . . . The trade route of truth no longer passes through thought: strange to say, it now seems to pass through things" (E, 122). This is the function of the signifier in its materiality. The "memory" in question is not a psychological faculty that recollects an image, perception, or thought, but must be located *outside* the psychological subject, at the level of the signifier.

Lacan explicitly marked the difference between the subject of psychoanalysis and the psychological category of subjectivity in schema L, in which the narrative of the ego was distinguished from the place of the subject as marked by symbolic debris.

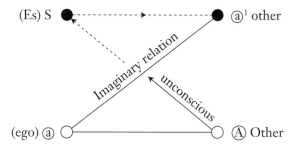

Here one sees clearly the distinction between the symbolic axis, in which the "non-sense" of the unconscious appears as the "discourse of the Other," and the imaginary axis, in which the narrative of the ego unfolds in the intersubjective relation of "I and Thou," not a relation of dialogue and mutual understanding, as our theorists of communication would wish, but a relation of deception and love, idealization and narcissism.

To ignore the symbolic, moreover, is to be forced, with Jules Masserman and his raccoon, to advocate a conception of "reality" in which the psychoanalytic understanding of the subject disappears altogether: "In analytic practice, mapping the subject in relation to reality, such as it is supposed to constitute us, and not in relation to the signifier, amounts to falling already into the degradation of the psychological" (SXI, 142). Thus, if we wish to follow the course of Freud's thought and assign a "true function to what, in analysis, is called recollection or remembering," we must not confuse it with the return of an image from the world of "reality": "Recollection is not Platonic reminiscence—it is not the return of a form, an imprint, an *eidos* . . . from the beyond. It is something humble . . . at the level of the signifier" (SXI, 47). We have dropped the thread that would lead from perception to recollection, along the path of the image.

No Labyrinth in the Beehive

Indeed, Lacan writes in the early seminars that memory is not really a property of the living being, the organism, but only appears with the symbolic order, the nonliving machinery of the signifier, the primal technology that, as so many myths tell us, was originally a gift (or curse) of the gods, since it is clearly not a tool in human hands, an invention stumbled upon one day by the supposed signifying monkey. A long humanist tradition would be pleased to think of the human being as a clever animal, capable of using language like any other tool (a cultural acquisition), or as an innate faculty "belonging" to humanity (a natural endowment). These are the only two currently rational alternatives, the "innate" and the "acquired": the former orients us biologically, the latter by a humanistic historicism in which "man makes himself." It would be unscientific and even superstitious to revert to mythology and say that language is "a gift of the gods," as many religious accounts do, suggesting, furthermore, that only this alien gift allowed the human to become "human"—not to rule over nature as the dominant or most evolutionarily successful animal, but rather to be separated from nature, to plunge into the maladaptive and perverse course of history. All this is an affront to our narcissism, our image of man as the most competitive and rational monkey, a "naturalism" perfectly in keeping with the humanistic idea that only the human being develops "culture." "Is psychoanalysis a humanism?" Lacan asks. "People tell us about the autonomous ego," but "nothing in experience gives us the slightest hint of it . . . we are told that man is the measure of all things. But where is his own measure? Is it to be found in himself?" (SII, 68). As he says in the "Rome Discourse," "it can be seen that I do not shrink from seeking the origins of symbolic behavior outside the human sphere" (E, 62).

It should come as no surprise that the same two impoverished alternatives govern current theories of sexuality: on the one hand, we speak of *gender*, determined by cultural practices that codify "masculinity" and "femininity" as *historically* formed; on the other hand, we use the term *sex* to name the *biological* order of "male" and "female." Given this alternative between naturalism and historicism, "sexuality" in Freud's sense would belong *neither to nature nor to culture* (like the incest taboo in Lévi-Strauss).[9] From the standpoint of psychoanalysis, sexuality is neither a natural fact nor a human invention, a convention "instituted" in the course of history, but an *imperative of division* that lies at the origin of history, the rending open of a time that destines the human for an unnatural and perpetually contested embodiment. Thus, in the Freudian universe, sexual difference is neither reduced to a biological fact, grounded in anatomy, nor explained as a historical product, constituted by social practices. This is the great conceptual difficulty, but also the theoretical importance, of psychoanalysis: on the one hand, the facts of anatomy are insufficient to determine sexual identity, which is understood in terms of identification and is therefore no longer a question of biology; on the other hand, sexual difference cannot be reduced to a purely historical and socially constructed phenomenon, since it is tied to the fact that every subject, regardless of social conventions and historically variable laws, is born of a woman, from the union of two sexes, into a body that will be *like* one of these two sexes, and *not like* the other. The child's identification with one or the other of these two sexes is certainly variable and subject to a number of social conventions that are historically contingent, but the fact of sexual difference itself is not the product of convention: it is not an arrangement invented by human beings, like democracy or capitalism, an institution that might be true only in a particular place and time (a convention that the human subject might freely manipulate, in accordance with the humanistic idea that man is the maker of all things). Like the imperative of death, the law of sexual embodiment is not a human law. This does not mean, however, that sexual difference can be reduced to a fact of nature: the question of sexual identity for the human subject is not automatically answered by the fact of anatomy, as it is for the animal, who is simply born male or female, and whose sexual identity is therefore given biologically. This is the fundamental enigma and the central theoretical interest of psychoanalysis: sexual difference is neither reducible to a natural fact nor explicable as a product of history. From the point of view of psychoanalysis, therefore, historical investigation and natural science are both theoretically inadequate when it comes to sexual difference.

Thus, contrary to a long tradition of "natural philosophy," which would ascribe to all the higher animals a psychological faculty of memory grounded in the recollection of images and thus an ability to "learn from experience," to "adapt to the environment," and to "modify behavior," Lacan almost perversely suggests that memory does not belong to nature, while insisting that it is not a human technology.[10] Only the "animal in possession of the signifier" (*zōon logon echon*, a definition profoundly altered by its translation into the Latin *animal rationis*, or our biological *Homo sapiens*) is subject to memory, which must therefore be located, not in the organism, but at the level of the symbolic machine. The ego doesn't like it and wants to deny it, but it's true:

> You've been told, you've understood, and you don't believe it—the adding machine has a memory . . . the sort of memory it has is destined to put all the images of memory which up to now we've given ourselves into question. The best thing we've found for giving an image of the phenomenon of memory was the Babylonian wax seal, a thing with a few little reliefs and some lines which you roll out onto a wax plaque. . . . The seal is also a machine, only no-one notices that. (SI, 88)

Lacan goes on to argue that the memory in question can only be understood as a message, "a message inside a machine," "something articulated, of the same order as the fundamental oppositions of the symbolic" (SI, 89). What is more, the symbolic machinery does not circulate in a harmonious, adaptive way, correlated with "external reality" or the "internal pressure" of need, like the dance of the honeybee described in the "Rome Report," which signals "the existence of nectar and its relative distance," as well as "the direction to be followed, determined in relation to the inclination of the sun" (E, 84). No Babylonian confusion of tongues, no Greek labyrinth in the beehive, for "the other bees respond to this message immediately," setting off for the honey of their desire.[11] They do not stop to wonder, "yes, this is what the messenger says, but what does he really want?" Animal society is thus to be distinguished from *groups formed in accordance with language*. Lacan addresses this question in "The Agency of the Letter" when he remarks that psychoanalysis has brought about a reorganization of the sciences, challenging the familiar distinction between nature and culture: "the ethnographic duality of nature and culture is giving way to a ternary conception of the human condition—nature, society, and culture—the last term of which could well be reduced to language" (E, 148). Lacan also remarks in "The Freudian Thing" on the difference between society and culture: "it is this," he writes, "that distinguishes a society founded in language from an animal society," adding that an animal society must be distinguished from "groups formed in accordance with language," since "the inmixture of subjects makes it a group with quite a different structure" (E, 127). One can see here, in the terms *structure* and *group*, the initial bearings that orient Lacan's work in topology.

Beyond the developmental time of either learning or evolution, we have the *time of history*, which is unique to the animal in possession of language, a time not of development or linear chronology, but of memory, retroaction, and the intersubjectivity that is formed in accordance with language, which cannot be understood as a tool in the hands of the learned or adaptive organism, since it *constitutes* the being who then—in a narcissistic delusion—pretends to be its master. Human history, then, far from amounting to the celebrated "adaptive advantage" of the most clever monkey (as the current theorists of cultural evolution maintain), is, rather, the trauma of the signifier upon the organism, the opening up of the subject to an Other law that goes beyond the pleasure principle, beyond the mechanisms of survival and reproduction.[12]

In short, we may be tempted to call instinct a type of "memory," by which the animal recalls its phylogenetic inheritance and "remembers" how to sing the appropriate song, how to defend itself or join in the ritual of mating. But properly speaking, "memory" does not occur in nature and even goes against the grain of nature, "instituting" a kind of machinery that may even repeat itself at the cost of the organism's need, trammeling life in a chain of dead desire: "this comes very close to what we can conceive of as *Zwang*, the compulsion to repeat . . . the form of behavior staged in the past and reproduced in the present in a way that doesn't conform much with vital adaptation" (SII, 89). "The human being," Lacan adds, "is in part outside life, he partakes of the death instinct" (SII, 90). The Fort-Da game, the child's "great cultural achievement" (SE, 18:15), is also a wager with death.

We have passed from the image to the symbolic function and also from the sanguine time of learning and adaptation to the time of the signifier and its memory, alien to nature, perverse and maladaptive. Insofar as our thought is still split between the *naturalism* of organic medicine and the *historicism* that takes the symbolic order to be an invention, a set of institutions by which the human being perpetually reinvents itself, it can be said that we remain pre-Freudian, committed to nineteenth-century models that have been exhausted for almost a century. What trauma maintains our thought within the orbit of this obsolescent division between organic medicine and psychology, a division that amounts to a refusal of the symbolic?

Looking Backward

At first glance perverse and exceptional, an affront or disruption that contradicts the entire tradition of "natural philosophy" by separating memory from organic life, Lacan's claim may turn out to be the norm.[13] Nietzsche, at least, was equally perverse in his text on history, itself a radical contestation of the "philosophy of life," the "vitalism" with which it has so often been confused. Nietzsche, too, separates memory from nature at the beginning of his "untimely" text, starting with the human's inability to forget, and stressing the derangement of pleasure that results: "Consider the herd that is feeding yonder. They know not the meaning of yesterday or today; they leap and feed, rest, digest, and leap again; and thus from morning to night, and from day to day, they are fettered to the moment and their pleasure or displeasure, and therefore neither melancholy nor bored."[14] "Thus the animal lives *unhistorically*," Nietzsche adds, not only because it is contained in the present, but also because it *does not speak*. Nietzsche's remarks are thus organized not simply around the image, but around *the articulation of a question*:

> This is a difficult sight for man to see, for though he thinks himself better than the animals because he is human, he cannot help envying them their happiness. . . . A human being may well ask, "Why do you not speak to me of your happiness but only stand and gaze at me?" The beast wants to answer, "Because I always forget what I wanted to say." But he forgets this answer too and is silent, and the man is left to wonder.

Humanity is thus left hanging on the *question* of happiness, for "he cannot learn to forget but clings relentlessly to the past," as if bound eternally to the return of the signifying chain. Nietzsche adds: "however far and fast he runs, this chain runs with him. And it is a matter for wonder: a moment, now here and then gone, nonetheless returns as a ghost [*als gespenst weider*] and disturbs the peace of a later moment."

To say that memory (this "return" of the ghost from the past) does not belong to nature would seem to contradict a long tradition, for Aristotle, the good biologist (at least this is how we have come to remember him), situated memory within a hierarchy of living beings, differentiated according to their lack or possession of certain faculties—the need for nourishment and reproduction (shared by plants and animals), the capacity for locomotion (given only to animals), the potential for memory distinguishing the higher animals (those capable of learning), and finally the "rational soul" of the human, who is able to "decide," to exercise "judgment" and "will." Didn't Aristotle *locate* memory this way, assigning it a *place* on the great chain of being? We read in *On the Soul*, for example: "not everything that has sensation has movement also," for "plants seem to live without sharing in locomotion or in perception, and many living animals have not power of thought (*dianoia*)" (410b20f). This is the tradition we remember, and yet one may begin to doubt, as one looks back.

At first glance perverse and exceptional, a disruption of "natural philosophy" and "the tradition," the link between memory and the signifier may already belong to Aristotle. We said that Aristotle associates memory with the image or perception, as the faculty that recalls these things after the fact, belonging to "that part of the soul to which imagination belongs." We said that "the tradition" (a singular noun) confirms, through Wordsworth, that the "remembrance of things past," "emotion recollected in tranquility," is the principal gift and debt of imagination. A ghost returns, beckoning: perhaps we have gone too quickly. Let us retrace our steps. If memory is of the image, if memory is said to recall the "image" or "perception" or "thought," bringing back an "impression" after the fact, *what* exactly is being remembered if this "impression," as David Krell has shown, concerns "perception" (*aisthesis*) but also "thought" (*hypolepsis*), and perhaps some other things as well, such as "affects" (*pathēmata*). Addressing this plurality, Aristotle's formulation is striking: "for when a man is exercising his memory he always *says in his mind* (*en tēi psychēi legei*) that he has *heard, or felt, or thought* this before" (449b23, my emphasis).

We have remarked on the question of place: *Where* is memory if it is of the body, rooted in the sensory apparatus, but also of the mind, recalling ideas or thoughts? And *where* is the affect if, like "guilt" or "anxiety," it is difficult to call such a bodily phenomenon "sensory" and absurd to call it an "idea"? Now, the question also arises as to *what*, exactly, is remembered in memory—*the thing itself* (idea or affect or perception) or rather some *re-presentation* of the thing ("mistakes are frequent on this point"; 449b10). It must be observed, Aristotle says, that in remembering we do not return to the things themselves, but only have a "memory" of them: "it is only the affection that is present, and the fact [*pragmatos*] is not" (450a26). This creates a new difficulty for the relation between the present and past, perhaps, since Aristotle asks whether a memory is actually *the thing that was*, or whether it is *a thing of its own*: "Is what one remembers the present affection [*to pathos*] or the original from which it arose [*hē ekeino aph' hou egeneto*]" (450b13–14)? At this point in his discussion, Aristotle returns to an image—or metaphor—he has already used, in which a memory is compared with a picture. In one sense, he suggests, the memory is like a picture, which represents what was, and in this sense it can be said that one is able to "remember the absent fact" (15), to "remember what is not present" (18). But in another sense, a memory is a separate thing of its own, "just as the picture painted on the panel is at once a picture and a portrait, and though one and the same, is both" (21–22). Consequently, "we must regard the mental picture within us both as an object of contemplation in itself and as a mental picture of something else" (24–26). There are a host of problems, even at the level of our traditional, "imaginary" memory, even before we wind our way to the unconscious.

To this plague of questions, we would add one more: When we speak of memory as recalling a perception—idea or affect or sensation—that has passed away, when we speak of memory as "re-presenting" something that was once present, terminology that revolves around the image is easily displaced by another terminology, one that is closer to "inscription" than to images. Here too, the term *representation* seems to lead in more than one direction. When Aristotle writes of memory as "being like a portrait" (*hoion zōgraphēma*, 450a29–30), his vocabulary is no longer that of the image that served as his starting point, but rather links together two references: the living being (*zōon*) and the verb for inscription or writing (*to graphēma*).[15] (When Lacan speaks in *Seminar XI* of the "gaze," that peculiar object of the scopic drive beyond the visible field, he says "I am photographed"; SXI, 106.) In spite of our initial direction, then, we wind our way to the symbolic, that field about which Aristotle seems already to have been speaking. We know Aristotle as the good biologist, but these ghostly remarks return to us now: What is it that "the tradition" wants us to recall; what has our memory of "the tradition" concealed? What indeed *is* "the tradition" (a singular identity)? One is easily disoriented by these recollections: What route would lead us back to the Greek origin, the natural philosopher, as we try to recall him, the father, who has been such a decisive part of our destiny?

Doesn't Wordsworth also say that the imagination, while certainly a faculty bound to the image, is nevertheless constitutively structured by words? In his famous note to "The Thorn," he suggests that the signifier, far from simply re-presenting or "remembering" an image or experience that took place somewhere in "reality," on the contrary plays a constitutive role in imagination itself. "It was my wish in this poem," Wordsworth writes, "to show the manner in which men cleave to the same ideas," to present characters who have been afflicted by some trauma, and are compelled perpetually to return to this trauma: "I had two objects to attain; first, to represent a picture which would not be unimpressive . . . secondly, while I adhered to the style in which such persons describe, to take care that words, which in their minds are impregnated with passion, should likewise convey passion to Readers."[16] Moreover, Wordsworth remarks, in treating the sort of character who speaks in this poem, in showing that tendency by which "men cleave to the same ideas," he also wished to illustrate how "an attempt is rarely made to communicate impassioned feelings without something of an accompanying consciousness of the inadequacies of our own powers, or the deficiencies of language." As a result, in the midst of the imagination's effort to speak, Wordsworth says, "there will be a craving in the mind, and as long as it is not satisfied the speaker will cling to the same words." All of which indicates "the interest [the investment or cathexis, perhaps] which the mind attaches to words, not only as symbols of the passion, but as *things*, active and efficient, which are themselves part of the passion." Here again, the imagination veers off from the start, diverging from its natural origin.

A similar trajectory is evident in Freud. When he comes to the analysis of the sexual drive in the *Three Essays* (SE, 7:135–243), Freud does not speak of a "masculine" and "feminine" drive ordered as if by nature. One might wish to find two forms of sexuality, one for each of the sexes, but, as Lacan says, giving Freud's observation its most extreme and counterintuitive force: "there is only one libido." Thus Freud, unlike Ernest Jones and Karen Horney, does not speak of a "masculine" and "feminine" form of the drive, but rather of an "active" and "passive" drive that, far from being divided between the two sexes according to nature (thus confirming the conventional "passive" female and "active" male), rather characterizes human sexuality as such *along the lines of grammar*: "active and passive," "subject and object" are grammatical functions (SXI, 177, 192, 200). This "sentence structure" organizes Freud's reflections on the relations between sadism and masochism, voyeurism and exhibitionism (SXI, 170). Freud's text "A Child is Being Beaten" (SE, 17:177–204), which deals with primary masochism, is equally clear on this point, the fantasy it explores being ordered by a series of variations: "My father is beating the child (whom I hate)"; "I am being beaten by my father"; "A child is being beaten (I am probably looking on)," and so on. Perhaps even more intriguing is Freud's remark in "Some Points for a Comparative Study of Organic and Hysterical Motor Paralyses" (SE, 1:155–72), where the displacement from the image to the symbol is central. Pointing out that the hysterical symptom does not follow the lines of anatomy as a neurologist might expect, Freud remarks that "in its paralyses and other manifestations hysteria behaves as though anatomy did not exist or as though it had no knowledge of it" (SE, 1:169). The part of the body that is affected in hysterical paralysis corresponds, not to the biological unit, but to the *idea* of the body, the *popular conception* of the body. We come to a crossroad here: Does the part of the body correspond (in this representation, this correspondence theory) to the *image* of the body, in defiance of medical knowledge, or does it correspond to the *concept*, the *common name*? The problem is explicit in Freud's text: hysterical paralysis, he writes, "takes the organs in the ordinary, popular sense of *the names they bear*: the leg is the leg as far up as its insertion into the hip, the arm is the upper limb *as it is visible under the clothing*" (SE, 1:169, my emphasis). When the symptom is a "reminiscence" in some way, does it follow the image or the word?[17] Let us consider more closely some elements of this symbolic memory.

THE SYMBOLIC: DOUBT, NEGATION, SYMPTOM

We have stressed the lapsus, the dream, and the forgotten word—symbolic debris that has no apparent meaning, "material" that is "nonsense" from the point of view of the speaker. Appearing as a mistake or accident that interrupts discourse, the lapsus is nevertheless not error but the truth of the unconscious.

THE LABOR OF SYMBOLIZATION

If the first hysterics "suffer mainly from reminiscences" instead of purely organic conditions, it is also the case that their symptoms could be relieved—against all biomedical causality—by purely symbolic means (voodoo or magic, rather than "science"): "nothing can be grasped, destroyed, or burnt, except in a symbolic way, as one says, *in effigy, in absentia*" (SXI, 50; Lacan is citing SE, 12:108). What is more, this symbolic intervention upon the bodily symptom is not accomplished through *conscious memory* but through *verbalization* (the "talking cure"), a speech that the early patients would articulate under hypnosis, but often *would not remember* upon being awakened—which suggests that the work of symbolization is not a psychological process of recollection, but a labor that operates *outside* the psychological subject, at the level of the signifier. "The psychological prejudices of Freud's day were opposed to acknowledging any such *reality* in verbalization," but the fact remains that one does not "have to *know* whether the subject has remembered anything whatever from the past," Lacan says. "He has simply recounted the event . . . verbalized it . . . made

it pass into the *verbe*" (E, 46, my emphasis). Thus, the labor of symbolization is not accomplished *at the level of knowing* or by "making the unconscious conscious." This fact should carry more weight than it does with
analysts who believe that their task is to go back through the past and
discover "what really happened," as if an appeal to prediscursive "reality"
would be sufficient for addressing what, at the same time, they admit to
be "psychological" difficulties. Freud himself, in *Studies on Hysteria*, tells
of his early discovery of this point, when, having been given a diary by the
mother of his patient in which all the facts of the past were written down,
he tried to accelerate the patient's memory, to hand her the "truth" when
she stumbled, only to find that it impeded the patient's progress.

DOUBT

Following the "Rome Discourse," we have stressed the symbolic manifestation of the unconscious. In *Seminar XI*, Lacan turns to a quasi-Cartesian
formula, adding doubt to the lapsus: where the subject doubts, or denies,
or is uncertain, that is where Freud pricks up his ears. "It is here that
Freud lays all his stress—doubt is the support of his certainty" (SXI, 35).
If the subject doubts ("This is probably irrelevant, but it occurs to me
that . . ."), Freud is sure: "Freud places his certainty, his *Gewissheit*, only
in the constellation of signifiers" (SXI, 44). To be more precise, then, it is
not only in symbolic detritus, but also in "doubt," wherever there is an
element of negation and the subject *no longer knows*: that is where Freud tells
us, like Descartes to a certain extent, that "it thinks" behind my doubt.
"Descartes tells us—by virtue of the fact that I doubt, I am sure that I
think" (SXI, 35). The uncertainty of the ego is thereby distinguished from
the *locus of the subject* and its peculiar "memory," a "thinking" that is
lodged outside consciousness and the imaginary order, in the machinery
of the signifier. Descartes, according to Lacan, thus establishes a radical
disjunction between the "I" of doubt (where it is a question of asserting a
particular content, intended—or put in question—by the conscious ego),
and the locus of the cogito (where a certain *formal place* is opened). The
Freudian "subject" is not a psychological phenomenon, a conscious subject, or a storehouse of images, a faculty of will or recollection. The "subject" is, rather, this *empty place* opened by Descartes, the *locus* of a cogito
that suspends all its certainties, a place from which all knowledge has been
evacuated. This locus, the gap of the unconscious, is momentarily held
open not only by symbolic detritus, material that disrupts the narrative of

the ego, nor only by sentences punctuated with doubt, but also by the symptom, insofar as the symptom "remembers" what memory forgets.

MEANING AND BEING

For Lacan, this place of the subject beyond knowing, a locus marked by "non-sense," apparently devoid of meaning, is a *locus of being*, as the *"ergo sum"* of Descartes might suggest. Accordingly, Lacan links the symbol and being in the pun *l'être*. Lacan's early Schema L, distinguishing the ego from the subject, also suggests this distinction between knowing and being, aligning the position of the unconscious subject, not only with the lapsus and the debris of the signifier (*lettre*), but with the "question of being" (*l'être*) posed by the symptom. In "The Agency of the Letter," Lacan takes up the distinction between the knowing (or doubt) of the ego and the being of the subject, noting that the symptom itself can be strictly formulated *as a question*, so that it has a purely symbolic rather than organic form. The two central modalities of this "question of being" articulate the two "imperatives" of sexed embodiment and mortality—"Am I a man or a woman?" being the fundamental question of hysteria, "Am I living or dead?" that of the obsessional.[18] The symptom itself thus has a symbolic form and can be understood as a question: "the neurosis is a question that being poses for the subject" (E, 168). This question, however, is not asked *by the ego*, but is located *outside*, in a locus of being: "the 'being' referred to is that which," Lacan says, "poses its question for the subject. What does that mean? . . . It poses it *in place* of the subject, that is to say, in that place it poses the question *with* the subject, as one poses a problem *with* a pen" (E, 168). The place of the subject, therefore, is not general and neutral, finally Cartesian, like the transcendental ego revealed after all the reductions have been performed, but is "in each case mine," as Heidegger's formula has it, marked by symbolic material that is *particular* to the subject, the debris of a singular history: "this truth of his history is not at all contained in his script, and yet the place is marked there" (E, 55). Such history is inconceivable along imaginary lines and cannot be reduced to the history one "remembers," for it is not contained by the narrative of the ego, but appears in the exteriority of the symbol. Thus, if we follow Freud's path of thought: memory, repetition, and the "reminiscence" of the symptom; doubt, error, and other phenomena of negation, which, as Hegel says, cancel out nature and introduce nonbeing, the movement and labor of the negative; the very concept of the Freudian subject and its peculiar history—all would have to be located in relation to the signifier.

The Cartesian reference to doubt highlights more clearly than the lapsus a number of points organized around the symbolic function of *negation*—a phenomenon that does not function at the level of the image, but only with the "murder" or "lack" introduced by the Fort-Da game, the presence-in-absence of the symbol, which Lacan links to the "negativity" of the paternal function, the *non/nom du père*, which is murder and substitution, death and metaphor. To begin with, the Cartesian reference, by establishing a homology between the lapsus and doubt, bears on free association. Freud gives examples to elucidate the fundamental analytic rule, the principle of free association, which is to *verbalize* everything that "comes to mind," whether you think it relevant or not: "This is probably stupid and *I don't know why I think* of it," or "I doubt this matters, but I am reminded that . . ." Such a "memory," lodged in words that are spoken without being understood, without even being intended, is not an active faculty employed at will, but a sort of *passive memory*, a "being-reminded," a thought that comes "when it wants, not when I want," as Nietzsche says. What does "it want" with us?

Given Freud's distinction between cognitive remembering and the apparent autonomy of the symbol, one cannot help recalling that Aristotle also distinguishes two forms of memory: in addition to the active faculty of recollection (*to anamimnēskesthai*), there is a passive memory (*to mnēmoneuein*), something that comes when "it wants." Aristotle remarks that the former is an attribute of "good learners" (*eumathes*) and is thus linked to knowledge, while the latter often characterizes "the slow-witted" (*oi bradeis*), who, even if they do not exercise their faculties voluntarily, may nevertheless be, so to speak, in the possession of excellent memories. "Those who learn easily are better at recollecting," he says, but "the slow-witted have better memories" (449b7–8). We are thus confronted with a distinction between the adaptive function that belongs to higher animals, destined for enlightenment, and another memory, alien to nature, a memory that comes when "it wants," in its own time. Aristotle also notes that if "recollection" is an *activity* of the soul, a faculty guided by the will, this other memory is an *affection* of the soul—as in "the case of the melancholic" (*tous melancholikous*), for example, "for these are especially affected by mental pictures" (453a19–20). Here, memory is a *pathos*, something the subject suffers. In addition to those who remember helplessly, as if under the affliction of an autonomous memory, there are even those who remember *a past that was never present*, "as happened to Antipheron of Oreus, and other lunatics; for they spoke of their mental pictures as if they had actually taken place, and as if they actually remembered them" (451a9–11). The "Other" memory of Freud would seem to be already present in the tradition, in spite of the "natural" way in which we are taught to remember it. But let us take up our thread again, lest we become distracted.

DIE VERNEINUNG

We have seen Lacan stress the relation between the lapsus and doubt (a link, then, between what is "forgotten" and what is "repudiated," both of which "return" in the signifying chain). Lacan also notes the *element of negation* lodged in doubt, following Freud's observation that often the material deemed unimportant or dubious by the ego will be specifically negated, "marked off" by reservations that identify and reject a given association as "beside the point" ("I doubt this matters," or "This is stupid, but . . ."). The negation exercised by the ego *repudiates*, but does not *conceal*, the place of the subject, any more than conscious forgetting eliminates the evidence of the lapsus or the "reminiscence" of the symptom. Only the symbolic order has this character of presence-in-absence, this aspect of negation that does not simply destroy or reduce to nonbeing, but on the contrary "preserves" and "shows" what is negated, forgotten, or repressed. Freud therefore suggests that when someone claims, "it is not my mother in the dream" (or, e.g., "the deconstruction of logocentrism is not a psychoanalysis of philosophy"),[19] we are dealing at one level with a "judgment," an assertion or proposition, an intended meaning, yet at another level we are justified in disregarding the negative and concluding that an unconscious thought has emerged under the cover of censorship. "The unconscious knows no negation," Freud says (SE, 14:186; see also 5:661). We may therefore follow the "constellation of signifiers" rather than the judgment of the ego. Thus, the ego doubts and says "no," yet this negation does not simply cancel out and annihilate, but rather *shows* the place of the subject beyond doubt.[20]

TRANSFERENCE

The Cartesian formulation, adding doubt to the lapsus, has a further bearing on free association, for the analytic discourse is not a purely logical one, concerned with propositions and knowledge, doubt and certainty, but is structured by the peculiar human relation to the Other, which is not an alter ego. Accordingly, beyond the expression of *doubt* or *uncertainty* previously mentioned, negation takes another turn that bears on the transference. The moment at which the subject's discourse is punctuated by denial will often have a further characteristic, Freud says. In the essay "Negation" (SE, 19:235–39), he gives the example of a client who says: "Now you will think what I'm about to say is insulting, but I've really no such intention." Let us look at the elements of this discursive structure, which (like the symptom) has features that go beyond those of the image. In such a case, Freud argues, we not only have a refusal by consciousness ("I've no such intention") of the thought that has nevertheless emerged ("what I'm about to say is insulting"). We also find a sentence governed by an intersubjective relation ("you will think, but let me tell you"). Lacan points out that we are faced here with an *attribution of knowledge* that "transfers" the thought that has been negated and locates it in the other, thereby establishing a homology between the place of the unconscious thought (the Other) and the place of the analyst ("you will think"). As Russell Grigg points out, such a "transference" of sense or meaning was the original use of the term *Übertragung.*[21] We can see here why "psychological intersubjectivity," as a model of two subjects (persons) who engage in dialogue, should not be confused with the analytic operation, which takes its bearings from "the beyond," the position of the Other, the unconscious discourse, even if this example makes clear how easily the two are intertwined and confused. The "subject supposed to know" is nothing but this support that the analyst provides for an unconscious knowledge, an "it thinks" that, to be sure, does not belong to the analyst, but that is nevertheless "supposed," attributed to the analyst, thereby *opening a position or place* that it is the function of the analyst (as Other) to maintain. In this sense, the analyst's position is not a position of *knowledge* so much as an *obligation.* This is why Lacan speaks of the ethics of psychoanalysis, at the limit of "science."

NEGATION AND LACK: *URVERDRÄNGUNG*

But this "revealing" negation is not the most fundamental issue. Like doubt and symbolic debris, denial *shows* what the ego does not recognize and wishes to avoid. One might therefore be tempted to think that the signifier is able to *bring everything to light,* as if analysis were an entirely symbolic operation. On the basis of such a "productive" negation (*Aufhebung*), it would be tempting to see here a dialectical process, in which the ego's negation brings to light a "truth" that might be integrated into consciousness. Analysis would thus be understood as the process of "making the unconscious conscious"—as if its task were that of *complete recollection* or *absolute knowledge*, its telos a harmony between the exteriority of symbolic material and the interior act of reflection, an "adaequatio rei et intellectus" (cf. E, 131, 296; SXI, 49). But Lacan insists that there is a *limit* to the work of consciousness, a limit to remembering, a limit to symbolization, which is designated as the real. In *Seminar XI*, Lacan addresses this limit to symbolization and modifies the transference as a result, orienting it with reference to a nondialectical "object," a primordial lack.

For the moment, let us simply note the negation that operates productively through the signifier, giving evidence of what the ego did not wish to say and wished not to say, distinguishing this negation ("denial") from another, more radical feature of negation, an irrecoverable absence. Even as early as the first seminar, we have a clear version of this difficulty. It would be tempting, Lacan says, to follow Freud's remarks on the doubt exercised by the ego and to conclude that if the "no" of denial can be understood as a "yes" in the unconscious, then the unconscious may be construed as the dialectical reversal of consciousness.

> The question is—is there an equivalence to be found between these two systems, the system of the ego . . . and the system of the unconscious? Is there an opposition like that of a yes and a no, of a reversal, of a pure and simple negation? Doubtless, the ego makes a great many things known to us by means of the *Verneinung*. Why, while we are at it, couldn't we simply go on to read the unconscious by changing the sign of everything that is said? (SII, 58–59)

To follow the path of the symbol would be to suppose that analysis is a matter of "making the unconscious conscious," as if there were no limit to self-knowledge and as if alterity could ultimately be eliminated through the labor of symbolic recollection. But if it is true that denial "makes a great many things known to us," allowing a repressed thought to emerge into the light, nevertheless Freud's essential discovery lay elsewhere. The "nucleus" of the unconscious is essentially irretrievable, exterior to the laws of the signifier. This is the difference between primary and secondary repression: "originally, for repression to be possible, there must be a beyond of repression, something final, already primitively constituted, an initial nucleus of the repressed, but which . . . is the center of attraction, calling up all the subsequent repressions" (SI, 43). This fundamental, irretrievable lack, which constitutes the subject, makes possible the secondary repressions that "return" in the signifier, but this nucleus itself is beyond recollection, an origin that belongs to "time immemorial." "I'd say that is the essence of the Freudian discovery" (SI, 43).

THE LOGIC OF LOGIC

Following the path from the "error" of the lapsus and the "non-sense" of the dream to doubt, and thence from doubt to negation, we have been led, within negation, to a divergence between that which "shows" (repression, which "returns" in the signifier, through doubt or denial) and that which does not show (primary repression, where lack is given a place). This final aspect of negation introduces an element of lack rather than negation, something that is separate from the affirmation and denial of logic, alien to the level of "judgment" and "thought" that characterizes propositional discourse. Freud argues that the "no" of denial can be converted into a "yes" in the unconscious, and that the repressed is able to "return" in symbolic form, but if, as Lacan says, the "nucleus" of the unconscious cannot finally be revealed by the laws of symbolization, by "changing the sign" from yes to no, this is because the unconscious is not entirely captured in the oppositions of the signifier, the plus and minus of its calculation. As we shall see, what is not captured, what remains outside representation, as a trauma impossible to signify and irreducible to the image, has a relation to *sexuality*.

Here, it is enough to notice that in this primordial lack, we encounter one of Freud's most far-reaching claims, according to which the entire work of rational judgment, predication, and truth claims, is said to depend upon another "logic," a logic of lack that is prior to the yes and no of judgment, a constitutive lack that must be *allowed a place* if the symbolic work of conscious thought, truth and error, even the denial of the ego, is to be possible.[22] At the level of conscious thought, then, we find logic, judgment, the full range of propositions that affirm and deny, but the plus and minus that operate symbolically, the binary calculus of language, seem to depend on a primary repression that cannot be manifested. The logic of this lack is elaborated by the *non/nom du père*, the first substitution that

Lacan finds in the "paternal metaphor," by which the subject's being-toward-death is registered. Here is a "place" beyond the oppositions of the symbolic, the no of the ego that can be translated into a yes: a primordial negation that is not a denial but a void, a fundamental lack to which the subject says "yes" in a more fundamental way, thereby opening up the world of negativity and judgment by way of a trauma that is not so much a historical event, something one might recall, as the opening of history itself. This absolute past is the origin of human time.[23]

THE OTHER AND THE OBJECT

Beyond the pleasure of symbolization, separate from the productive work of negation that is accomplished in speech, prior to the yes and no of judgments, there is a fundamental lack which is not really a "negation" but a place of *primordial affirmation*, deeper than any counterposing opposite, a *Bejahung* or "yes" that is the precondition for any positing of logic (Foucault speaks of "non-positive affirmation").[24] This "yes" is not the assertion of any content, a logical judgment or conscious thought, but the foundation of consciousness, what Freud calls "primal repression," a yes that is the affirmation, for Lacan, not of any proposition, but of lack as such, which is the precondition for the advent of the law of the signifier (Derrida speaks of "the logic of logic").[25] This yes can be witnessed in the *jubilation* of the child playing at the Fort-Da game, not the pleasure of the ego, but rather the obscure pleasure of a primary masochism, a constitutive repression, the foreclosure of which leaves a hole where affirmation would have brought the subject into being.[26] Insofar as the child's game refers us to this trauma, "the exercise with this object refers to an alienation, and not to some supposed mastery" (SXI, 239). In this game with the "cotton-reel," we witness the "self-mutilation on the basis of which the order of the significance will be put in perspective"; consequently, "this reel is not the mother reduced to a little ball," as is often said by those who see here a game of mastery, but "a small part of the subject that detaches itself from him," the lack that is the cost of the subject's coming into being (SXI, 62). This is why Lacan insists that, in the Fort-Da game, behind the jubilation and mastery it seems to promise, there is the institution of the void and that "no subject can grasp this radical articulation" in which the object a is originally lost, so that speech can be born (SXI, 239).

We are now at the heart of the "twist" that separates the Other from the object, distinguishing the "Rome Discourse" and its emphasis on the symbolic order from *Seminar XI*, where the real is decisively thematized. However much the speech of the subject may bring to light, however much the dominion of the ego may be brought into doubt by the slave labor of free association, however much the unconscious may thus be "re-membered" and "integrated" into conscious thought, there is a *place* beyond symbolization that constitutes the nodal point of the subject. The transference, which is in part dedicated to supporting a labor of symbolization, thus also has the aim of enacting this "encounter with the real." As a result, when the analytic discourse approaches the "nucleus," it approaches a domain that, however much it is manifested by symbolic debris, is not, finally, a symbolic phenomenon. "At the end of *Studien über Hysterie*," Lacan writes, "Freud defines the pathogenic nucleus as what is being sought, but which repels the discourse—what discourse shuns" (SI, 36; cf. E, 78–80). Psychoanalysis is not, finally, a hermeneutic science. The distinction between the symbolic and the real is the decisive focus of *Seminar XI* and marks its opening words: "When the space of a lapsus no longer carries any meaning (or interpretation), then only is one sure that one is in the unconscious" (SXI, vii). Is the unconscious therefore in some sense real? Is this not why Lacan revises the concept of the transference, isolating this element of the real that cannot be grasped by the labor of symbolization? Is this not why he provides a new definition of the transference in *Seminar XI*, saying that "the transference is the enactment of *the reality of the unconscious*" (SXI, 149, my emphasis)? "The transference is what manifests in experience the enacting of the reality of the unconscious, insofar as that reality is sexuality" (SXI, 174). Before we turn to this final concern, let us consider how the "Other place" of memory emerges in Freud's work, for here too one finds a limit to symbolization.

THE IMPASSES OF THE PERCEPTION-CONSCIOUSNESS SYSTEM

In *The Interpretation of Dreams*, Freud presents a diagram of the "perception-consciousness system," in which, like Aristotle, he aims to account for the relation between the sensory apparatus and our conscious awareness. But Freud encounters difficulties in his effort to explain the connection between the immediate impression given through the senses and the representation of these impressions in the mind. Freud's schema presents three basic parts: the data given with "perception" at one end of the diagram, the product (so to speak) of "consciousness" at the other end (the synthesis of awareness that is somehow organized out of perceptual material and internal impulses), and a middle portion, in which Freud locates "memory," a series of layers connecting the two extremities of the diagram, proceeding from the perceptual image or impression, through intermediate stages of integration or synthesis, layers in which various impressions come to be associated with one another, eventually to be organized as "consciousness."

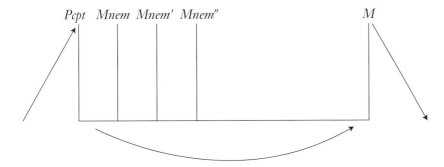

We know that Freud was tempted to treat these intermediate layers anatomically, as neurological pathways, guiding, with greater or lesser "facilitation," the energy of sense through the labyrinth of the mind. But if he wanted to say this, if it would have pleased the neurologist to *locate* memory thus, it is not what he ended up claiming: "What is presented to us in these words," Freud writes, "is the idea of a psychical locality" (SE, 5:536), but "I shall carefully avoid the temptation to determine the psychical locality in any anatomical fashion." Commenting on this passage in his first seminar, Lacan notes that, between the perceptual data at one end of the apparatus and the product of consciousness at the other, in the intermediate layers of "memory," Freud would situate the unconscious and preconscious, those residues of past experience that influence, organize and channel a perception as it moves into consciousness. (This is presumably how "memory," generally speaking, can include "sensation," but also "thought," "affect," and other heterogeneous elements, which are difficult to locate in relation to the terms *body* and *mind*.)

Now in refusing to locate memory anatomically, Lacan points out, Freud resorts instead to the model of optics, the psychic apparatus "resembling a compound microscope or a photographic apparatus, or something of the kind" (SE, 5:536). We thus find an analogy with the production of an image, which comes into focus in stages (in a compound microscope, it is realized through a series of lenses), these stages being located in no "anatomical" part of the instrument, but at "ideal points" within it: "On that basis, *psychical locality* will correspond to a point inside the apparatus at which one of the preliminary stages of an image comes into being. In the microscope and telescope, as we know, these occur at ideal points, regions in which no tangible component of the apparatus is located" (SE, 5:538, my emphasis; SI, 75).

Without proceeding too far down this path, let us simply make two remarks. First, when it is a question of images and their recollection, Freud no longer maintains the space of the natural body, the organization given by anatomy. Second, what strikes Lacan about Freud's account is the disruption it brings about in the "perception-consciousness system" that it was meant to elucidate (as if, in speaking, Freud found that "what is presented to us in these words," as his passive formulation has it, were something other than what Freud's luminous "project" had anticipated). If, in the beginning, we were inclined to view memory as the faculty that recollects an image or perception after it has passed away, thereby understanding "consciousness" as a product that includes both perception and memory, integrating body and mind, we find Freud saying that perception and consciousness are *separated* from one another, disjoined by the memory-traces that intervene between them.

In Freud's text this disjunction is unmistakable. Perception, in order to be free of influence and able to receive perpetually new impressions, must "retain no trace," and thus perception, strictly speaking, has no memory: "the very front of the apparatus receives the perceptual stimuli but retains no trace of them and thus has no memory" (SE, 5:538). The second layers, in which we are to locate "memory," by contrast *do* retain a trace, and thus constitute "a second system which transforms the momentary excitations of the first system into permanent traces" (ibid.). For the disjunction to be complete, of course, there would also have to be a separation, at the other end, between memory and consciousness. But to say this would be to contradict the entire tradition which views "consciousness" as the faculty that "remembers," synthesizing experience and mobilizing memory in a voluntary, adaptive way. However much it may violate the tradition (as we remember it), Freud is willing to take this step: "At this point," he writes, "I will interpolate a remark of a general nature which may perhaps have important implications": "our memories—not excepting those which are most deeply stamped upon our minds—are in themselves unconscious. They can be made conscious; but there can be no doubt that they can produce all their effects while in an unconscious condition" (SE, 5:539). Freud is thus led to wonder whether "it could be confirmed" that *"memory and the quality that characterizes consciousness are mutually exclusive*" (SE, 5:540, original emphasis). A footnote to this passage, added in 1925, re-marks: "I have since suggested that consciousness actually arises *instead of* the memory-trace." It is almost as if consciousness, far from being the finished "product," the end-point of a synthesis, were rather a "by-prod-uct," a sort of residue, not a "faculty" of memory but something that is left over and serves as an illusion, arising *instead of* memory, and covering up the fact by speaking and thinking, while the memories "produce all their effects" without being remembered.

In the second seminar, Lacan takes up Freud's schema again: "the way in which the diagram is constructed has the singular consequence of repre-senting as dissociated, at the two terminal points . . . perception and con-sciousness" (SII, 140). As Vallabrega says in the discussion, if the schema accomplished what Freud apparently intended, if it presented the "unity" of the perception-consciousness system, the line ought to have been a cir-cle, closed upon itself. There is no circle here, but an open-ended system, split in the center. Freud comes to the same conclusion somewhat differ-ently in another text, Lacan adds, in which "Freud describes a well-known little apparatus, a slate board," the "mystic writing pad" (SE, 19: 227–32), which likewise shows us the "peculiar dissociation of perception and mem-ory" (SII, 140).[27] Thus, in this second discussion, Lacan notes that "Freud recognizes here that the system perception-consciousness," which is "the nucleus of the ego," presupposes "a unity" that the schema itself disrupts. To presuppose such a unity would be to conclude that "consciousness" is able to remember "perceptions"—a notion one might have liked to arrive at (and some analysts are satisfied to think that analysis allows the client to remember the past and "integrate" unconscious memories and past ex-periences into consciousness). "We won't be satisfied with this," Lacan says, for this very schema "obliges Freud" (there is an ethics to Freud's way of thought) to confront the "dissociation of perception and memory" (SII, 139–40). In summary, Freud's starting point, like Aristotle's at first sight, lies in sensory data; "for him, the organism is essentially impression-able" (SII, 143). Setting out from the neurological, organic unity of the perception-consciousness system, however, Freud is led away from anat-omy through optics, only to find himself at a dead end, with a system that amounts to a series of heterogeneous parts: "the ease with which he abandons this task, to which more naive people are known to devote them-selves, is in itself an education" (SII, 138). Reading Freud's discussion, Lacan is thus led to the following question: "Can what happens at the level of the phenomena of consciousness be in any way purely and simply assimilated to the elementary phenomena of perception? What may be said in Freud's favor, is that even at this naive level . . . he doesn't evade the difficulty of the existence of consciousness as such" (SII, 143).

The Invention of the Other

Let us venture a little further. Lacan underscores, in his second discussion of Freud's schema, one further point, a question concerning time. Freud's diagram appears in a section of *The Interpretation of Dreams* devoted to the topic of "regression" (closely bound, of course, to memory), and Freud says that the elements of his construction must not be given a spatial order but regarded as a temporal succession (SE, 5:537). Perceptual excitations, as such, come and go, and have no memory in themselves, but they leave a trace (this is Freud's word) in the memory system. Now, the diagram posits several memory systems, and sensations that occur together in time will be associated in one memory system, while sensations that are associated in some other way—by similarity for example—will be grouped together in another memory system ("the same perceptual material," Freud writes, "will be arranged in the later systems in respect to other kinds of coincidence"; SE, 5:539). Lacan recognizes in Freud's account that these memory systems are not to be construed as though an initial image, stamp, or impression were simply being retained, but as systems that organize and gather associations according to the *categories of language*—similarity, contiguity, and so on. Thus, if Freud wants us to take his schema as a temporal one, its time must be that of language and not the linear chronology of nature. Memory is not the record of events in "real," sequential time, but their symbolic organization.

Having set forth to locate all the levels of the apparatus, having been led to replace anatomy with an optical model, and having eventually abandoned optics and talked himself into acknowledging the heterogeneity of the apparatus itself (thus confronting "the difficulty of the existence of consciousness as such"; SII, 143), Freud is now led to "hint at a theory of a more radical kind," and to speak of the relations between these memory systems in terms of "degrees of conductive resistance" (5:539). When he abandons the schema as inadequate, therefore, he is not only showing that the perception-consciousness system cannot be presupposed as a unity, the one simply representing the other, nor is he simply indicating that the problem of recollection and consciousness leads to a "psychical locality" that is irreducible to anatomy; according to Lacan, he also recognizes that "memory" is organized according to the laws of language. What is more, Freud is realizing, according to Lacan, that one cannot generate the categories of language by *deriving* them from perception, by basing them on the "experience of reality," or by seeking to itemize them in isolation, one at a time (similarity, contiguity, and so on). Contrary to common sense, the system of linguistic syntheses is not derived from the "reality" of perception, as though names were born a posteriori and served the function of representing a "psychological" experience. This is what is ultimately at stake in the separation of perception and memory: the structures of the latter cannot be *genetically* produced from a "pre-linguistic reality," or derived from the perceptual elements that might be thought to comprise them; on the contrary, the memory systems introduce an "other" law, one whose mechanisms are not built up, piece by piece, from sensory input, nor governed by the laws of anatomy and neurology, or even reducible to the optical mechanics to which Freud appeals along the way.[28] For Lacan, this is, of course, one of the elementary aspects of structuralist thought: the system cannot be generated out of its parts, for the system as a whole exhibits properties that exceed its elements taken together atomistically. We can see here the full force of Lacan's difference from genetic psychology and also the reason he first appealed to the idea of the *Gestalt*, a concept whose originality "consisted in contesting the existence of 'sensation as such,'" arguing that "the compounding of mechanical forces lacks *Gestalt* character precisely because such compounding *is* additive."[29] Like a magnetic field, a *Gestalt* is a totality that *determines* its elements rather than resulting from their combination, and in this sense the whole is logically prior to its parts. In Saussure's terms, the laws governing the signifier as an autonomous systemic order cannot be built up on the basis of what an individual signifier or act of speech might be thought to accomplish "individually." In short, when he abandons the model, "Freud realizes the foolishness of any attempt at trying to recreate all the categories of language by schematizing the various ways in which the elements of reality, atomistically conceived, are organized" (SII, 138). The symbolic order does not represent reality, or derive from it, but reorganizes it retroactively, from the moment it is introduced. From the moment there is language, pleasure and pain will no longer be governed by the laws of nature.

Why does Lacan stress language here if not to indicate that Freud is in the process of refusing to situate memory organically, somewhere between the perception of immediate "reality" and its representation in consciousness? The phenomenon of "memory" does not support the supposedly continuous and unified relation between perception and consciousness, the image and its recollection, the immediacy of the senses and the reflective act of mind. In *Seminar XI*, Lacan returns to this schema a third time, asking once more Freud's question of where to locate unconscious memory. Now Lacan is explicit: "it is not, says Freud, a spatial, anatomical locus," but is rather "an immense display, a special specter, situated between perception and consciousness [and] one should not forget the interval that separates them, in which *the place of the Other* is situated, in which *the subject* is constituted" (SXI, 45, my emphasis). Freud seems to corroborate the Lacanian reading later in his text. He remarks that his account of the "transcriptions" from one system to another (the same word is later translated as "transference") "must be carefully kept free from any idea of a change in locality" (SE, 5:610). The "transcription" *Übertragung* from one memory system to another is not a change of place: such "images," Freud says, are "derived from a set of ideas relating to a struggle for a piece of ground" and "tempt us to suppose" that we are "literally" concerned with a "change of locality" (ibid.). But the question of memory is, rather, one of how "unconscious thoughts" (affects, ideas, images, sensations, signifying chains . . . ?) are *activated or left latent*: "What we are doing here" Freud says, is "to replace a topographical way of representing things with a dynamic one" (ibid.).

Thus, some seventy pages after he was first led merely to "hint at a theory of a more radical kind" and to speak of the relations between these systems in terms of "degrees of conductive resistance" (SE, 5:539), we now find Freud returning to the same issue with systematic determination. What before was elaborated as a hint, necessary in the collapse of the perception-consciousness system, where the position of the Other was encountered, is now decisively taken up as a shift from a "topographical way of representing things" (conscious, preconscious, unconscious) to a "dynamic" one (the Id, Ego, and Superego conceived as conflictual forces). What before was elaborated (in spite of the spatial locality suggested by Freud's "topographical" diagram) as an explicitly *temporal* problem, in a chapter devoted to the enigma of *regression* (the process of going back that occurs in analysis), is now taken up as a question of "dynamics." It is now a question, Freud says, of understanding how "some particular mental grouping has had a cathexis of energy attached to it or withdrawn from it, so that the structure in question has come under the sway of a particular agency or been withdrawn from it" (SE, 5:10). We might conclude that Freud, faced with the collapse of the earlier diagram, is retreating here to *dynamis*, energy, the materialism of Freud's greatest predecessors in psychology, just as, in the earlier passage, he claimed to hint at a more radical theory, yet spoke of "degrees of conductive resistance." But since Freud is speaking of how a group of associated ideas—a linkage of signifiers that are not conscious—comes "under the sway of a particular agency," it would seem that the language of energy, to which Freud remained devoted, cannot conceal the discovery that is being made despite that language. Lacan's view is that the "agency" in question—Freud wrote of his diagram that he would "give the name of 'agencies' [*Instanzen*]" to its "components" (SE, 5:536–37)—brings us up against the *agency of the letter*. This view seems to be confirmed by the note Freud adds to this passage in 1925. The text says, "What we regard as mobile is not the psychical structure itself but its *innervation*" (SE, 5:610–11, my emphasis), what seventy pages earlier he had called "degrees of conductive resistance." Despite the vocabulary of energy, the note adds: "It became necessary to elaborate and modify this view after it was recognized that the essential feature of a preconscious idea was the fact of its being connected with the residues of verbal presentations" (SE, 5:611).

Resistance and Regression: The Symbolic and the Real

Thus, if we follow Freud's "hint" toward "a theory of a more radical kind," concerning "degrees of conductive resistance," we will be led to conclude that, far from returning to the "energetic" model of biology, he is approaching an organization of "mental pathways" that are not so much *anatomical*, located in organic space, or *neurological*, governed by currents of force, quantities of energy, a "physics" of libido, but internal to the signifier itself, the Other that inhabits the human animal, with a parasitic logic beyond all nature's conjuring. If we recall that the chapter which presents Freud's diagram is devoted to regression, we may recognize more adequately that what is at stake is a question of time, above all, the peculiar temporality given with the symbolic order. When Lacan speaks of "regression," when he speaks of "resistance," the principal point distinguishing his work is his isolation of the symbolic function. But at this point, the trajectory of our discussion must take another turn, for with these two terms it is not only the symbolic order that confronts us, but also the *limit* of symbolization, a limit that takes us in the direction of the real. In order to follow this twist, let us take these two terms briefly.

With respect to regression, the analytic task of "going back," the essential point is perfectly clear in the "Rome Discourse." Here, the question of history will be decisive: "Regression is simply the actualization *in the discourse* of the phantasy relations reconstituted by an *ego* at each stage in the decomposition of its structure. After all, *this regression is not real*" (E, 44, my emphasis). The consequences for our conception of the past are momentous. It is commonly said that "regression" names the process in which the patient is led back to remember the earliest "stages of life." Lacan has only scorn for those who take this regression to be *realistic*, a return to "what really happened." Similarly, analysis is often thought to amount to a repetition, in the here and now of analysis, of events that happened in the "real" past, as though the client might *act out again* stages of life that were lived through previously, with parents, for example. Again, Lacan finds this to be conceptually vague, collapsing repetition into the very different idea that in analysis, the past is somehow "reproduced." In *Seminar XI*, he writes, "repetition is not reproduction. There is never any ambiguity on this point: *Wiederholen* is not *Reproduzieren*" (SXI, 50).

Thus, the idea that one might really reproduce the past, or return to it through regression, is not only nonsense, but short-circuits the effect of the symbolic order in structuring reality. "To reproduce is what one thought one could do in the optimistic days of catharsis," when the trauma was relived during analysis and everything turned out fine. Unfortunately, Freud discovered that the trauma is not so easily grasped and that, far from being a "real event" that might be "reproducible," the trauma turns out to have a different status, to belong, not so much to the order of "historical events," located in chronological time, but rather to the original rending open, the splitting in which the subject is constituted. The trauma is therefore not so much an *event in history* as the *origin of history itself*, the detachment of the human animal from the order of nature and its birth as subject of the signifier. For Lacan, therefore, regression can only be understood if it is given its symbolic dimension. Psychoanalysis discovered the peculiar relation between the past and the signifier, and it would be absurd for analysis to pretend that it might circumvent the symbolic function by aiming to lead the subject back "to a transcendent reality" (E, 120), in which the origins of the subject might be found or in which the earliest object-relations might be recovered, "namely, the objects of the pre-Oedipal relation, shit and nappy rash" (E, 120). Freud's theory allows no such conception of the past, for even the much-discussed "object-relation" is already bound up with the function of the symbol, as the Fort-Da game suggests. We should not be misled, then, into seeking a "pre-symbolic reality" in the pre-Oedipal world. Lacan thus stresses "the contradiction between the pre-Oedipal intrigue, to which, in the opinion of certain of our modern analysts, the analytic relation can be reduced, and the fact that Freud was satisfied with having situated it in the position of the Oedipus complex" (E, 120). This remark from "The Freudian Thing" is clarified in the essay on psychosis, where Lacan remarks that Melanie Klein saw clearly, in spite of some of her followers, that the "object" (in particular, the mother), could not be adequately conceptualized as a "real" object (in the ordinary sense of the word *real*), above all not as an object of need, because of the role of the signifier in constituting reality. Thus, even with the earliest objects, it is a question "of relations that refer not to pre-Oedipal stages, which are not nonexistent of course, but which cannot be conceived in analytic terms (as is sufficiently apparent in the hesitant but controlled work of Melanie Klein), but to the pregenital stages insofar as they are ordered in the retroaction of the Oedipus complex" (E, 197).

With this remark on the retroactive function of the symbolic, one sees the full force of Freud's own insistence that his perception-consciousness schema is, in the final analysis, concerned, not with spatial relations, but with the problem of time.[30]

As for "resistance," this concept is only superficially understood if it is taken to be an activity of the conscious ego, a "defensive" refusal of unconscious desire, which it is the task of the wise analyst to overcome by "breaking down the resistance." Such a view, by centering the analytic dialogue on the (aggressive/sympathetic) relation of ego to ego, and by remaining oriented toward "understanding" rather than toward the radical alterity of the unconscious, can only remain trapped in the order of the ego and defense: this is "our critique of an analysis that claims to be an analysis of resistance and is reduced more and more to the mobilization of defenses" (E, 143). Once again, it is a question of ethics: "this is what makes our responsibility so formidable when, along with the mythical manipulations of our doctrine, we bring [the client] one more opportunity to alienate himself" (E, 71). Far from being an act of the ego, according to Lacan, "resistance is the inflection *the discourse* adopts on approaching the unconscious" (SI, 36, my emphasis), a movement within discourse itself, a turning away that occurs when speech approaches "what Freud called the *verbal nucleus* of the *ego*" (SI, 174). In *Seminar XI*, Lacan formulates this point as follows: "What eludes the subject is the fact that his syntax is in relation with the unconscious reserve. When the subject tells his story, something acts, in a latent way, that governs this syntax and makes it more and more condensed. Condensed in relation to what? In relation to what Freud, at the beginning of his description of psychical resistance, calls a nucleus" (SXI, 68). "We must distinguish," he goes on to say, "between the resistance of the subject and that first resistance of discourse . . . for the expression *resistance of the subject* too much implies the existence of a supposed ego, and it is not certain whether—at the approach of this nucleus—it is something that we can justifiably call an ego" (ibid.). On the contrary: "the nucleus must be designated as belonging to the real."

Thus, when the fountain of speech suddenly runs dry, it may indeed be because the client has *consciously* thought of something that is then defensively censored, but this is a superficial phenomenon, a simple failure to follow the "fundamental rule," which is to say everything that comes to mind. In such a case, the thought held in abeyance is bound to emerge at another point: repressed, it will return. At this level, the repressed thought can indeed be symbolized and even brought into consciousness. In its most fundamental aspect, however, resistance is not an activity of the ego, the holding back of something that will eventually be *manifested*; at a more fundamental level, resistance is a signal of something essentially unspeakable, a domain that is not only incapable of being translated into consciousness, "recognized" by the ego (we have passed beyond the dialectical movement of self-consciousness), but that is also beyond all symbolization, the realm, Lacan says, *of the unborn* (SXI, 23). This is a difficult place to approach, easily misunderstood: "it is always dangerous to disturb anything in that zone of shades," though "perhaps it is part of the analyst's role" (ibid.). It is also not clear that a public, theoretical discourse, which operates at the level of knowledge, can bring such an unspeakable thing to the clear light of day, whether it can be grasped in the form of a proposition (it is also the question of whether analysis is a "science," in the sense of being something one can teach in the classroom): "There is a danger in public discourse . . . Nietzsche knew this, a certain type of discourse can only be addressed to those furthest away" (ibid.). The "thing" in question is not a general category, but a *particular* element, and far from having the status of an entity, far from being an object in the usual sense, it is a gap, something that "does not lend itself to ontology," though "with this gap one is dealing with an ontological function," the "structuring function of a lack" (SXI, 29). One can see here that, in *Seminar XI*, the symbolic order that so dominates Lacan's early work encounters its limit, which Lacan designates as the real.

As Lacan's earliest remarks on "resistance" suggest, then, one does not have to wait for *Seminar XI* to see this category emerge. In a section of "The Freudian Thing" entitled "Resistance to the Resisters," Lacan writes, "it is as well to remember that the first resistance with which analysis has to deal is that of the discourse itself" (E, 130), not something the person "knows" and is "hiding," but something that appears *in the discourse*, as that from which the discourse itself turns away, as the unsayable. There have been many complaints that, with his abstract, theoretical concerns, Lacan has led analysis away from "reality," as if reducing everything to language (similar things are said about Derrida). In "The Direction of the Treatment," where it is a question of the transference, Lacan writes: "I can already hear the apprentices murmuring that I intellectualize analysis: though I am in the very act, I believe, of preserving the unsayable aspect of it" (E, 253). Even the concept of desire, however much it is submitted to the law of the signifier, located by the movement of the signifier as it cuts across the discourse of the ego, is not thereby reduced to a symbolic phenomenon. This is why Lacan does not accept the historicist position, according to which the subject is a "product of the symbolic order."[31] Lacan says it again and again: "it is precisely because desire is articulated that it is not articulable. . . . I mean in the discourse best suited to it, an ethical, not a psychological discourse" (E, 302). In this sense the subject is not *present* in the signifying chain, though it is *represented* there—which "makes it easier to understand why it was necessary to question oneself regarding the function that supports the subject of the unconscious, to grasp that it is difficult to designate that subject anywhere as subject of a statement" (E, 314), as Lacan says in "The Subversion of the Subject." Such a fading of the subject does not mean that desire "does not exist," but rather that its mode of being is not to be an entity, but rather to ex-sist. "Ontically," Lacan says, "the unconscious is the elusive—but we are beginning to circumscribe it in a structure, a temporal structure" (SXI, 32). Let us conclude, before we lose our way: the "theory of a more radical kind" to which Freud has led us, in spite of its language of energetics, is in fact an effort to explain phenomena of memory by a "dynamic" model, by the idea of "conductive resistance," terms that are dedicated not so much to the (spatial) pathways of neurology, as to the (temporal) reordering of organic life according to the intervention of an Other memory.

Time Immemorial: Law and Cause

Yet in the very network of the signifying chain, something appears as missing. Consequently, if the "truth" is manifested in the lapsus or other symbolic material, this does not mean that the truth can be given a symbolic form. In "The Freudian Thing," where Lacan remarks that "the trade route of truth . . . seems to pass through things," appearing materially in the error of the signifier, he also writes: "But there is no need to . . . keep a closer watch on yourselves" (E, 122), for "I am the enigma of her who vanishes as soon as she appears" (E, 121). Speaking in the name of truth, he taunts the good detectives of analysis: "Seek, dogs that you become on hearing me. . . . Enter the lists to howl at my voice. There, you are lost already, I contradict myself, I defy you, I take cover: you say I am defending myself" (E, 123). But the truth is not something one can grasp by breaking down the defense, in the service of total enlightenment: "have we not overstepped the limit when we admit that the drive itself may be led to consciousness?" (E, 118).[32] Again, in "The Subversion of the Subject," we find that it is not a question of reducing the unconscious to a purely symbolic phenomenon: "we must bring everything back to the function of the cut in discourse . . . a bar between the signifier and the signified. . . . By which we would arrive at the paradox of conceiving that the discourse in an analytic session is valuable only insofar as it stumbles or is interrupted" (E, 299). It is not a question of the *manifestation* of material that might be interpreted in accordance with a hermeneutic of deciphering, a therapeutics of knowing; it is rather a question of the *limit* that is posed to such a project, a *limit of symbolic formalization* that *is* the subject itself: "This cut in the signifying chain alone verifies the structure of the subject as discontinuity in the real" (E, 299).

If we have marked the radical split that separates Darwin from Hegel, distinguishing the time of development or evolution from the time of the signifier, we may now see why Lacan insists upon the historical rupture that occurs between Hegel and Freud, since, for the former, "the dialectic is convergent and attains the conjunction defined as absolute knowledge," which "can only be the conjunction of the symbolic with a real" (hence all that is real is rational). "I would to heaven it were so," Lacan says, but in spite of Hegel, history itself displays a different logic: "the history of science itself . . . presents itself rather in the form of *detours* that comply very little with this immanentism" (E, 296, my emphasis). Thus, psychoanalysis, for all the guidance it takes from linguistics, runs headlong into the question of the "limits of formalization."[33] Despite linguistics, and the temptation to grasp the totality of truth within the circuit of the signifier, construing analysis as a hermeneutics in which symbolic material would be progressively "interpreted," Lacan tells us this is a dead end. *The Lacanian subject does not belong to the symbolic order*: its *place* may be manifested by the debris of the signifier, but at a more important level, the place of the subject is real: "As we know, this *limit* and this *place* are still well outside the reach of [Freud's] disciples" (E, 124).

In *Seminar XI*, Lacan distinguishes the "linguistic" formulation of the unconscious from this "place" of the real, and the central theme of the "Rome Discourse," the "law" of the signifier, leads off in another direction. "The unconscious is structured like a language," he insists at the outset, and "it is this linguistic structure . . . that assures us that there is, beneath the term unconscious, something definable, accessible and object-ifiable. But when I urge psycho-analysts not to ignore this field . . . does this mean that I hope to include the concepts introduced historically by Freud under the term unconscious? No, I don't think so" (SXI, 21). The Freudian unconscious, the "subject," cannot be reduced to the linguistic field that manifests it, making it "accessible and objectifiable," for the symbolic order is *not the whole* truth (*pas tout*). "I always tell the truth," Lacan says in *Television*, "but not the whole truth, for there's no way to say it all," to bring the totality within the circuit of the signifier. "Yet it's through this very impossibility," he adds, "that truth holds onto the real" (T, 3). *Seminar XI* seeks to approach more clearly this limit to formalization, the impossibility of enclosing the totality within the network of the law, by addressing the element of the real. Let us summarize, before we become distracted: the terms *resistance* and *regression* not only move beyond the model of energy by which Freud has often been interpreted, introducing the (temporal) reordering of organic life according to the intervention of an Other memory; what is more, this law of the Other is itself founded on the lack of an "object" that *never was*, until it was missing, an absolute past that is the opening of human time.

This is why, in *Seminar XI*, Lacan insists that even if the law of the symbolic order is essential, our path must turn elsewhere, toward the "cause": "Cause is to be distinguished from that which is determinate in a chain, in other words *law*. By way of example, think of what is pictured in the law of action and reaction. . . . There is no gap here" (SXI, 22). "Whenever we speak of cause, on the other hand, there is always something anti-conceptual, something indefinite" (ibid.). The problem of the subject thus leads beyond the law of the signifier to the object a, the cause of desire. We must therefore confront this element which, in "The Freudian Thing" he calls an element "of death, the quasi-mystical limit of the most rational discourse in the world, so that we might recognize the place in which the symbol is substituted for death in order to take possession of the first swelling of life" (E, 124). The path of the symbolic order thus reaches a dead end, for if the formations of the unconscious (lapsus, dream, symptom) belong to the network of the signifier, it is quite another thing to speak of the "formations of fantasy," which are not reducible to the symbolic order. In Freud, the isolation of the fantasy meant the encounter with something beyond the suffering of the symptom, a more primordial formation that did not yield to the work of interpretation, that was not resolved by symbolization—something that led Freud to conclude with dismay that the subject did not want to get better, but clung to suffering as if to life itself. Thus, the symbolic resolution of the symptom, accomplished through speech, was not sufficient. Beyond the symptom, there lay a level of fantasy, a *jouissance* that was not susceptible to resolution, to which the subject remained attached. In Freud's account, fantasy is linked to primordial masochism, a concept that "was only accepted by Freud once he had put forward the hypothesis of the death instinct."[34] This is why, in *Seminar XI*, Lacan's formula for fantasy is written $ \lozenge $ a, a formulation that indicates the heterogeneous relation binding the subject of the symbolic chain ($) to the object of fantasy (a), which is not contained within the symbolic order. Beyond the "formations of the unconscious" (lapsus, dream, symptom) that are grasped dialectically through the labor of symbolization, one finds the "object" of fantasy, which is neither specular nor symbolizable, but real.

We see here that the famous "division of the subject" is not simply the "alienation" that occurs when the subject identifies with an image, nor merely the familiar "division by language" that marks the subject upon entry into the chain of representation ($); it also includes the relation between these two heterogeneous elements of the fantasy. The enigmas of "sexuality" are most at issue for Freud in this last relation, in that the fantasy "binds together two very different things, the satisfaction of an erotogenic zone and the representation of a desire."[35] The paradox is not only that, whereas the symptoms in Freud's early cases could be resolved by the labor of speech, a more fundamental, "symptomatic" domain (that of the fantasy) emerged beyond resolution; what is more, the symptom in its classical form brings suffering, while the fantasy appears to do the opposite, to bring a peculiar sort of pleasure. Even masochism is thus paradoxically said to involve a kind of pleasure, something Lacan therefore formulates as distinct from the pleasure of the ego, namely *jouissance*—not, as is so often said, the "orgasm" it appears to name, but the obscure satisfaction that looks out from the Rat Man's eyes as he tells the part of his story that is most tortuous to him. This is why Freud says the patient clings to suffering, or seems to enjoy the symptom, or more precisely, to enjoy something "in" the symptom that is beyond the suffering it entails. When Lacan develops what Freud understands as the death drive, he uses the term *jouissance* to designate that primordial suffering, that punishing enjoyment to which the subject clings, beyond the symbolic and resolvable construction of the symptom.[36]

The Desire of the Analyst

In order to take our final steps, let us retrace the path that led Freud to diverge from the first miraculous accomplishments of speech to the impasses that led to sexuality. Let us return to the "chimney-sweeping" technique, the early revelations in which the "talking cure" took shape. "This was fine in the beginning," Lacan says: "How convincing the process of remembering was with the first hysterics . . . one remembered things right down to the dregs" (SXI, 49–50). But Freud found something beyond the pleasure of symbolic labor, something real, a limit to the signifier and the work of memory, something that manifested itself as repetition: "in the recalling of his biography," Lacan writes in *Seminar XI*, the subject "goes only to a certain limit, which is known as the real" (SXI, 49). "Freud's discovery of repetition" thus points out "the relation between thought and the real" (ibid.). But this limit, Lacan adds, could not have been expected by Freud, for in the very process of symbolization, in this dramatic point of departure, something was at issue that Freud himself could not have divined, something that, according to Lacan, may even bear on the question of the father: "what is at issue in this remembering could not have been known at the outset—one did not know that the desire of the hysteric was the desire of the father" (SXI, 50). Is the "return to Freud" in some way an attempt to retrace some steps that Freud himself passed over too quickly? Or a return to passageways that Freud explored, but that his followers mistook for a detour?

Here we run headlong into the enigma of the transference: Freud, the good doctor, used every means at his disposal—hypnosis, suggestion, even the manipulation of the televangelist ("Now, when I remove my hands from your forehead, you will then remember . . .")—to enable symbolization. And the patient, eager to please, and quite unwilling to have the sympathetic physician's efforts come to naught, suddenly began to speak: "for the benefit of him who takes the place of the father," Lacan says (SXI, 50). Thus, the most surprising successes, in which a simple recounting of the concealed event brought about an alleviation of suffering, suddenly came to a halt in the relation to the other, which, although it should have been a *means*, abruptly turned into an *obstacle*. The patient, Freud concluded with dismay, evidently did not want to get better, but clung to suffering as if to life itself. Clinicians began to speak of resistance, and defense, a series of technicalities bound up with the transference. In spite of the claims that link the unconscious to the laws of language, then, in spite of the fact that "the unconscious of the subject is the discourse of the Other," we must not be tempted by the closure of the Law, the completeness of the signifying system so often attributed to Lacan whenever his work is reduced to the "structuralist" position of Saussure or Lévi-Strauss. We must proceed slowly at this juncture, in order to see clearly where we are going.

These remarks are made in the chapter of *Seminar XI* entitled "Of the Network of Signifiers." Later, Lacan returns to this issue, and the chapter is now entitled "Sexuality." Here Lacan writes that there is a remainder, something missing from the circuit of the signifier, an "object" that must be distinguished from the Other. And in this sense, the unconscious is not simply a symbolic order phenomenon, but is *real*: "the nodal point by which the pulsation of the unconscious is linked to *sexual reality* must be revealed. This nodal point is called desire" (SXI, 154, my emphasis). Here it is a question of the relation between what shows up in the field of speech, "the field of demand, in which the syncopes of the unconscious are made present," and the field of "sexual reality" (SXI, 156), a dimension that, though it cannot be understood by recourse to the biological functions of mating and reproduction, nevertheless does not reduce to the level of the signifier. "Look again," Lacan says: "It was in the case of Anna O. that the transference was discovered. Breuer was quite delighted with the smooth way the operation was going. At that time, no one would have challenged the signifier. . . . The more Anna provided signifiers, the more she chattered on, the better it went. It was a case of the chimney-sweeping treatment" (SXI, 157). And of course the good doctor was quite happy. But "there was no trace, in all of this, of the least embarrassing thing. Look again. No sexuality." Now Freud always claimed that the essential point in the unconscious, however much it might be linked to symbolization, was sexual. But as Anna dutifully provided signifiers ("for the sake of him who takes the place of the father"), no trace of sexuality appeared.

"Yet sexuality was nevertheless introduced by Breuer" (SXI, 157), who had begun to wonder about his preoccupation with this interesting patient: "Thereupon, the dear man, somewhat alarmed, good husband that he was, decided that things had gone quite far enough," and set off for a vacation in Italy with his wife—"in response to which, as you know, [Anna] O. displayed the magnificent and dramatic manifestations of what, in scientific language, is called *pseudo-cyesis* or, more familiarly, she blew up with what is called a nervous pregnancy" (SXI, 157). The question Lacan poses at this point concerns the transference. The symptom in this case, tied to sexuality, is not one that brought the patient into analysis, but is produced in the relation to the analyst. But how, exactly, are we to understand this symptom, as it opens beyond biology onto the relation to the Other? One thing is clear: in the "Rome Discourse" (and elsewhere), Lacan had said that the symptom can be understood in terms of the symbolic order and resolved by means of symbolization, but now there is something beyond the symbolic, a factor that links the symptom to sexuality, which is not reducible to the happy days of chimney sweeping, when one remembered "right down to the dregs"; it is this factor, moreover, that disrupts the concept of the transference. The symptom is no longer understood as a signifier "written in the sand of the flesh" (E, 69): "the nervous pregnancy is a symptom, and, according to the definition of the sign, something intended for someone. The signifier, being something quite different, represents a subject for another signifier" (SXI, 157). The symptom here is not something she brought with her into analysis: in different language, we might say that it is not her memory, not her reminiscence.

Parallel to this transformation of the symptom (from signifier to sign), one finds a second shift, in keeping with the peculiar twist that has taken us from the symbolic to the real. Following Freud, Lacan has stressed the voodoo of the "talking cure," the magical effects that detached the symptom from its place in organic medicine, adding that since the symptom is symbolic, so also the operation of the talking cure is symbolic. Lacan says, citing *The Interpretation of Dreams*: "nothing can be grasped, destroyed, or burnt, except in a symbolic way, as one says, *in effigy, in absentia*" (SXI,

50). But the symbolic order is "not the whole truth." And Freud says in "The Dynamics of Transference" that "when all is said and done, it is impossible to destroy anyone *in absentia* or *in effigy* (SE, 12:108; Lacan cites this remark as well, SI, 38). Are we simply faced with a contradiction, or is it not rather that, as Russell Grigg says, "something beyond the signifier is at work in the transference," something Freud will elaborate as "transference-love," an *identification* that binds the subject to some "thing," outside the network of signifiers?[37]

Faced with this remarkable turn of events, Freud speaks to his colleague about the case. "Let us observe what Freud says to Breuer—*What! The transference is the spontaneity of the said Bertha's unconscious. It's not yours, not your desire*," Lacan writes, adding "I think Freud treats Breuer as a hysteric here" (SXI, 158). Now, for Lacan, this is the beginning of the end, the first foothold of a movement that *forgets* the Freudian discovery, a movement that has its source in Freud himself. Freud exonerates Breuer, certain that this is really a manifestation of Bertha's desire, since after all it is *her* symptom. We must notice the distribution of responsibility here: Breuer's action, after all, was entirely philanthropic, and surely merits no guilt. "The curious thing is," Lacan observes, that Freud's response "does not make him feel less guilty, but he certainly makes him feel less anxious" (a decisive opposition: less anxiety, but more guilt). "This brings us to the question of what Freud's desire decided, in diverting the whole apprehension of the transference in a direction that has now reached its final term of absurdity" (SXI, 158).

Still later in *Seminar XI*, as it reaches its end, Lacan returns to this issue once more, claiming that Freud appealed to "a kind of rapid sleight of hand when he said—*after all, it is only the desire of the patient*—this should reassure one's colleagues" (SXI, 254). But "why not consider Bertha's pregnancy rather, according to my formula *man's desire is the desire of the Other*," that is to say, recognizing that Bertha's symptom was "the manifestation of Breuer's desire . . . that it was Breuer who had a desire for a child?" (SXI, 158). It might be confirmed if we remembered that Breuer, on vacation with his wife, "lost no time in giving her a child"—a child who, at the very time Jones ("the imperturbable Welshman") was writing this history, had just committed suicide, thereby demonstrating the profound and unnatural force of unconscious desire, and the indestructibility that preserves it from one generation to the next.

We cannot stop here, with the platitude that would conclude "it is not her desire, but his." Such a view would end up with a mere reversal, by which we would be encouraged to admit the "counter-transference," the fact that the analyst, too, has feelings. Lacan writes: "You must follow my thinking here. It's not simply a matter of turning things upside down" (SXI, 158). For if Breuer was unable to sustain the position of the Other, if he abandoned the position that would support the elaboration of her unconscious, if he was reduced to finding *himself* caught up in the "inter-subjective relation" with his patient, and if this failure to maintain the position of the analyst leads to "the final term of absurdity" and modish remarks about the "counter-transference" (simply turning things upside down, along the imaginary axis), we must nevertheless acknowledge that, whatever may have been Breuer's desire, Bertha ("Anna O.") *identified* with this desire, put herself in the role of *completing* the other, as if throwing herself, dutiful daughter, into the void that showed itself in the disconcerted doctor. Thus, behind whatever may be expressed as "Breuer's counter-transference," we must acknowledge what is at stake in Bertha's desire, or, more precisely, in the *abdication of desire* that she suffers in *identifying* herself as the object that will complete what is lacking in the Other. In this sense, something in the symptom would indeed appear to belong to the patient, not so much as a reminiscence, but as a repetition.

It is this identification that the analysis ought to encounter. The desire of the analyst is radically distinguished from that of "the other person," which Breuer manifested, thereby abdicating the position of the Other which allows the patient to play her cards. If something is nevertheless revealed about Bertha's own desire, or more precisely her *identification with the object* of the Other's desire, this should allow us to recognize that the position the analyst occupies, the "place" of the analyst, is not ultimately reduced to that of the Other, supporting the discursive formations of the unconscious, but is a position that obliges the subject to relinquish this identification with the Other. The twist that concerns us is to be found here: if the analyst assumes the position of the Other, the one whose silence or supposed knowledge supports the discourse of the unconscious, the unfolding of the signifying chain in its alterity, this symbolic operation is not the end of analysis, for this Other is not the whole truth and must emerge as lacking, in order that the lack in the subject be *given its place* in turn.

Lacan is therefore not ultimately concerned with Breuer and *his* desire, relevant as it may be in demonstrating that Breuer's desire was precisely *not* what Lacan calls "the desire of the analyst." Lacan's focus is, rather, on what we may learn about the direction of the treatment. If the analysis were taken further, then, it would have to show, not only that the pregnancy is the expression of Breuer's desire (contrary to Freud's sleight of hand), and not only that Bertha was herself prepared to answer this desire, to dedicate herself to this unconscious labor of love, a symptomatic, incestuous labor "for him who takes the place of the father," a labor in which her desire is lost—if the analysis continued, it would have to proceed to the point where this identification with the object lacking in the Other could be broken. As long as this identification is maintained, the question of her desire will remain closed.[38] As long as the lack in the Other is not given its place, the lack that brings her own desire into being will be refused, *in the name of love*. "It is from this idealization that the analyst has to fall in order to be the support of the separating *a*." (SXI, 273) Thus, the analytic action would proceed from the labor of symbolization supported by the analyst's position as Other, to the point at which the analyst occupies the position of the object, by virtue of which the Other comes to be lacking. In this way, the analysis would be brought to bear on the identification which Anna O. maintains, in which her desire disappears. "The fundamental mainspring of the analytic operation is the maintenance of the distance between the I—identification—and the *a*" (ibid.).

In "crossing the plane of identification" (SXI, 273), the analyst emerges as helpless to do anything on behalf of his dear patient. The analyst is finally useless, a castoff, a reject. In the end, analysis has this depressive aspect, a dimension of mourning and even death. Human emotions tend in the other direction. They hope for a homeland that the community could share in common, recognizing themselves in one another, in keeping with the "best part" of human nature, love and philanthropy, those passions by which our moral being would be guided. Such a community has a dark side that its promises conceal, according to Lacan, "something profoundly masked" (SXI, 274), a sacrificial character that rears its head "in the most monstrous and supposedly superseded forms of the holocaust," the "drama of Nazism" being the culmination of a long history of sacrificial identification in which the People was formed—and formed, we must acknowledge, in just this dutiful labor of love on behalf of "the desire of this Other that I call here *the dark God*" (SXI, 275). Perhaps we can see here the intervention "that analysis makes possible in relation to the many efforts, even the most noble ones, of traditional ethics" (SXI, 276). If the position of the analyst, at the limit of communication, at the limit of science and law, is an ethical position, this is not because it culminates in a moral law (prohibition, taboo) that would bind us all within the symbolic unity of the human community, a law by which desire might be given its limit, but because it confronts the pathology of such a law, insofar as this law always entails an "offering to obscure gods" (SXI, 275).

CHAPTER 6

Human Diversity and the Sexual Relation

> Imitation is natural to man from childhood, one of his advantages
> over the lower animals being this, that he is the most imitative crea-
> ture in the world, and learns at first from imitation.
>
> —ARISTOTLE, *Poetics*

> What follows is speculation.
>
> —FREUD, *Beyond the Pleasure Principle*, cited in Derrida, *The Post Card*

The concept of "race" has received considerable attention in recent years, both as a theoretical category and in its historical development. In both respects, difficulties arise that may lead to some surprising connections between race and psychoanalysis. On the conceptual axis, we must ask whether race is a biological or a cultural category, while on the historical axis, we must consider the very formation of this alternative—the specific configuration it has assumed in modernity, and also the relation between this alternative and the emergence of Freudian theory, which breaks with the inherited division between nature and history. Any comprehensive thesis on "psychoanalysis and race" must bear on both these difficulties at once. Accordingly, I will suggest that the concept of race as it functions today can no longer be grasped in terms of the distinction between nature and culture, and that it is precisely because psychoanalysis refuses this distinction that it may cast light on our physical diversity without perpetuating sterile debates between biological science and historicist theories of discursive construction.

The Limits of Historicism

For more than a century, appeals to race as a biological concept have been subject to strenuous criticism, not only because of the history that has bound scientific definitions of race to eugenics, colonialism, and the Holocaust, but also because biological definitions of race have proven difficult to sustain even on scientific grounds. It is therefore not only for political and ethical reasons, but also for reasons internal to science that the biological category of race remains problematic. And yet, while research has made us profoundly and rightly suspicious of the uses to which racial science has been put in the past, it has not been possible simply to dispense with the question of "race" as it bears on our *bodily or physical diversity*. The distinction between cultural and natural aspects of human identity thus *appears* to remain intact, and worthy of attention.

A growing mass of scientific literature advocates the legitimacy of continued interest in the biology of racial differences, especially in genetics and medicine, but even in the arena of social theory, the popular terms race and ethnicity tend to suggest that we can still distinguish—and perhaps need to distinguish—between those aspects of identity that can be attributed to culture (learning, tradition, religious practice, kinship systems, language, etc.), and those aspects that are due to a natural or genetic endowment. A Caucasian who is adopted at birth by a Native American family, who shares the customs and beliefs of the Ojibwa, who thinks and dreams in Algonquin, and who cherishes the values embodied in that language and community might well be considered *ethnically* Native American, but it is less likely that we would regard such a person as *racially* Native American. And certainly the current legal system, which obliges citizens to identify themselves as "Hispanic," "Pacific Islander," and so on, would classify such a person as "Caucasian."

It is therefore not only from a biological point of view, but also from the standpoint of social and political theory that our physical differences continue to receive terminological attention and to play a conceptual role that is distinguished—however obscurely and inadequately—from purely cultural and historical differences. Thus, in spite of the extreme vigilance we have been taught to maintain with regard to the biological category of race, human diversity seems to remain open to both cultural and biological analysis.

This difficulty is not limited to sociopolitical theory, where (despite the distinction between "race and "ethnicity") the term *race* refers ambiguously to both social and physical differences. The same conceptual impasse and the same need for an analysis that would bear simultaneously on bio-logical and social factors arise in a number of fields—in physical anthro-pology (which encounters the problem of how various cultural phenomena, such as agriculture and medicine, have affected the human body, to the point of altering its genetic makeup), but also in disciplines like linguistics (where the question arises as to whether language, properly speaking, belongs only to the human species, and if so, whether it is learned or innate, a cultural invention or a natural endowment). The prob-lem thus goes well beyond our everyday use of the word *race*, wherein the term seems to designate something more than cultural difference.

Recent medical literature has likewise relied on the distinction between "social" and "biological" identity, while making it especially problematic. Differences in morbidity, heart disease, cancer, and many other conditions have been explained in part by reference to social factors (economic condi-tions, diet, "behavior," access to medical care, etc.), but research has also given increasing attention to "genetic predispositions" and other "inher-ited factors," which point, not only to the "family" (a group that is both a social institution and a biological relation), but also to a larger group iden-tity, and thus to something like "race."

It has been suggested, to cite only the most familiar examples, that Na-tive Americans do not metabolize alcohol as easily as Caucasians, that there is a genetic basis for depression among the Amish, that sickle cell anemia tends to appear only in certain populations (among "blacks," or rather, as Sander Gilman says, "actually only those individuals who inhabit or whose ancestors inhabited malarial water areas"),[1] and so on. Prior to AIDS, Kaposi's sarcoma appeared largely among people whose anteced-ents lived in the Mediterranean basin, and many other diseases circulate, not randomly, but in a way that distinguishes some human populations from others.[2] Debates rage fiercely as to whether these distributions are due to social or biological factors, and obviously there is no single answer, since not all diseases circulate according to the same logic or the same routes of transmission. In the case of diabetes and hemophilia, which are not contagious, genetic factors appear to predominate, whereas in the case of tuberculosis, which is airborne, and cholera, which passes through the water supply, social structures (or their lack) are directly correlated with the spread of disease. In each case, the social and biological factors must be weighed; but again, as with the term *race*, both factors seem to merit attention, even though the difficulty of distinguishing them remains.

Like some forms of medical knowledge, the concept of race thus points to a question of identity that cannot be entirely resolved at the level of social or symbolic identity, even if we tend to resist purely biological arguments. This difficult border between nature and culture is negotiated not only in medicine and in popular discussions of race, but in anthropology, psychology, linguistics, and many other fields that deal with human diversity and address the fact of our physical embodiment. Any discipline that touches on the peculiar border between nature and culture—any discipline that deals with the body, as psychoanalysis does—seems to require some way of distinguishing the "biological" and "social" dimensions of identity, however problematic and unsatisfactory this distinction may be.

Cultural criticism has tended to avoid this problem. To the extent that it leaves our bodily diversity to one side in order to concentrate on the meanings and interpretations that are imposed upon it, cultural criticism has handed over the fact of our physical embodiment to the natural sciences, as though it were entitled to address only the sociohistorical aspects of our diversity—our cultural differences. Discussing various *representations* of the body, and the changing *conceptions* of the body that have arisen at different historical moments (as, e.g., when Thomas Laqueur describes the shift from the "one sex" model to the "two sexes" theory of post-Enlightenment medicine),[3] cultural criticism often appears to abandon the body itself to the arena of nature. One might almost suggest that cultural criticism thereby maintains a tacit alliance with the very naturalism it so frequently denounces. The denunciation of "pre-discursive reality" or "naturalism" can thus often be read as a denegation, which tacitly takes sides with the very "realism" it condemns. To be sure, we are warned that every *observation* or *theory* of the body is embedded in a complex network of symbolic conditions, such that even a scientific account, while promising to describe "the thing itself," is a contingent discursive construction that cannot provide unmediated access to reality. Feminist theorists like Donna Haraway and Anne Fausto-Sterling, and historians of science like Nancy Stepan, have shown us in convincing detail how the purportedly objective and neutral discourse of science is unwittingly burdened by preconceptions that are drawn from other domains. On these grounds, "race" may be rejected as a valid biological concept, and the focus shifted to *racism* as a social and political issue that can be placed alongside class and gender, and regarded as a cultural effect. Psychoanalysis has often contributed to these forms of social critique by exploring the fantasies that support racist ideologies, and the narcissistic underpinnings of prejudice, hatred, and aggression. As Foucault points out,[4] Freud himself took pains to break with the theories of "degeneracy" that supported racism and homophobia in the early twentieth century.

Such arguments are extremely valuable, and we have no wish to contest them here. In a sense, we only wish to deepen the historical question, in order to render the terms of the debate more problematic. We might ask whether every phenomenon can be historicized in precisely the same way, or be given the same "discursive" status, when it is construed as a historical construction. We may speak of "the Renaissance theory of madness" or the modern invention of the nation-state, but it is not clear that all phenomena have the same historical status or should be placed at precisely the same conceptual level when we address their historical formation. Nor should we immediately suppose that race can automatically be situated at the same level as class or gender—regarded as a historical product and analyzed with the same conceptual tools that we bring to the analysis of national identity and other social categories. The difficulty is conspicuous in the case of AIDS. Here, we are faced with a phenomenon that is embedded in the most vicious and prejudicial representations; it cannot simply be detached from this discursive horizon in the name of pure biological knowledge. So powerful is the network of representation that it has affected not only the progress and funding of research, but the very course of the disease. AIDS itself is therefore not a purely natural phenomenon which representation would render in a merely secondary way. And yet, this should not lead us to suppose that AIDS is a purely symbolic effect or that it is "historical" *in the same way* that gender and national identity are said to be, when they are regarded as social constructions.

If we question the limits of historicism, then, it is not in order to propose a return to the reality of empirical facts or in the name of biological truth, but rather because the historicity of various phenomena—what one might call their modes of temporalization—have often been prematurely reduced to a single form by the discourse of social construction. In this sense, the body, like race itself, perhaps, cannot be adequately grasped if it is regarded as a discursive effect or a purely symbolic formation. It is this deficiency in much of our theoretical work that Judith Butler, in *Bodies That Matter*, and many other writers have recently sought to rectify by exploring in more detail the concrete relation between language and the flesh—what one might call the material effects of discourse.

In this respect, race has much in common with the term *sexual difference*, which plays a notorious role in psychoanalytic theory. We often speak of "gender" as a network of social and symbolic meanings, imposed on the "sex" of the subject, which we regard as anatomical fact. On the basis of this vocabulary, readers are frequently encouraged to decide whether "sexual difference" refers to sex or gender—that is, whether psychoanalysis is a disguised form of naturalism, a version of essentialism, or whether it regards sexual difference as a "symbolic formation," thereby coinciding with historicist theories of gender. In fact, however, neither is the case. In psychoanalysis, "sexual difference" is neither a symbolic construction nor a biological reality. We should therefore be led to acknowledge that the vocabulary of psychoanalysis cannot be grasped in its own theoretical specificity if it is forced to coincide with a conceptual alternative that effaces its most elementary terms from the outset.

The relevance of psychoanalytic theory to contemporary discourses on race should therefore be clear in a preliminary way. Like sexual difference, our racial differences are clearly bound up with the most heavily invested symbolic values, but the social formation of those values cannot lead us to treat racial diversity itself as the invention of a particular culture or the product of a specific historical moment. This does not mean that we can regard race or sexual difference as natural phenomena, reducible to biological facts. But it does mean that we cannot adequately conceptualize these things if we treat them like laws, or theories of selfhood, or economic policies. Like sexual difference, race is not a human invention, and there is a sense in which arguments for social construction, insofar as they fail to theorize these differences, remain bound to a humanistic tradition in which "man is the maker of all things."

This brings us to the historical axis of our argument, for the fact that this conceptual problem arises today with such regularity, across such a wide variety of disciplines, including medicine, psychology, anthropology, linguistics, and the entire range of social theory, suggests that the inherited configuration of our knowledge has reached an impasse: the very distinction between nature and culture to which we appeal so frequently in our discussion of race and many other issues is no longer adequate to the phenomena it seeks to address. What can current developments in psychoanalytic theory contribute to this discussion—not only to the concept of race, but to the ancient question of human physical diversity?

The Nature/Culture Debate

Before we turn to the historical question, let us consider the conceptual issue more closely. As a concept, "race" designates an obscure and contested domain, seeming to refer to both natural and cultural aspects of human identity. In certain contexts, the term *race* has a strictly biological sense (and one can endorse or denounce such usage), but it can also designate a group identity that is based on a common cultural and historical inheritance. Although some writers simply take one of these senses for granted, ignoring or dismissing the other, many accounts of race employ the term in all its ambiguity, without distinguishing these two registers of meaning. In such cases, *race* is used to indicate a cultural inheritance, a form of social identity, while also referring to features that are not entirely social and that cannot be acquired by education and upbringing, such as skin color and ancestry in a biological sense. Discussions of the term *race* often lead back to this ambiguity, and thus to a single, decisive question concerning its status as a biological or social category.

One might seek to avoid this difficulty by terminological fiat, insisting that "race" *really* designates a biological fact, or that it is *really* a social invention, a product of history that might be equated with class or religion or national identity and analyzed with the same conceptual tools that we bring to the discussion of other cultural phenomena, asserting thereby that race is a human invention, a social phenomenon no different from architecture or parliamentary representation. It is tempting, perhaps, to insist on a terminological division of labor, in the hope of removing ambiguity and placing the term *race* on one side or the other of this conceptual divide. But the "ambiguous" and (one might say) "careless" use of the term gives us a more accurate grasp of the problem than the "cleansed" or policed usage of experts, which offers to secure the term within a purely biological or purely symbolic arena. Ordinary language tells the truth in this case, indicating something about *race itself*, in its very oscillation between nature and culture, its excess over the conceptual alternative we continue to use in our efforts to address it. In Lacan's language, we might say that race is something *real*, not in the sense that it refers to a prelinguistic *reality*, but in the sense that it exceeds our symbolic grasp.

Lucius Outlaw has stressed this conceptual instability in the following way: "For most of us that there are different races of people is one of the most obvious features of our social world." The careful precision of this formulation lies precisely in its simultaneous presentation of the evidently simple "fact" ("that there are different races") as a feature "of our social world." These differences, he continues, are evident "in our encounters with persons who are significantly different from us particularly in terms of physical features (skin color and other anatomical features), *but also, often combined with these*, when they are different with respect to language, behavior, ideas, and other 'cultural' matters."[5] If we stress the words "but also, often combined with these," it is because they provide an initial orientation for the problem that concerns us here, since it is a question of recognizing, at one and the same time, a *difference* between two distinct domains ("physical features . . . *but also* . . . 'cultural' matters"), and yet also a *mixture* (the one being "*often combined with*" the other). As a result, these two domains, which can and must be distinguished from each other, and which demand to be analyzed in different ways without being reduced to a common ground or too quickly collapsed into one another, nevertheless also combine in a manner that calls for theoretical clarification.

We thus have a first indication of our difficulty: cultural critics today might be tempted to insist that race has no biological validity, but is merely a symbolic effect, a contingent product of discursive practices that is wrongly naturalized as a biological fact. Across from these critics and directly opposed to them—though in perfect keeping with the same conceptual framework—the scientific community today increasingly celebrates "the revival of interest in the biological roots of human nature,"[6] claiming that race is simply a biological reality, and offering to demonstrate that such things as intelligence, the incest prohibition, and many other phenomena, including war and religion,[7] in fact have a biological basis. We know how heavily this debate is invested today.

The notorious incest taboo is the example that, according to the historian Carl Degler, will finally allow us to dismiss Freudian theory altogether. Degler asks us to recognize that this apparently cultural law, whatever may be its peculiar manifestations in the human world, is a genetically inherited mechanism that aims to prevent "inbreeding." Citing authorities who have established "the avoidance of incest among animals," Degler argues that "the incest taboo could not be an invention of human beings."[8] He enlists Norbert Bischof's claim that it is "an empirical fact that in the whole animal world with very few exceptions no species is known in which under natural conditions inbreeding occurs to any considerable degree."[9] We are thus faced with "a growing and often enthusiastic interest among social scientists in looking at the history of the incest taboo from a biological point of view." Freud would indeed seem obsolete, when "the ethological evidence, mounting each year, renders the avoidance of incest within the family or basic social unit no longer a peculiarly human activity."[10]

Freud, Lévi-Strauss, and other social theorists were therefore wrong to believe that this law or prohibition is a social institution, or the dividing line that separates nature from culture. They lacked our advanced scientific knowledge and fell prey to the anthropocentric illusion that humanity is somehow an exception to nature, refusing to admit that this prohibition only reinforces an already "natural avoidance."[11] But we now know "that culture evolved in accordance with genetic advantage" and "that incest avoidance was genetically based."[12] We thus have "new support for the Westermarckian hypothesis" that "family members do not have a strong sexual attraction,"[13] and new ammunition against Freudian theory, Lévi-Strauss, and others who share the prejudice of the social sciences.

A long period of philosophical naiveté would thus be brought to a close, with consequences that bear on race and a number of other issues, which can now receive the biological treatment they deserve. As Peter Bowler notes, "The collapse of evolutionary race theory came not because it was scientifically disproved but because the social sciences turned their backs on the whole evolutionary viewpoint."[14] This period of repressiveness, which began early in the twentieth century, was characterized by a turn from evolutionary explanations to an emphasis on "superorganic" forces, which were thought to organize culture—historical and symbolic forces that could not be reduced to nature or explained by biological mechanisms. For these sociologists, Bowler laments, "Cultural forces alone account for the differences; and, as A. L. Kroeber (1917) proclaimed in his paper on the 'superorganic,' these forces have nothing to do with biological differences."[15] It is this theory of purely "symbolic" differences that the new biological discoveries will finally discredit.

In the course of his triumphant discussion, however, Degler notes that the theory he defends, while confidently asserting an innate repulsion against any "intra-familial erotic attraction," may "leave some elements unaccounted for."[16] He mentions (in passing) "the question of father-daughter incest," which (it must be admitted) not only occurs, but appears to be forty times more frequent than mother-son incest. But this small detail seems to present no obstacle to the theory of "innate avoidance," for it remains confined to one sentence and a footnote, while the argument for genetic predisposition and innate avoidance proceeds. Indeed, there is no time for philosophical naiveté, or culturalist prejudice. It is no longer possible to avoid the conclusion, based on evidence that is mounting every year: "Westermarck's conception of the lack of intra-familial erotic attraction seems to be more accurate than the assumption that among human beings there is a natural urge to incest."[17]

The point here, however, is not to assert a familiar counterargument, turning from nature to history in order to claim (as Degler puts it) that the incest prohibition is a social construction, "an invention of human beings."[18] For Degler, these are indeed the only possibilities: the avoidance of incest is either a natural mechanism or a cultural institution, like democracy or abstract expressionism—something invented by human beings, which can therefore be confined to a particular culture or a specific historical moment. And yet, for Freud, the incest taboo is neither a biological fact nor a human invention. It would be more accurate to say that *the human is an invention of the incest taboo*, and that is why Freud situates it, not *in history*, but at the origin of human time—the time of the subject and the human community. The taboo thus cannot be grasped in terms of the alternative Degler proposes.

This also means that, when Degler ascribes to Freud the belief that the prohibition is a "law" like other human conventions, he has already refused the most radical and philosophically important aspect of Freud's work. He not only presupposes that Freud can be read sociologically (so that the entire problematic of the *constitution* of the subject is eliminated and the discussion is displaced onto the field of sociohistorical *construction*), but he also avoids the question of *what "incest" means*. For the biologist, "incest" simply concerns the actual sexual union of two *organisms*, and not the union of a "subject" and a sexual "object" (terms that receive extended discussion throughout psychoanalysis—but there is no time for semantic quibbling); it simply designates the union of two individuals viewed as carriers of genetic material that will either mix ("inbreeding") or not ("avoidance"), so that animals who do not breed with their immediate biological relatives may also be said to avoid "incest." For Freud, however, incest cannot be understood at the level of genetic substance. And to speak of the taboo as a cultural invention aimed at preventing "inbreeding" is thus equally beside the point. The entire conceptual framework demands to be rethought.

And yet, Degler opposes psychoanalysis in precisely these terms, drawing Freud's work back into the very debates he intended to reconfigure: "Psychoanalysis required the taboo to be cultural rather than innate."[19] Freud wrongly assumed that, in the face of incestuous desire (and here, too, the most basic terminology is simply avoided, as if "desire" were the same as "instinct" and simply meant the natural urge to copulate), an institution had to be developed to prevent by law or custom—indeed "from an apparently rational decision"[20]—what would otherwise naturally take place. There is no time for psychoanalysis: we can simply conclude that the Freudian theory of "incestuous desire" designated a "rational decision" to avoid incest, which was mistaken, because we now know that animals also avoid it. Between "biological laws" and "human institutions," the entire field of psychoanalysis is made to disappear. It is therefore not a matter of insisting, against Degler, that the taboo is in fact a cultural construction, like table manners or the modern form of the prison—the contingent effect of a given social order. Yet this is the alternative frequently proposed in contemporary debates, in regard to a number of widely disparate phenomena, including race, homosexuality, schizophrenia, and many other things: the object in question is either grounded in biological causes, like hormones or skin color, or viewed as a social construction that is destined to pass away, like democracy, or the nation-state, or atomic weapons.

An enormous problematic could be opened at this point, for the difficulties that arise over the term *incest* will reappear at many other points. When Degler speaks of incest between *brother* and *sister*, when he uses the terms *mother* and *father*, these words simply designate organic beings in a certain biological relation. And yet, it should be obvious that terms such as *mother* have a highly developed sense in psychoanalysis and cannot simply be translated back into the vocabulary of "natural relations" without misconstruing the entire theoretical field (as if *woman* and *mother* and *female* were all equivalent terms). Given a biological reduction of all this vocabulary, in which it is always a question of "genetic mixing," how could one speak of the mother-daughter relation as "incestuous"? The question cannot even arise.

Freud, by contrast, explicitly points out in *Totem and Taboo* that the essence of the prohibition is not biological: following Frazer, he notes that, among the aboriginal people of Melanesia and the Solomon Islands, a man will avoid not only sexual intercourse, but any physical contact, even the exchange of glances, with a woman who bears the same name, *even if she is no biological relation whatsoever* (SE, 13:12–13). The biologist may claim that in such cases these "primitive people" do not understand how conception works and that they have extended a natural principle in a symbolic way, taking it beyond its true and proper function. The "incest taboo" would thus continue to perform its (obviously natural) function, while humans in their misunderstanding simply extend the "natural" avoidance in a symbolic way (for reasons that must remain mysterious). For Freud, however, *this apparently excessive and perverse case of symbolic displacement reveals the actual nature of the prohibition itself*—not an aberration of its proper biological purpose, but the very heart of the taboo: it brings to light the discontinuity between biology and the name. "Kinship terms," Freud writes, "do not necessarily indicate any consanguinity, as ours would do" (SE, 13:7). As a result, the prohibition of incest must bear on a structure—a relation between subject and object—that is distinct from biological relations. According to Freud, this structure confronts us with "a peculiarity which remains obscure to us—of replacing real blood-relationship by totem kinship" (SE, 13:6). Nor should this structural relation be confused with a social or "tribal" identity: "An Australian's relation to his totem is the basis of all his social obligations: it overrides on the one hand his tribal membership and on the other hand his blood relationships" (SE, 13:3).

In rejecting biology, then, Freud does not regard the taboo as a historical institution, an "invention of human beings." The very universality of the prohibition suggests to him that the structure of the symbolic order brings with it a number of features that are decisive for subjectivity as such. These features cannot be grasped if they are confused with biological mechanisms or reduced to historical conventions and placed at the same level as other social phenomena. Contrary to Degler, the prohibition against incest is neither a natural mechanism that one might analyze at the level of genetic mixing nor a cultural invention that one might explain via the methods of sociohistorical research. Like desire itself, it cannot be regarded as the exclusive possession of a particular culture, or equated with the biological concept of "instinct" and regarded as a natural "urge." It is this very alternative that Freudian theory calls into question.

The historical axis of our argument is now clear: when two discourses arise simultaneously, promising to explain so many varied and diverse phenomena, when such a wide variety of objects (from schizophrenia, alcoholism, and depression to homosexuality, anorexia, and male violence, extending even to perception itself) are regarded as the "discursive effects" of a particular social network, the invention or construction of a specific symbolic order, while at the very same moment science promises to provide us with their "true biological causes" at the level of our genetic determination, the genealogist can only suspect that these two modes of explanation, however fervently they may denounce one another, are simply two faces of one and the same conceptual formation and that their opposition to one another—so public and so heavily invested with our moral passion today—is the sign of a deeper commonality, a sign that they have a common birth.

We might take our direction from Foucault at this point: "What often embarrasses me today," he says:

> is that all the work done in the past fifteen years or so . . . functions for some only as a sign of belonging: to be on the "good side," on the side of madness, children, delinquency, sex. . . . One must pass to the other side—the good side—but by trying to turn off these mechanisms which cause the appearance of two separate sides . . . that is where the real work begins, that of the present-day historian.[21]

This is why the *theoretical* ambiguity of the term *race*—its obscure position with respect to the distinction between nature and culture—cannot be approached as a purely logical or conceptual problem, but must also be articulated in terms of the *history* that has given rise, not only to the term *race* as it functions today (in a manner that is far from unified), but also to the *disciplines* that promise to explain it, whether they draw on the techniques of contemporary cultural theory or on the latest developments in genetic analysis. This also means, however, that if psychoanalysis offers to contribute to current discussions of race on the basis of its own theoretical perspective, by drawing on its unique vocabulary or procedures, it cannot simply respond to the conceptual impasses of contemporary debates, but must also bear on the historical development of race as a concept—and thus on *the very history that gave rise to psychoanalysis itself.*

From a genealogical perspective, then, the impact of psychoanalysis is historical as well as theoretical: if the fundamental concepts of psychoanalysis (such as "incest" or "sexual difference") are irreducible to the opposition between biological and historical models, that is not only for conceptual reasons. In one sense, this opposition is very ancient, but it took a particular form in the nineteenth century, when the biological sciences and the discipline of history were both organized. It is this disciplinary heritage that psychoanalysis disrupts, but that paradoxically continues to organize our understanding of psychoanalytic theory (as Degler's account of incest suggests), distorting it from the very outset. And yet, it should be clear that the incest prohibition is neither the invention of a particular culture, a phenomenon that can be located in historical time, nor a biological fact, the result of instinctual forces.

The same point can be made for many other basic concepts. When Freud speaks of the ego, he is not speaking of a biological phenomenon, an anatomical part of the living being, but neither is he speaking of an institution that can be attributed to a specific culture. To be sure, each culture may provide different rituals or symbolic props to regulate the ego in various distinctive ways; but this does not mean, for Freud, that the ego itself is a human invention. Similarly, when Lacan speaks of the imaginary body, it is clear that each culture will negotiate corporeality in different ways, but the body itself cannot be confined to a particular historical moment—any more than madness, as Derrida has shown, can be simply historicized.[22] This does not mean that the body, or madness, can be handed over to the natural sciences or situated at the level of the organism—a thesis the "imaginary body" explicitly opposes. It simply means that the basic concepts of psychoanalysis cannot be grasped in terms of this familiar alternative. We have suggested that "sexual difference" itself falls outside the opposition between nature and culture and that, as a result, when readers try to determine whether the term refers to "sex" or "gender," the entire vocabulary of psychoanalysis has already been abandoned. Thus, when Degler offers to resolve the debate over the incest taboo by deciding once and for all whether the prohibition is a social institution or a biological phenomenon, his question is simply anachronistic. It proceeds in terms of an alternative that is, from a genealogical perspective, strictly pre-Freudian, drawing the entire debate back onto the conceptual field that Freudian theory intended to displace.

These remarks should have an effect on race and many other concepts, for when we are asked to decide whether the object in question (be it race or incest, homosexuality or sexual difference) is a discursive effect or a biological phenomenon, it is clear that neither alternative confronts the two compelling difficulties that Outlaw's formulation puts before us: first, that both dimensions of human existence have a distinctive character and should not too quickly be absorbed by one another (as if culture could simply be derived from natural laws, or as if nature could be reduced to a cultural construction), and second, but even more important, that we can approach this very distinction *only through a certain mixture*, a "combination" that would finally oblige us to detach race from the two alternatives still promising to explain it today and demanding our allegiance so loudly.

As a result—and this is what we will now try to suggest—*race itself* would no longer belong to this horizon of debate. Instead of asking whether race is a biological fact or a cultural construction, a natural phenomenon or a purely ideological formation disguised as scientific truth, and instead of allotting some justice to "both sides" of the debate, might it not be more accurate to say that race is *neither*, just as "sexual difference" is neither sex nor gender? The historical aspect of the difficulty should therefore be clear: if we speak of race, or the body, or sexual difference today (and we can no longer think without addressing them), and if all these concepts prove irreducible to the nature/culture debate, surely these particular difficulties arise for us not because of their intrinsic and eternal importance, as the "great questions" that have always been asked, but rather because the history of our thought has reached an impasse at precisely these points, so that these specific questions dominate and weigh upon us today, even as our conceptual resources remain inadequate to them.

Imaginary Physiology and Genetic Diversity

We have said that the biological concept of race is problematic not only from an ethical and political perspective but also for reasons internal to science. Without entering into an extended discussion, let us consider a few of these difficulties more closely.

The most common and popular markers of racial difference (such as skin color, hair, and facial features) are also the most superficial from an evolutionary point of view, in the sense that they are "surface" phenomena, expressions of phenotype that lead to "racial" classifications that do not correspond to the divisions of the population given by the international genetic maps that are currently under construction.[23]

Although opponents sometimes suspect biological accounts of automatically subscribing to the most familiar and prejudicial stereotypes, representatives of the Human Genome Diversity Project have pointed out that the very opposite may well be the case: a more accurate account of human genetic diversity, far from confirming traditional racial categories, would in fact run counter to them, since "patterns of variation that appear at the genetic level cut across *visible racial divisions*."[24] Thus, Luca Cavalli-Sforza, a professor of genetics at Stanford University, claims that "only genes . . .

have the degree of permanence necessary" to produce a historically adequate account of the evolution of human populations, in relation to which phenotype expressions (visible physical traits) are relatively superficial.[25]

For the geneticist, the point may be simply that "good science" should restrict itself to its proper object, without relying on traditional "typologies" of race.[26] But for the intellectual historian, the mistakes of "bad science" are not simply errors that the progress of knowledge will overcome, like the medieval doctrine of humors (which is either regarded as a "primitive" form of biology or dismissed as a spurious metaphor inherited from the ancient theory of elements). On the contrary, these "mistakes" have their reasons and must therefore be explained as positive phenomena in their own right. In Foucault's words:

> Genealogy does not resemble the evolution of a species and does not map the destiny of a people. On the contrary, to follow the complex course of descent is to maintain passing events in their proper dispersion; it is to identify the accidents, the minute deviations—the errors, the false appraisals, and the faulty calculations that gave birth to *those things that continue to exist and have value for us*.[27]

Will our current rage for "genetic science" not one day appear in precisely the same light as the doctrine of humors does today? And is our passion for revealing the discursive construction of all things not equally one of these "accidents" that give rise to our current and momentary truth? May we not already consider both these discourses with the same cold gaze that the genealogist brings to the extravagant mythologies of the past, instead of blinding ourselves with the illusion that we have finally emerged into the light?

Given the distinction between visible racial differences and genetic diversity, the scientist may wish simply to dismiss the traditional classification, regarding it as an error of the past, but another conclusion seems to follow. The most familiar racial groups, the four or five "types" found in traditional physical anthropology since the time of Linnaeus—the "Asian," "African," "Caucasian," "American Indian" and perhaps two or three others, such as the "Capoid" or "Koisan" people, commonly known as "Bushmen," the "Australoid" group, and the "Polynesians,"[28] as well as two groups added by Linnaeus,[29] which he called *ferus*, for "wild" children, and *monstrosus* to describe "hairy men with tails, and other travelers' confabulations"—may be regarded, not as *mere mistakes*, which genetic science will rectify, but as groups based on *visible features*, which generate classifications that are quite distinct from those obtained by reference to other genetic traits. Those genetic traits may be more fundamental from an evolutionary perspective, but it would be premature to dismiss the visible racial groupings, as if the order of the visible had no bearing on the history of human genetics. Without simply abandoning the errors of the past, we may therefore posit a discontinuity between what one might call *the imaginary physiology of race* and *human genetic diversity*.

This taxonomic discontinuity is not the only difficulty, of course. Genetic diversity gives rise to a number of problems even when taken on its own terms, and apart from traditional typologies, because the classifications one obtains by focusing on one trait do not correspond to those that result from considering other features:[30] for example, populations in which adults share a genetic lactase-deficiency include a number of "different" groups, including people from Southern Europe, most African blacks, East Asians, and American Indians,[31] while in the case of differences in ear wax, genetic analysis puts Caucasian and black populations in one group, contrasting them to East Asian populations.[32]

Efforts to resolve these difficulties of classification by focusing on groups of traits rather than single features, far from stabilizing the familiar racial taxonomies, will only yield greater internal variation within apparently unified groups. Since features such as fingerprint pattern, dental characteristics, and hair color are inherited independently (and not genetically linked), a more rigorous table of differences will only produce a more diverse and complex map of human diversity, in which the familiar races conceal more than they show. Nor are the difficulties limited to group taxonomy, for individual genetic traits present their own difficulties: in the case of organ donation, where genetic considerations are frequently crucial, an African-American will often turn out to be a better match for a Caucasian, and vice versa, than someone of the "same" race.[33] Here again, *genetic proximity* cuts across received categories of racial type.

These difficulties can be multiplied, for the diversity of the human blood pool remains notoriously problematic from a biological point of view and variations in the antigens of the human immune system (which is based on bone marrow as well as blood) are similarly obscure, though knowledge of these differences is essential for transplants, transfusions, and other medical reasons. As for skin color, even aside from its relatively superficial status in evolutionary theory, this too remains highly problematic from a biological perspective. Although differences in pigmentation are commonly attributed to varying degrees of exposure to the sun over many generations, this "adaptive" explanation has not proved satisfactory to the scientific community. As Jared Diamond notes:

> anthropologists love to stress the dark skins of African blacks, people of the Southern Indian peninsula, and New Guineans, and love to forget the pale skins of the Amazonian Indians and Southeast Asians living at the same latitudes. . . . Besides, when one takes into account cloud cover, peoples of equatorial West Africa and the New Guinea mountains actually receive no more ultraviolet radiation or hours of sunshine each year than do the Swiss.[34]

Arguments based on exposure to sunlight have been sufficiently problematic, he notes, that researchers "have proposed at least seven other supposed survival functions of skin color, without reaching agreement."

Differences in human skin color thus continue to escape arguments based on adaptation to the environment, posing a problem for accounts that rely on the theory of natural selection. Faced with these difficulties, arguments often turn to "sexual selection" as a supplementary mechanism, as Darwin himself did in a short but crucial section of *On The Origin of Species* that has recently been given a considerably broader role in evolutionary theory.[35]

Sexual Selection and Intersubjectivity

Let us look at the question of sexual selection more closely. Whereas natural selection concerns the individual's *relation to the environment and other species* (survival), sexual selection concerns *the relation between individuals* (procreation). The latter appears to obey different principles, and perhaps to yield different consequences, than those that the principle of natural selection would entail. "Sexual selection theory suggests that much of the behavior and some of the appearance of an animal is adapted not to help it survive but to help it acquire the best or the most mates."[36] The two might seem to coincide, for as Darwin himself said, "the best adapted individuals . . . will tend to propagate their kind in greater numbers." And yet, he immediately distinguishes the two: "This leads me to say a few words on what I have called Sexual Selection. This form of selection depends, not on a struggle for existence in relation to other organic beings or to external conditions, but on a struggle between the individuals of one sex, generally the males, for the possession of the other sex."[37] In Darwin's view, moreover, the principle of sexual selection is "*less rigorous than natural selection*," because "the result is not death to the unsuccessful competitor, but few or no offspring."[38]

Classical evolutionary theory recognizes this fact, since there are many cases when an animal faced with the choice between survival and reproduction will choose the latter, at the cost of its own life, but for the sake of its genetic perpetuation—as the spawning of salmon suggests, or, to take an example more dear to Lacan, as when the male praying mantis joins with its partner, only to be devoured when his function has been fulfilled (SVIII, 249–54). Thus, sexual selection would explain such things as the peacock's tail and his ritual display, and indeed many "social" phenomena in the animal world that have no direct adaptive function in relation to the environment. In each case, the given phenomenon can be considered from two perspectives: the songs of birds, for example, may be regarded from the standpoint of survival, as marking out and claiming territory, but they may also be regarded from the standpoint of sexual selection, as a means by which the individual relates to others of its kind.

It is on this basis, moreover, that theorists of cultural evolution have offered to give a biological account of many phenomena that social theorists usually regard as cultural inventions. Sexual selection thus differed from natural selection, but it thereby became the means by which evolutionary theory could extend its theoretical grasp into territory that had previously been claimed only by social theorists (as if "sexual selection" were the adaptive advantage of biology). In short, evolution no longer would explain only the physical characteristics of animals, but also their social structures and behavior: "By 1980 no detail of animal courtship mattered unless it could be explained in terms of the selective competition of genes. And by 1990 the notion that human beings were the only animals exempt from this logic was beginning to look ever more absurd."[39] War, religion, technology, even stories and ancestral myths can thus be regarded—like the incest taboo—as mechanisms by which genetic material is able to circulate.[40] For advocates of genetics like Matt Ridley, these apparent "institutions" actually have a biological foundation, and have been "selected for" in the ancestor. A word to the wise psychoanalyst, then: "you are descended not from your mother but from her ovary."[41]

Nevertheless, these cultural institutions, however genetically determined they are said to be, already broach a extremely complex question of representation, a question concerning the function (or malfunction) of language. This effort to reconcile culture and nature on evolutionary grounds, although at first glance it would seem to regard the human animal from a strictly biological perspective (abandoning the "humanism" of social theorists, which naively regards man as able to transcend nature), nevertheless accomplishes precisely the opposite, for it already gives humanity a peculiar and strangely eschatological position—precisely that ascribed by Foucault to modernity. For theorists of cultural evolution, "man" would be that animal who lives not by nature alone, but by stories and symbolic forms that provide a supplementary means by which the human population would *regulate itself.* The ambiguity of this gesture is extreme, and we must not move too quickly in deciding whether it should be taken as evidence of a "cultural uniqueness" or as a confirmation of evolutionary models. Even if "man" is, as Aristotle already said, a unique animal—"the most imitative creature in the world," who "learns at first from imitation," acting not only from instinct, but on the basis of an acquired and traditional wisdom—it is nevertheless perfectly possible, from the perspective of cultural evolution, to consider these institutions from a strictly biological perspective, as the means by which the human animal evolves. Culture is the adaptive advantage of the human species, and all our symbolic diversity, whatever historical differences it may produce, can be viewed (like the peacock's display) as the expression of evolutionary forces. If we choose to create prisons or to experiment with various welfare programs, this is not fundamentally a psychological or political matter, but rather the effect of a genetic commandment that forces the most effective forms of life to survive. "Why then," Ridley laments, "does social science proceed as if it were not the case, as if people's natures are the product of their societies?"[42]

It is precisely here, however, that we must consider the status of representation more closely, for even biology seems to endorse a familiar humanism at this point. It is as if, at the very moment when culture is finally to be grasped in terms of the mechanisms of sexual selection, so that even symbolic conventions are revealed to have a grounding in genetic distribution, an unexpected humanism erupts within the discourse that would seem to eliminate it. As the great biologist Theodosius Dobzhansky wrote in 1962:

> The most important point in Darwin's teachings was, strangely enough, overlooked. Man has not only evolved, he is evolving. This is a source of hope in the abyss of despair. In a way, Darwin has healed the wound inflicted by Copernicus and Galileo. Man is not the center of the universe physically, but he may

be the spiritual center. Man and man alone knows that the world evolves and that he evolves with it. By changing what he knows about the world man changes the world that he knows; and by changing the world in which he lives *man changes himself.*[43]

Thus, "Evolution need no longer be a destiny imposed from without; it may conceivably be controlled by man, in accordance with his wisdom and his values."[44]

One could hardly hope to find a clearer expression of the framework in which "man" was invented—the very framework that Freudian theory found to be inadequate. As Foucault puts it, in modern thought "man" is *that creature who lives by means of representation*. In attempting to formulate a "science of man," therefore, one does not elaborate a simple *object of knowledge*: it is not a question of developing empirical sciences of "wealth," or "language," or "production." Nor is it a matter of *describing* the various forms of life, the historical values and systems of belief that have characterized human existence in all its mysterious and bizarre diversity. In order to arrive at a properly human science, we must, rather, isolate a *relation* between culture and nature, so as to suture them in a functional hierarchy. "Man" is therefore not automatically given in the objective world as a possible object of research. On the contrary, "man" appears whenever a biological need is regulated through representation, by means of which the human animal will live; whenever the scarcity of goods available in the market is managed and redistributed through the symbolic codification of economic values; or whenever the representation I make of my words gives me access, not to the linguistic object, but to the essence of my subjectivity, my thought in its full consciousness and self-presence.

Thus, "biology, economics, and philology must not be regarded as the first human sciences."[45] "Man" for the human sciences is not a living being, the human creature in its natural immediacy, but rather "that living being who, from within the life to which he entirely belongs . . . constitutes representations by means of which he lives";[46] "man" is not that creature who labors in an alienated but unnaturally productive way, whose existence takes form in a surplus that extends beyond nature, but rather that creature who, faced with a finite set of resources, and with demands that go well beyond need, is brought into unnatural conflict with his own kind, but is nevertheless able to form groups that can "represent to themselves the partners with whom they produce or exchange," so that these conflicts can be regulated by "the manner in which they represent to themselves the society in which it takes place."[47] In each case, "man" appears as a being who is forced into a denatured life, dominated by external conditions and subjected to the environment of labor, embodiment, and language, but who is able to master that very dislocation *precisely to the extent that he is able to represent, and thereby take in hand,* the very forces that deprive him of any natural existence: "man appears as a being possessing *functions*—receiving stimuli (physiological ones, but also social, interhuman, and cultural ones), reacting to them, adapting himself, evolving . . . having, in short, conditions of existence and the possibility of finding average *norms* of adjustment which permit him to perform his functions."[48] This "self-regulating" animal, whose external conditions of existence can be manipulated by norms of adjustment, precisely because of the power this animal has to represent them, is the "man" invented by modern thought—the "man" that is presupposed and confirmed by the discourses of biology and social theory alike.

It should come as no surprise, then, that biology and historicism were born at the same time in European culture and that their present antagonism only hides a deeper commonality. Social theory may regard symbolic norms and cultural modes of regulation as the product of human imagination and as evidence of cultural diversity, but the same differences in symbolic existence can be taken by the theorist of cultural evolution as proof of the biological forces that lead humans, like other animals, to elaborate mechanisms that will maximize their genetic proliferation. What cannot be doubted, however, is that man is the being who represents. And it is at this point that the humanism of the biologist—which is to say, a very precise theory of representation—becomes clear. The fact of cultural and historical difference presents no difficulty for the biologist who is willing to recognize "human nature" in terms of this unique capacity to represent and thereby to take in hand and manage the very forces that would otherwise be imposed from without. "Man and man alone knows that the world evolves and that he evolves with it. . . . Evolution need no longer be a destiny imposed from without; it may conceivably be controlled by man" (346–47). This is the dream of genetic engineering so precisely expressed by Dobzhansky, well before it became the reality it is today. The forces of exteriority—the language I am given to speak, the conditions of production I must inhabit, the organism in which I live—all these determinations, both natural and historical, can be regulated by the very being who is subject to them, insofar as that being has the power to represent, "in accordance with his wisdom and his values."[49] Language would thus be a tool in the hands of man, and not irremediably Other. Cultural critics who appeal to the symbolic order as a uniquely human possession, the inventive capacity giving human existence it peculiarly contingent and historically diverse character, do not occupy a different conceptual field, but remain tightly bound to the same discursive arrangement, of which "man" is but one effect. Needless to say, this arrangement no longer holds much interest for us. It is an old fantasy now, and hides as much as it shows about the possibilities of desire.

The Organism and the Ego

What, then, may we conclude with respect to the enigma of "sexual selection"? How is the notorious "sexuality" of psychoanalysis distinguished from the biological accounts that promise to explain such things as incest avoidance? And what is the link between "sexuality" in the psychoanalytic sense and human physical diversity? Let us take up our thread again. As we have seen, while sexual selection is distinguished from natural selection and even regarded as "less rigorous" in some sense, the relation between individuals can still be explained, according to the biologists, by appeal to genetic determination, as a matter of "instinct." Thus, a highly codified mating ritual or a distinctive song will be instinctively produced, even when the animal has never previously seen this ritual or heard such a song before.

But perhaps this principle of sexual selection, though regulated in the case of most animals by a strict biological mechanism, is less regular, less normal and uniform, and indeed still "less rigorous" in the case of the human animal than it is in the rest of the animal world. Do we not find here an opening toward Freud's distinction between the "instinct" and the "drive" (in *Three Essays on the Theory of Sexuality*), and thus toward the idea that, whereas the instinct is governed by the laws of nature (survival and reproduction), the drive is detached from its natural foundations, displaced into an Other domain, where it is governed by representation, indeed, by a "principle of pleasure" that cuts against the grain of nature, so that "satisfaction" is obtained not by the organism and its needs, but by the ego and its demands? Do we not in fact confront a discontinuity, in the human animal, between this "principle of pleasure" and the "reality principle," the "external world" to which the animal would appear to be far more harmoniously adapted?

The order of mating may thus follow a biological law with a strict and mechanical regularity in cases such as the one Lacan mentions in "The Mirror Stage," in which "it is a necessary condition for the maturation of the gonad of the female pigeon that it should see another member of its species, of either sex; so sufficient in itself is this condition that the desired effect may be obtained merely by placing the individual within reach of the field of reflection of a mirror" (E, 3). But the image may have a different function in the human world, such that mating is governed not by the *relation between organisms* (which is all that counts from the standpoint of genetic science), but also by the *relation between egos*, a relation that is conspicuously maladaptive and deprived of the regular rituals that govern the animal world.

In the human world, organisms only manage to meet *through their representatives*, through the mediation of their egos (including all the social identifications this entails), so that the imaginary is indeed the pivotal point at which the entire relation between the organism and the subject is denatured, deprived of the regularity that instinct affords in the animal world. This also means that the image no longer opens on a world of "reality" and no longer functions as a natural "perception" that provides access to things themselves, but rather gives rise to representations that *reconfigure* the entire order of intersubjectivity. Accordingly, it is not only a question of distinguishing the principle of natural selection from that of sexual selection, but above all of distinguishing, *within the principle of sexual selection itself*, between the image as it functions in nature and the imaginary domain in which the human lives its life. The question therefore arises, not only of distinguishing, with Darwin, between natural selection and sexual selection, that is, not only of demonstrating how the *relation to the other* (in mating) differs from the *relation to the environment* (in survival); it also becomes necessary to ask whether—within the arena of sexual selection—this famous "relation to the other" obeys laws in the human world that can be distinguished from those that obtain in the "state of nature." If the rupture *within* "sexual selection" is thereby clarified, what are its consequences for human "racial" diversity?

Let us take up our thread again. We have suggested that the traditional typologies of race are a "mistake" from the standpoint of genetics (since "patterns of variation that appear at the genetic level cut across *visible* racial divisions"[50]). But it would be a mistake to follow the geneticist, believing that the proper scientific conclusion would therefore simply be to *dismiss* this level of superficial visibility, condemning it to the dustbin of historical "errors" and *replacing* it with the truth of genetic analysis. At the level of sexual selection, visibility is not a matter of indifference. We may return here to Outlaw's remark that physiological differences are "often combined with" cultural matters. In fact, while the scientific community may often proceed as if the "natural" dimension of the body were independent of all cultural overlay—as if the biological domain were autonomous and *prior* to any merely "symbolic" matter—we have good "scientific" reasons to object.

Human genetic diversity does not coincide with visible typologies of "race," and yet this does not mean that visible differences (such as skin and hair color) are simply a scientific mistake. On the contrary, the impact of the imaginary on sexual selection, and thus on genetic diversity, must make itself felt at this point. But the genealogist will also turn a cold gaze on the pieties of cultural studies, for if the humanist is tempted to claim that race has no biological validity, concluding that it is only imaginary, a product and a doctrine of cultural practice, the difference between imaginary physiology and genetic diversity is not so easily resolved. The imaginary physiology of race is not reducible to a discursive phenomenon, whether one seeks, with the scientist, to dismiss it as an error, or conversely, with the social theorist, to reduce it to an ideological formation: in short, if such things as skin color and facial features have some genetic basis, while nevertheless being insufficient for classifying human populations from an evolutionary perspective, then perhaps its specific character, within the arena of genetic diversity, can be identified more precisely.

It may well be that many of the features that are commonly enlisted in the traditional racial classifications belong, not to the domain of survival, but to the "less rigorous" domain of sexual selection. The question must then be asked whether such features may exceed not only the adaptive function of *natural* selection, but also the less rigorous principle of *sexual* selection. For the "imaginary physiology of race" may well, in the case of the human subject, contradict or pervert what one might expect from the visual image in the natural world. Far from dismissing the imaginary as a scientific mistake (the erroneous classical typologies of race) or reducing it to an "imaginary" formation, in the sense of a "mere" representation, the product of ideology, one would have to confront *the impact that the imaginary has on human genetic diversity*. Outlaw, who has no particular interest in advancing the claims of psychoanalysis, has put this point quite clearly: "When we classify a group as a 'race,' then, at best we refer to generally shared characteristics derived from a 'pool' of genes. Social, cultural, and geographic factors, in addition to those of natural selection, all impact on this pool, thus on raciation."[51]

This brings us to a final complication of recent genetic science, one that takes us from the imaginary domain (as distinct from natural "perception") to the symbolic order, where the impact of language on human embodiment can be seen. It must be stressed that the genetic differences that do in fact distinguish one person from another are not generally attributable to racial differences.[52] On the contrary, while the genetic differences between two individuals drawn from different racial groups may be visible to the eye (in terms of height, body type, sex, hair color, etc.), they are due to "racial factors" only to a remarkably small degree—about one hundredth of one percent. According to Paul Hoffman, "race accounts for only a minuscule .012 percent difference in our genetic material."[53] In other words, given a particular set of chromosomes with its large number of genes, two observations may be made: (1) virtually all of this genetic material will be shared by all other humans (allowing us to grow as mammals, with a spinal column, various internal organs, etc.), and (2) the portion that distinguishes us from others will also distinguish us individually from others who belong to the same genetic population—separating two pygmies or Germans or Lebanese from one another, as well as from all other humans. In short, if, as Jo Ann Gutin notes, "every human carries about 6 billion base pairs—the chemical rungs of the DNA ladder," only ".2 percent of the whole" will be distinct from that of another randomly chosen individual; and of that two-tenths of one percent, almost all variation occurs not between "races," but *within* any given group. Thus, "a random sample of people in any small group . . . from rural Sweden to the Ituri Forest to Tierra del Fuego—will turn up 85 percent of all the genetic variation our species contains."[54]

What happens, then, if we turn to the remaining 15 percent (namely, the 15 percent that remains of this .2 percent variation), which bears on differences *between* different genetic populations? Even here, the majority of this variation is due, not to "racial" differences, but to differences between "social" groups—that is to say, between those who belong to *different linguistic or ethnic groups*. "Of that 15 percent," Gutin adds, "almost 9 percent is reflected in differences among ethnic and linguistic groups *within any given race*."[55] We are thus faced, not with an absolute dismissal of any genetic analysis, but rather with *genetic differences that derive from ethnic and linguistic difference.* We may therefore posit a role for the symbolic order, in addition to the imaginary physiology of race. Perhaps genetic differences cannot be disregarded then, or dismissed on the grounds that such differences are too dangerous or too historically contaminated to contemplate—as if race could be recast as an entirely symbolic or ideological construction. But neither can our racial differences be reduced to a biological fact, separate from culture and language and from all the imaginary mechanisms that distinguish human existence from the world of animal life. Representation is not secondary to the biological domain, but appears to drive raciation as much as any factor scientists have identified:

> In conclusion, therefore, let us give the last word to the scientist of poetry: It is clear that the general origin of poetry was due to two causes, each of them part of human nature. Imitation is natural to man from childhood, one of his advantages over the lower animals being this, that he is the most imitative creature in the world, and *learns at first from imitation.* And it is also natural for all to *delight in works of imitation.* The truth of this second point is shown by experience: though the objects themselves may be painful to see, we delight to view the most realistic representations of them in art, the forms for example of the lowest animals and of dead bodies. (Aristotle, *Poetics* 1448b3–12, my emphasis)

Two features would thus mark out the peculiar destiny of the human animal, a creature that is by nature distinct from "the lower animals" and consequently subject to different principles of organization and change: first, "that he is the most imitative creature in the world" and that, as a result, he "learns at first from imitation," developing an understanding of the world, not from immediate contact with *things themselves*, or by adapting himself in response to the environment, but rather from *the representation of things*, which first gives him access to the world (since "he learns *at first* from imitation"); and second, that these representations afford the human animal with a certain "pleasure," a pleasure that is quite remarkable and perhaps even perverse, in the sense that this principle of pleasure would seem to run counter to nature, leading the human creature to *turn toward* the very objects that would lead the animal instinctively to *turn away*, since "we delight to view" representations of things even, and perhaps especially, "though the objects themselves may be painful to see," as if, in the very organization of our pity and fear, our love and hate—in our very relation to the other and the world—we are led away from nature, fatefully governed not only by a peculiar and unnatural pleasure, but also by a knowledge that comes from representation, and destines us for an Other domain—a domain that is not simply of "man's" making, like the various clever tools and institutions that human ingenuity has invented at different historical moments and that differentiate one culture from another, but is rather constitutive of the human in all its incarnations, a constitutive denaturing to which the human animal is subject, not only in one culture or one historical epoch, but in its very being—as such, or perhaps, as a race.

1. The Intimate Alterity of the Real

1. Miller, Jacques-Alain. "Extimité," in *Lacanian Theory of Discourse: Subject, Structure, and Society*, ed. Mark Bracher, Marshall Alcorn, Jr., Ronald J. Cortell, and Françoise Massardier-Kenney (New York: New York University Press, 1994), 74–87.

2. Juan-David Nasio, *Les Yeux de Laure* (Paris: Aubier, 1987).

3. For a fine short book on these issues, see Jeanne Granon-Lafont, *La topologie ordinaire de Jacques Lacan* (Paris: Point Hors Ligne, 1985).

4. See Kaja Silverman, *The Threshold of the Visible World* (New York: Routledge, 1996).

5. I have tried to make this argument in more detail (partly in reference to anorexia), in my "Adaequatio Sexualis: Is There a Measure of Sexual Difference?" in *From Phenomenology to Thought, Errancy, and Desire*, ed. Babette Babich (Dordrecht, The Netherlands: Kluwer, 1995), 447–73.

6. Jacques Derrida, "Structure, Sign, and Play in the Discourse of the Human Sciences," in Derrida, *Writing and Difference*, trans. Alan Bass (Chicago: The University of Chicago Press, 1978), 279.

7. See Mikkel Borch-Jacobsen's very useful discussion of this text in *Lacan: The Absolute Master*, trans. Douglas Brick (Stanford: Stanford University Press, 1991), 199–212, where he also corrects some deficiencies in the English translation.

8. Derek Attridge, "Language as History / History as Language: Saussure and the Romance of Etymology," in *Post-Structuralism and the Question of History*, ed. Derek Attridge, Geoff Bennington, and Robert Young (Cambridge: Cambridge University Press, 1987), 183–211.

9. Martin Heidegger, "The Thing," in Heidegger, *On the Way to Language*, trans. P. Hertz and J. Stambaugh (New York: Harper and Row, 1971), 165–86.

10. Slavoj Žižek, *For They Know Not What They Do* (New York: Verso, 1991), 99.

11. Michel Foucault, *The Order of Things: An Archaeology of the Human Sciences* (New York: Vintage, 1970), 237.

12. Marie-Hélène, Brousse, "La formule du fantasme?" in *Lacan*, ed. Gérard Miller (Paris: Bordas, 1987).

13. Judith Butler, *Bodies That Matter: On the Discursive Limits of "Sex"* (New York: Routledge, 1993).

14. Miller "Extimité," 85.

15. Ibid., 80.

16. Charles Shepherdson, "Vital Signs: The Place of Memory in Psychoanalysis," *Research in Phenomenology*, special issue, "Spaces of Memory," 23 (1993): 22–72, reprinted as Chapter 5 in this volume.

17. Miller "Extimité," 85.

18. Derrida, "Structure, Sign, and Play," 283.

19. Ibid., 289.

20. Ibid., 283.

21. Ibid.

22. Slavoj Žižek, *Tarrying with the Negative: Kant, Hegel, and the Critique of Ideology* (Durham: Duke University Press, 1993), 83.

23. Moustafa Safouan, *Pleasure and Being: Hedonism from a Psychoanalytic Point of View*, trans. Martin Thom (New York: Saint Martin's Press, 1983).

24. These categories are discussed in detail in Robert Samuels, *Between Philosophy and Psychoanalysis: Lacan's Reconstruction of Freud* (New York: Routledge, 1993).

25. Tim Dean, "Transsexual Identification, Gender Performance Theory, and the Politics of the Real," *literature and psychology* 39, no. 4 (1993): 1–27.

26. Slavoj Žižek has usefully explored the relationship between these two versions of the real and Kant's distinction between the *Ding-an-sich* and the *transcendental object*. See *Tarrying with the Negative*, 14–18, 150–51.

27. Samuels, *Between Philosophy and Psychoanalysis*, 7.

28. Richard Boothby, *Death and Desire: Psychoanalytic Theory in Lacan's Return to Freud* (New York: Routledge, 1991).

29. Samuel Weber, *Return to Freud: Jacques Lacan's Dislocation of Psychoanalysis* (Cambridge: Cambridge University Press, 1991), 106.

30. Jonathan Scott Lee, *Jacques Lacan* (New York: G. K. Hall, 1990), 136.

31. Borch-Jacobsen, *The Absolute Master*, 107.

32. Ibid., 109.

33. Ibid., 107.

34. Weber, *Return to Freud*, 106.

35. Michèle Montrelay, "The Story of Louise," in *Returning to Freud: Clinical Psychoanalysis in the School of Lacan*, ed. Stuart Schneiderman (New Haven: Yale University Press, 1980), 77.

36. Ibid., 81.

37. Ibid., 79.

38. Žižek, *For They Know Not What They Do*, 221–22.

39. See Charles Shepherdson, "History and the Real, in *Vital Signs: Nature, Culture, Psychoanalysis* (New York: Routledge, 2000), 153–85.

40. Butler, *Bodies That Matter*, 198.

41. Ibid.

42. Ibid.

43. Charles Shepherdson, "The Epoch of the Body: Need, Demand and the Drive in Kojève and Lacan," in *Perspectives on Embodiment: Essays from the NEH Institute at Santa Cruz*, ed. Honi Haber and Gail Weiss (New York: Routledge, 1996).

44. Butler, *Bodies That Matter*, 188.

45. Ibid., 189–90

46. Ibid., 199.

47. Derrida, "Structure, Sign, and Play," 294.

48. Samuels, *Between Philosophy and Psychoanalysis*, 18.

49. Ibid., 81.

50. Ibid., 82.

51. Ibid.

52. Ibid., 81.

53. Ibid., 83–84.

54. Butler, *Bodies That Matter*, 189.

55. Samuels, *Between Philosophy and Psychoanalysis*, 83, my emphasis.

56. Ibid.

2. The Atrocity of Desire: Of Love and Beauty in Lacan's *Antigone*

The first epigraph is from Pindar, *Nemean Odes, Isthmian Odes, Fragments*, ed. and trans. William H. Race, the Loeb Library (Cambridge, MA: Harvard University Press, 1997), Ninth Ode, lines 6–7.

The Second epigraph is from Sigmund Freud, *The Standard Edition of the Complete Psychological Works of Sigmund Freud*, trans and ed. James Strachey et al., 24 vols. (London: The Hogarth Press, 1953), 18:136.

1. Sophocles, *Oedipus the King, Oedipus at Colonos, Antigone*, trans. F. Storr, the Loeb Library (Cambridge, MA: Harvard University Press, 1962). Citations will be by line number, and the translation has often been modified to reflect Lacan's account

2. *Perseverance* is a word that explicitly calls attention to the father, indeed, to the "severity" of the father (*le père sévère*). This word designates not only the severity of a father whose fate is passed down to his daughter like a punishment or malediction, but also the very opposite, the desire that "perseveres" in spite of this inheritance, opening a path beyond fate (understood as a mere determinism), since Antigone chooses her fate in an explicit and even willful decision that her sister (who is less free in this respect) is not able to share. Antigone's paradoxical choosing of her fate would be the index of desire itself

(as contrasted with Ismene's willingness to comply with the demand of the Other). In addition, Antigone's choice also marks out the direction of the "ethics" of desire, for "perseverance" also means "responsibility," as Lacan is at pains to point out: "*Haftbarkeit*, which is perhaps best translated by 'perseverance' but has a curious resonance in German, since it also means 'responsibility,' 'commitment'" (SVII, 88).

3. In the lines in question, Antigone speaks of the irreplaceability of Polyneices (902–15), the singularity that distinguishes him from a husband or children, for whom she claims she would not have acted in the same way. If she would not insist upon burying her children or her husband, we cannot avoid recognizing that her attachment to Polyneices violates any claim that Antigone stands for the family in general, against the state (as her cruelty to her sister also indicates). The speech on the uniqueness of the brother thus disrupts what one might have taken to be the fundamental conflict of the play, the great agon that sets two equally compelling claims, the family and against the state, against each other. So disruptive are these lines that, as Lacan points out, Goethe hoped that they would one day be proved corrupt, so that the tragic conflict might be restored to its proper equilibrium (SVII, 255). See Michelle Gellrich, *Tragedy and Theory: The Problem of Conflict since Aristotle* (Princeton: Princeton University Press, 1988).

4. "For love *rather than* for hate": we must stress this formulation, for Lacan usually puts love and hate on the same axis, as two forms of imaginary intersubjectivity linking ego and alter ego. Here, following Antigone's own words to the letter, he says that she stands for love *rather than* hate. This love, suddenly detached from the axis of narcissism and rivalry—a love shorn of all imaginary investments—points out "the way of the gods," and gives Antigone her subversive and fascinating power as the heroine of the tragic drama.

5. "Choosing one's fate": Heidegger uses this formula in *Being and Time* to describe the form of Dasein's authenticity—linked to the terms "decision" (*Entscheidung*) and "responsibility" (*Schuldigkeit*, which also means "guilt" and "indebtedness")—as well as a mode of Dasein's temporalization, distinguished from "fear" (*Furcht*), which he characterizes as a turning away from mortality that compromises both the past and the future. "Choosing one's fate" is also the apparently contradictory formula (since one is simultaneously free and determined, if it still makes sense to use such terms) that we find in Antigone's own speech at the very start of the play, when she turns to her sister with the news of Creon's edict: "Do you see, dear sister, how through our lives Zeus would complete the fate of Oedipus? [1–3]. . . . Now you will show if you are well-born [*eugenes*] or not" (38). Cf. Heidegger: "Once one has grasped the finitude of one's existence, it snatches one back from the endless multiplicity of possibilities which offer themselves as closest to one—those of comfortableness, shirking, and taking things lightly—and brings Dasein into the simplicity

of its *fate*. This is how we designate Dasein's primordial historizing, which lies in authentic resoluteness and in which Dasein *hands* itself *down* to itself, free for death, in a possibility which it has inherited and yet has chosen." Martin Heidegger, *Being and Time*, trans. John MacQuarrie and Edward Robinson (New York: Harper and Row, 1962), 435.

6. George Steiner's survey of scholarly opinion about *Antigone* is, of course, heavily oriented by this interpretation, largely grounded in the Romantics, for whom the erotic relation between brother and sister is privileged on account of its supposed purity and intimacy, despite the incestuous barrier that ought to protect the love between brother and sister from all such erotic ties. See George Steiner, *Antigones* (New Haven: Yale University Press, 1984). I am suggesting that Lacan's account breaks with this reading.

7. See note 5. See also Heidegger's remarks on the *Augenblick*, the "moment of vision," in *Being and Time*, especially its bearing on time, on the way in which this "moment" disrupts the usual mode of being "in" time: "That *Present* which is held in authentic temporality and which thus is *authentic* itself, we call the '*moment of vision.*' This term must be understood in the active sense of an extasis. It means the resolute rapture with which Dasein is carried away to whatever possibilities and circumstances are encountered in the Situation as possible objects of concern, but a rapture which is *held* in resoluteness. The moment of vision is a phenomenon which *in principle* can *not* be clarified in terms of the '*now*' [*dem Jetzt*]. The 'now' is a temporal phenomenon which belongs to time as within-time-ness" (387–88). On this account, Antigone and Ismene would inhabit two different modes of time, and their relation to Creon's law, and to desire, could not be situated at the same level (one saying "yes," the other saying "no," both speaking, as it were, the same language). It is rather a question of two different modes of being, and it is from this that their "judgment" or "position" first arises.

8. For an argument distinguishing the tragic understanding of concepts such as "action," "agency," and "subjectivity" from the modern understanding of these terms, in which a particular appeal to "will" and "personal autonomy" tends to be presupposed, see Jean-Pierre Vernant, *Myth and Tragedy in Ancient Greece*, trans. Janet Lloyd (New York: Zone Books, 1988). For some brief but lucid remarks on the Aristotelian framework in which desire, deliberation, choice, and action are situated, see Gellrich, *Tragedy and Theory*, 104–7; Gellrich also provides a useful account of the way in which Aristotle's *Poetics* constitutes a "defense of poetry" aimed in part at Plato, in particular, justifying the affective and imaginative aspects of poetry against Plato's apparent claim that the emotional and imaginative dimension of art appears to mislead the judgment, allowing spectators to believe they have knowledge where in fact there is none (see 94–162). Though it is not Gellrich's point, her remarks lend weight to Vernant's argument that the conceptual framework for the

discussion of tragedy has altered significantly between the time of the tragic festivals and that of the philosophical academy. Finally, for some excellent remarks on the role of catharsis in psychoanalysis and its precursors in the history of science, see Léon Chertok and Isabelle Stengers, *A Critique of Psychoanalytic Reason: Hypnosis as a Scientific Problem from Lavoisier to Lacan*, trans Martha Noel Evans (Stanford: Stanford University Press, 1992).

9. See Jonathan Lear, "Katharsis," in *Essays on Aristotle's Poetics*, ed. Amelie Oksenberg Rorty (Princeton: Princeton University Press, 1992), 315–40. See also, in the same volume, Alexander Nehamas, "Pity and Fear in the *Rhetoric* and the *Poetics*," 291–314; and Martha Craven Nussbaum, "Tragedy and Self-Sufficiency: Plato and Aristotle on Fear and Pity," 261–90. For a broader account of the emotions in relation to the process of reasoning and making judgments, see Stephen R. Leighton, "Aristotle and the Emotions," in *Essays on Aristotle's Rhetoric*, ed. Amélie Oksenberg Rorty (Berkeley: University of California Press, 1996), 206–237; and, in the same volume, John M. Cooper, "An Aristotelian Theory of the Emotions," 238–57; and Martha Craven Nussbaum, "Aristotle on Emotions and Rational Persuasion," 303–23.

10. This is a curious and somewhat disturbing affirmation, as if Antigone were reduced—as woman so often is—to her beautiful image, and as if her words, her many speeches and all the arguments, principles, and affirmations they contain, could be circumvented, so that she is nothing more, for Lacan, than the "radiant image of the woman." This suspicion cannot but raise itself, and yet, as we will suggest, the function of the "image" in this case is not at all reducible to the familiar dimension of the "imaginary," but represents, on the contrary, an impasse in the symbolic order. The image of Antigone is therefore not to be equated with the images of women as "objects of the male gaze," as is sometimes argued in the context of Lacanian film theory. Antigone is not situated at the presymbolic level of an imaginary object; rather, she is aligned with the category of the real, insofar as she marks a point of malfunction in the symbolic law. The beauty of Antigone is thus not imaginary, but real—like the terrifying manifestation of the Medusa's head. What Lacan calls the "beauty" or "splendor" of Antigone (*l'eclat*) thus not only has (as we will show) a function of prohibition or restraint that resembles or supplements the law, but also a "real" aspect, which he will go on in 1964 to develop under the heading of the gaze. And if, in addition to this complex role, she is *also* "beautiful" (like the image in Kant's third *Critique*), this imaginary aspect of her presence functions as a veil, which covers the real that she contains and manifests—showing and hiding the Thing. Lacan's analysis thus aims to elaborate, in the figure of Antigone, the limit to the symbolic law. More precisely, it aims to do so by distinguishing, within the figure of Antigone, between her imaginary, symbolic, and real aspects, the latter being inaccessible without the former and yet not reducible to them. It would thus be premature to claim

that Lacan reduces Antigone to an imaginary object, nor does he ignore the speech of Antigone: "Let us not confuse this relationship to a special image with the spectacle as a whole. The term Spectacle . . . strikes me as highly problematic if we don't delimit the field. . . . On the level of what occurs in reality, an auditor rather than a spectator is what is involved. . . . Aristotle agrees with me . . . theater takes place at the level of what is heard, the spectacle itself being no more than something arranged on the margin" (SVII, 252).

11. This is the phrase of Philippe Lacoue-Labarthe, "The Caesura," *Heidegger, Art and Politics*, trans. Chris Turner (Oxford: Basil Blackwell, 1990), 41. See also Lacoue-Labarthe's "De l'éthique : à propos d'Antigone," in *Lacan avec les philosophes* (Paris: Albin Michel, 1991), 21–36.

12. "Au-delà des dialogues, au-delà de la famille et de la patrie, au-delà des développments moralisants, c'est elle qui nous fascine, dans son éclat insupportable, dans ce qu'elle a qui nous reteint et à la fois nous interdit, au sens où cela nous intimide, dans ce qu'elle a de déroutant—cette victime si terriblement volontaire" (SVII, 290).

13. It might be tempting to link the image of Antigone to Kant's thesis that "the beautiful is the symbol of the morally good," but this conclusion would clearly be hasty, for Lacan would not regard the image as a "symbol" in the Kantian sense, nor as the support of a common moral good. In fact, the very opposite would be closer to the truth, since Antigone's desire marks a breach in the order of the moral good, and bears on something "unwritten," something that cannot be inscribed in the order of symbolic law.

14. See *A Greek-English Lexicon*, compiled by Henry George Liddell and Robert Scott, revised and augmented by Sir Henry Stuart Jones with the assistance of Roderick McKenzie, with a supplement in 1968 (Oxford: Oxford University Press, 1968).

15. Though we cannot develop the point here, it is worth noting that the question of transmission runs persistently through this seminar, in connection, no doubt, with the transmission of psychoanalysis, as well as with historical transmission in general. "With the category of the beautiful," Lacan writes, "Kant says that only the example—which doesn't mean the object—is capable of assuring its transmission" (SVII, 257). And again, "Freud finds no other path adapted to the transmission of the rationalist Moses' message than that of darkness; in other words, this message is linked, through repression, to the murder of the Great Man. And it is precisely in this way, Freud tells us, that it can be transmitted and maintained" (SVII, 174). It is this transmission that we have tried to mark in the epigraph from Freud, which speaks of a certain creative work by means of which the individual—radically detached from the group—produces a mythical discourse that can be articulated and given over to the community, as is clearly the case with Antigone.

16. Carol Jacobs, "Dusting Antigone," *Modern Language Notes* 111 (1996): 889–917.

17. It is not clear that the judgment of the chorus actually changes upon hearing Antigone's lament, as Lacan appears to claim. It is notoriously difficult to glean a clear judgment from choral odes, which speak an archaic language, marked by notoriously empty and pious pronouncements (saying "woe is me," in effect, or "what disaster will come upon us next?"), and ridden with allusions to mythical figures, which function as a kind of allegorical commentary whose purport is often obscure. The clearest indication that the chorus's judgment has turned against Creon (which does not mean it was ever on his side) comes after the admonitory speech of Teiresias (line 1064 ff.), which Creon heeds too late.

18. Martin Heidegger, *Introduction to Metaphysics*, trans. Ralph Mannheim (New Haven: Yale University Press, 1959), 151–52.

19. One can see here the complex rearrangement that is taking place among imaginary, symbolic, and real, since the image of Antigone functions not exactly as a law, but as a support of the law, in a manner that no longer accords with the concept of the Gestalt. Furthermore, if her blinding image indeed prefigures the gaze, bringing into view a certain invisibility at the heart of the imaginary—a veil that covers, rather than showing—then a full account would have to rework this entire arrangement, not only in terms of the peculiar intertwining of the imaginary and symbolic, but also in terms of a newly emerging account of the real.

20. See Phillipe Lacoue-Labarthe, "De l'ethique: À propos d'Antigone," in *Lacan avec les philosophes* (Paris: Albin Michel, 1991), 21–36. Again Heidegger comes to mind, insofar as "hesitation" is a crucial category for the account of the mode of being wherein Dasein flees from its own destiny, through "indecision," "procrastination," and "hesitation"—temporal relations that could be correlated with Lacan's account of these terms in his note on "temporal tension" and "intersubjective time."

21. Disinterestedness, for Kant, is of course a characteristic of the judgment of taste. It would thus pertain to our aesthetic experience and not to the characters in the play—as if it were an attitude or attribute that one might ascribe to the tragic hero. Yet, if one follows the implicit logic of Lacan's account, it would seem that we must explore the relation *between* our "aesthetic" experience and Antigone's nonaesthetic relation to her brother, defined both a matter of desire and as an ethical act. As we have stressed, this very power in her position makes her the object of fascination for us.

22. David Grene, *Sophocles I: Oedipus the King, Oedipus at Colonus, Antigone*, 2nd ed., trans. with an introduction by David Grene (Chicago: University of Chicago Press, 1991), 1–8.

23. Heidegger, *Introduction to Metaphysics*, 151–52.

24. See Samuel Weber, Antigone's Nomos," in *Theatricality as Medium* (New York: Fordham University Press, 2004), 121–40.

25. Heidegger, *Introduction to Metaphysics*, 152.
26. Ibid., 249.
27. Ibid., 149.
28. Ibid., 149–50 (my emphasis).
29. Ibid., 150 (my emphasis).
30. Ibid., 150.

3. EMOTION, AFFECT, DRIVE

1. In *Group Psychology and the Analysis of the Ego*, for example (a text written at roughly the same time as the text on mourning), Freud famously describes what happens to the subjects who form the peculiar sort of bond that he explores in this text, a bond in which ordinary social belonging—what we might call the operation of the symbolic domain—is suspended in favor of a "group" formation. Absorbed into the "group" (such as the army or the church, Freud says), such subjects experience a loss of autonomy, together with a suspension of the usual functioning of moral conscience, and allow themselves to perform the most degrading or brutally violent acts under the guidance of a "leader." He functions, according to Freud, not in accordance with the laws of conscience, but in submission to an external authority that, Freud says, has a peculiarly disastrous and punishing effect, precisely insofar as it suspends the autonomy of the subject, who submits to an external authority. This, Freud argues, provides the model for an elaboration of the superego and manifests a discordance between the superego and the law that has occupied Lacanian theory greatly in recent years. A similar discordance appears in the splitting of the ego in melancholia.

2. To give only the smallest sample, see, for example, Richard Wollheim, *On the Emotions* (New Haven: Yale University Press, 1999); Martha Nussbaum, *Upheavals of Thought: The Intelligence of Emotions* (Cambridge: Cambridge University Press, 2001); Rei Terada, *Feeling in Theory: Emotion after the Death of the Subject* (Cambridge, MA: Harvard University Press, 2001); Charles Altieri, *Particulars of Rapture: An Esthetics of the Affects* (Ithaca: Cornell University Press, 2003); and countless neurobiological or "evolutionary psychology" texts that offer to explain the relation between emotion and culture.

3. See Charles Shepherdson, foreword to Roberto Harari, *Lacan's Seminar on Anxiety: An Introduction*, trans. Jane C. Lamb-Ruiz (New York: Other Press, 2001), ix–lxxix.

4. Does not Heidegger also distinguish, in *Being and Time*, between the "call of conscience" and the irruption of "guilt," the latter understood as a modality in which the subject falls away from itself into anonymity? What "subject" is posited in the emergence of guilt, as opposed to the subject of the call? Psychoanalysis might have allowed Heidegger to develop this distinction with greater efficacy, had he been less phobic about Freud's theory.

5. These issues are developed by Lacan in his seminar on anxiety, *Le séminaire, livre X: L'angoisse*, ed. Jacques-Alain Miller (Paris: Seuil, 2004). See also my foreword to Harari, *Lacan's Seminar on "Anxiety,"* ix–lxii.

6. For some English excerpts from Lacan's seminar on Hamlet, "Desire and Its Interpretation," see *Literature and Psychoanalysis*, ed. Shoshana Felman (Baltimore: The Johns Hopkins University Press, 1980).

7. Darian Leader, "Some Thoughts on Mourning and Melancholia," *Journal for Lacanian Studies* 1, no. 1 (2003): 4–37.

8. Jacques-Alain Miller has noted that Lacan initially took his conception of the object a from Abraham's account of the object of the drive (or, in the English of the Standard Edition, the "instinct"). "Where does the object *a* come from in Lacan? It comes from the partial object of Karl Abraham." "Extimité," in *Lacanian Theory of Discourse: Subject, Structure, and Society*, ed. Mark Bracher, Marshall Alcorn, Jr., Ronald J. Cortell, and Françoise Massardier-Kenney (New York: New York University Press, 1994), 85. I discuss this point at greater length in *The Epoch of the Body* (Stanford: Stanford University Press, forthcoming).

9. Literary examples of melancholia are numerous, and an entire tradition was constructed under the sign of Saturn. Let us only recall here the opening lines of Chaucer's "Book of the Duchess," which are spoken by a man afflicted with a great sickness, who can neither love nor hate, who keeps track of nothing, and who wonders how he is able to remain alive:

> I have gret wonder, be this lyght,
> How that I lyve, for day ne nyght
> I may nat slepe wel nygh noght;
> I have so many an ydel thought,
> Purely for defaute of slep,
> That, by my trouthe, I take no kep
> Of nothing, how hyt cometh or gooth,
> Ne me nys nothyng leef nor looth.
> Al is ylyche good to me—
> Joye or sorrow, wherso hyt be—
> For I have felynge in nothing (1–11)

10. See Bessel van der Kolk, "The Intrusive Past: The Flexibility of Memory and the Engraving of Trauma," in *Trauma: Explorations in Memory*, ed. Cathy Caruth (Baltimore: The Johns Hopkins University Press, 1995), 158–182.

11. Cathy Caruth, *Unclaimed Experience: Trauma, Narrative and History* (Baltimore: The Johns Hopkins University Press, 1996), 87.

12. Teresa Brennan, *History after Lacan* (London: Routledge, 1993), 16.

13. Ibid., 16–17.

14. I have discussed two possible readings of the "real" in more detail in "The Intimate Alterity of the Real," Chapter 1 in this volume.

15. I elaborate here some remarks already made in "The Elements of the Drive," *Umbr(a): A Journal of the Unconscious*, no. 1 (1997): 131–45.

16. For further discussion of this passage see André Green, *The Fabric of Affect in the Psychoanalytic Discourse*, trans. Alan Sheridan (New York: Routledge, 1999).

17. Teresa Brennan, *The Interpretation of the Flesh: Freud and Femininity* (London: Routledge, 1992), 83.

18. Ibid.

19. Ibid., 30.

20. Ibid., x.

21. Ibid.

22. Ibid.

23. Ibid.

24. Ibid., 35.

4. Telling Tales of Love: Philosophy, Literature, and Psychoanalysis

This essay was written at the invitation of David Goecocheia for a conference on Kristeva's *Tales of Love*, organized at Brock University. I was asked to comment specifically on her chapter on narcissism and have therefore limited my remarks to that particular horizon. I would like to thank the conference organizers for their hospitality. I would also like to acknowledge here the inspiration of Professor Claire Nouvet, whose scrupulous lectures on Ovid opened a far more labyrinthine path into this particular chapter of Kristeva's book than I would otherwise have taken.

1. The epigraph to this chapter of *Tales of Love*—a quotation from Ovid that Kristeva leaves in Latin—appears in the English text in a form ("the strangeness of his infatuation") that conceals the connection between Kristeva's title, "The New Insanity" and the original Ovidian line, *novitasque furoris*.

2. The whole of our question concerning Kristeva's exposition is already situated here: as Heidegger points out in *Being and Time*, one cannot avoid the problem of the relationship between this apparently obvious chronological "datability" and its internal possibility, "the structure of datability" (Martin Heidegger, *Being and Time*, trans. John Macquarrie and Edward Robinson [New York: Harper and Row, 1962], 460. This problem is especially pressing insofar as the relation between chronological datability and Heidegger's question—"wherein is such datability grounded, and to what does it essentially belong" (459)—will be replayed at the very heart of narcissism, since the structure of narcissism, in Freudian doctrine, articulates not merely a momentary

lapse, or a contingent pathological deviation, but the very coming into being of the subject.

3. As Kristeva's translator notes, there are "considerable discrepancies" (TL, 391 n. 3) between the French and English translations of Plotinus. In this case, Plotinus (*Enneads*, I, 6, 8, 26) is rendered by Kristeva as follows: "Echanger une manière de voir pour une autre" ("exchange one way of seeing for another").

4. I take this phrase, "the disaster of Narcissism," and some inspiration for my argument from Claire Nouvet, whose lectures at Emory University pushed me in directions I would not otherwise have taken. See Claire Nouvet, "An Impossible Response: The Disaster of Narcissus," *Yale French Studies*, no. 79 (1991): 103–34.

5. It should be clear that, in speaking of narcissism itself as a "trauma," we are not attempting to condense into a single form the actual experiences of trauma—those, for example, that are linked in contemporary psychological literature to the definition and diagnosis of PTSD—and the "structural" or "constitutive" trauma of narcissism. Following Freud, we are rather suggesting that specific events (such as World War I, and its analogues in the theory of PTSD), insofar as they reveal a peculiar temporal return, might lead us to consider that the very structure of the subject includes and even requires a peculiar traumatic dimension, something "beyond the pleasure principle" that must be theoretically developed beyond the contingent examples of actual historical trauma. Freud takes this very step in reformulating the theory of childhood incest in quasi-anthropological terms, as he does in *Totem and Taboo*, where the "original murder" of the father is cast, not as a real event, but as a structural characteristic that would account for the very emergence of historical time. See Monique Panaccio, "Notes on Freud's Concept of Trauma," *Clinical Studies: International Journal of Psychoanalysis* 2, no. 1 (1966): 55–63. As Slavoj Žižek also observes, the concept of "trauma" in Freud progresses from an initial grounding in reality (an actual rape or seduction or violent accident), to a more generalized account of the traumatic constitution of the subject, which leads Freud to regard the trauma not as an actual event (one that might be interpreted and symbolized) but as a logical "stage" that often can be only *constructed* and not *interpreted*. In this sense, the trauma corresponds to the second stage in Freud's presentation of the primal fantasy, "A Child Is Being Beaten"—a stage, Freud says, "that never had a real existence." See Slavoj Žižek, *The Plague of Fantasies* (New York: Verso, 1997), 119.

6. Maurice Blanchot. *The Writing of the Disaster*, trans. Ann Smock (Lincoln: University of Nebraska Press, 1986), 1.

7. A "fiction" or a "myth," I write, as if there were no difference, or as if these differences, which are ultimately differences in genre, were trivial, a matter of indifference, when in fact it should be clear that the entire burden of

our questioning may well come to rest on nothing other than this matter of genre—the forms of narrative (history, myth, fiction, and indeed developmental psychology, which is its own genre, and has its own narrative conventions) being precisely the many ways the subject has of relating to an impossible or traumatic origin.

8. Blanchot. *The Writing of Disaster*, 125.

9. See Jacques Derrida, *Memoirs of the Blind: The Self-Portrait and Other Ruins*, trans. Pascale-Anne Brault and Michael Naas (Chicago: University of Chicago Press, 1986), 17.

10. For an extended discussion of the relation between the ideal ego and the ego ideal, see SI, esp. 107–42.

11. Jacques Derrida, *The Gift of Death*, trans. David Wills (Chicago: University of Chicago Press, 1995), 95–96.

12. Ibid. See also Blanchot, who writes of the peculiar way in which the Law produces this impossible situation, such that the Law must be covered over by ruses of narrative construction, which forget the Law they claim to represent, while preserving something of what they forget, just as Kristeva's history allows us to read, in spite of everything, the impossible structure of narcissism through it, is veiled by the tale she seems to tell us. Blanchot thus writes: "Laws—prosaic laws—free us, perhaps, from the Law by substituting for the invisible majesty of time the various constraints of space. Similarly, rules suppress, in the term 'law,' what power—ever primary—evokes. Rules also suppress the rights which go along with the notion of law, and establish the reign of pure procedure . . . a manifestation of technical competence." In Blanchot, too, we find not only this peculiar relation between the Law and laws, structure and history, but also an inevitable turn toward the question of genre: "Kafka's trial can be interpreted as a tangle of three different realms (the Law, laws, and rules). This interpretation, however, is inadequate, because to justify it one would have to assume a fourth realm not derived from the other three—the overarching realm of literature itself." *The Writing of the Disaster*, 144.

13. Derrida, *The Gift of Death*, 94.

5. The *Place* of Memory in Psychoanalysis

The first epigraph is from, first, Jacques Derrida, "Let Us Not Forget—Psychoanalysis," *Oxford Literary Review* 12, nos. 1–2 (1990): 3. The second is from Aristotle, *Parva Naturalia*, Loeb Classical Library, vol. 8, trans. W. S. Hett (Cambridge, MA: Harvard University Press, 1975), 285–313. This text contains the pieces which have been titled "On Memory and Recollection," and "On Sense and Sensible Objects." The same Loeb volume also contains *On the Soul*. References to all these will be given in the text according to the

Bekker numbers, in this case, 449b9–10. Translations are occasionally modified. The third epigraph is from Freud, SE, 20:59.

1. These remarks in the "Rome Discourse" are developed in Lacan, "Logical Time and the Assertion of Anticipated Certainty: A New Sophism," trans. Bruce Fink, in *Écrits: The First Complete Edition in English* (New York: Norton, 2006), 161–75. The text, as well as some later remarks on time from *Seminar XI*, are discussed by John Forrester, *The Seductions of Psychoanalysis: Freud, Lacan and Derrida* (Cambridge: Cambridge University Press, 1990), 168–218.

2. I am indebted to David Krell's discussion of Aristotle in *Of Memory, Reminiscence, and Writing: On the Verge* (Bloomington: Indiana University Press, 1990).

3. William Wordsworth, preface to *Lyrical Ballads* (1850 edition), in *The Prose Works of William Wordsworth*, ed. W. J. B. Owen and J. W. Smyser (Oxford: Oxford University Press, 1974), 1:138.

4. We find here the constitutive ambiguity of memory, the original bifurcation by which imagination, buried in the past, opens towards both empiricism and idealism. The poet cannot see, in the most wild frenzy of speculation, something that has not been seen *before*; the child cannot learn, Plato says, something that it does not *already* know in some way; it is impossible, Locke remarks, for the most extravagant fancy to compose anything new, since even the monstrous Gorgon or Manticore are composed of elements all of which have been encountered somewhere *previously*. This gesture has a long history. But does this doctrine that binds the imagination to recollection amount to a Platonism of transcendent Forms, in which the "most real" objects of recollection would reside Elsewhere, or is it a doctrine of empiricism in which, as Locke seems to suggest, the senses provide all our information? To which "reality" is the imagination bound, in being bound to recollection?

5. William Wordsworth, *The Prelude; or, Growth of a Poet's Mind*, ed. Ernest de Selincourt (Oxford: Oxford University Press, 1926), 1805 edition, book 1, 416–27.

6. An excellent example of such a complaint about Lacan's purported refusal of "reality" and his favoring of "linguistics" may be found in Mikkel Borch-Jacobsen's *Lacan: The Absolute Master* (Stanford: Stanford University Press, 1991), a book that speaks of the "evolution" of Lacan's work, separating an "imaginary stage" from a later "symbolic phase," which is interpreted in such a way that the body disappears entirely, thereby giving the author the opportunity to lament that "reality"—particularly the reality of "affect"—is neglected, as if affect were entirely prelinguistic. A peculiar reading, since it appeals to Heidegger in its critique of Lacan, apparently without recognizing Heidegger's own remarks that "having a mood is not related to the psychical in the first instance," that "State-of-mind" is "characterized equiprimordially

by *discourse*" (original italics), and that while "'affects' and 'feelings' . . . have always been under consideration in philosophy," these things are "not treated in the framework of 'psychology,'" but in the context of the signifier, since "Aristotle investigates the *pathe* [affects] in the second book of his *Rhetoric*." Martin Heidegger, *Being and Time*, trans. John Macquarrie and Edward Robinson (New York: Harper and Row, 1962), 172–78.

7. A splendid example of this interpretation can be found in Peter Dews, *The Logics of Disintegration: Post-Structuralist Thought and the Claims of Critical Theory* (London: Verso, 1987).

8. The remarks Derrida has made about chance and law should be referred to this passage in *Seminar XI*, where Lacan claims that "according to Freud nothing is left to chance," though as we shall see there is a limit to the law in Lacan, a limit, it should be said, that poses problems for the "scientific" status of psychoanalysis. This problem is explicit in *Seminar XI*, though it is given less attention in Derrida's analysis than it warrants. See Jacques Derrida, "My Chances / Mes Chances: A Rendezvous with Some Epicurean Stereophonies," in *Taking Chances: Derrida, Psychoanalysis, Literature*, ed. Joseph Smith and William Kerrigan (Baltimore: The Johns Hopkins University Press, 1984), 1–32.

9. See Jacques Derrida, "The Violence of the Letter," in *Of Grammatology*, trans. Gayatri Spivak (Baltimore: The Johns Hopkins University Press, 1976), 101–40, and "Structure, Sign, and Play in the Discourse of the Human Sciences," in *Writing and Difference*, trans. Alan Bass (Chicago: University of Chicago Press, 1978), 278–93.

10. If Lacan locates memory—at least the specific form of memory that concerns psychoanalysis—only within the speaking being, if the human being is radically distinguished from nature, as would already be suggested by the distinction between the instinct and the drive, one might worry that psychoanalysis is a humanism. It should be clear that things are not so simple, since language is not conceived as a tool in the hands of the "culture-making animal." This would be one place to initiate an encounter between Lacan and Derrida, insofar as Derrida has posed questions regarding Heidegger's apparent "vestigial" humanism, focusing on (1) the privilege of the *question* (and *Rede* in general) in Heidegger, as well as (2) the role played by *the hand* (as a "signifying" dimension of embodiment, a first index, something that shuttles *Dasein* between *Vorhandenheit* and *Zuhandenheit* and also opens the space of the question of being as such). See Jacques Derrida, "*Geschlecht* II: Heidegger's Hand," trans. John P. Leavey, in *Deconstruction and Philosophy: The Texts of Jacques Derrida*, ed. John Sallis (Chicago: University of Chicago Press, 1987), 161–96.

11. On bees in Heidegger and Agamben, who address the questions of animal language, see Giorgio Agamben, *The Open: Man and Animals*, trans. Kevin Attell (Stanford: Stanford University Press, 2004), 40 and 52.

12. What is striking in the theory of cultural evolution is that despite its adherence to an adaptive, functionalist model of history, the "inheritance" in question is no longer simply genetic, but linguistic. Thus, what gives the human animal its unique place in evolution, the "historicality" that distinguishes it from the rest of the animal world and gives it an adaptive advantage, is its inheritance of the signifier. See L. von Bertalanffy, *General Systems Theory: Foundations, Development, Applications* (New York: Braziller, 1968); T. Dobzhansky, *Mankind Evolving* (New Haven: Yale University Press, 1962); and more recently, Robert Boyd and Peter J. Richarson, *Culture and the Evolutionary Process* (Chicago: University of Chicago Press, 1985). A useful summary is John Paul Scott, *The Evolution of Social Systems*, Monographs in Psychobiology: An Integrated Approach, vol. 3 (New York: Gordon and Breach Science Publishers, 1989). Some of these remarks are based on a seminar on Cultural Evolution at the University of Virginia's Commonwealth Center for Literary and Cultural Change in the spring of 1991.

13. See Jean Laplanche, *Life and Death in Psychoanalysis*, trans. Jeffrey Mehlman (Baltimore: The Johns Hopkins University Press, 1976), 23.

14. Friedrich Nietzsche, *Untimely Meditations*, trans. R. J. Hollingdale (Cambridge: Cambridge University Press, 1983), 60–61. Translation slightly altered.

15. See Krell, *Of Memory*, 16.

16. William Wordsworth, note to "The Thorn," in *Wordsworth: Poetical Works*, ed. Thomas Hutchinson, rev. ed. Ernest de Selincourt (Oxford: Oxford University Press, 1936), 701.

17. Lacan indicates the relation between the symbolic, the organism and the image in a passage we have already cited, saying that "speech is driven out of the concrete discourse that orders the subject's consciousness, but finds its support either in the natural functions of the subject . . . or in the images that organize at the limit of the *Umwelt* and the *Innenwelt* their relational structuring." This "makes of the illness the introduction of the living being to the existence of the subject" (E, 69).

18. For specific analyses of obsessional and hysteric structures, as governed by these questions, see *Returning to Freud: Clinical Psychoanalysis in the School of Lacan*, ed. and trans. Stuart Schneiderman (New Haven: Yale University Press, 1980). See also *Psychoanalysis, Creativity, and Literature: A French-American Inquiry*, ed. Alan Roland (New York: Columbia University Press, 1978).

19. Derrida, "Freud and the Scene of Writing," *Writing and Difference*, 196.

20. For an extended analysis of negation, see Wilfried Ver Eecke, *Saying "No": Its Meaning in Child Development, Psychoanalysis, Linguistics, and Hegel* (Pittsburgh: Duquesne University Press, 1984). The terms we have been following are *Verneinung* (denial or repudiation, in the psychoanalytic sense,

though the word in ordinary German also means a logical judgment of negation, and Freud sometimes uses it in this way, occasionally using *Verurteilung* as well); *Verleugnung* (for "disavowal," a term specifically referring to the rejection of maternal castration and being radically distinct from "denial" in that the latter entails an implicit recognition of what is denied); *Verdrangung* (repression); *Urverdrangung* (primary repression); and, finally, *Verwerfung* ("foreclosure," which bears specifically on the name of the father and designates the absolute blocking of all registration of the lack that binds the subject to the signifying chain, hence the "lack of lack," in Lacan's phrase). My remarks do not coincide entirely with Ver Eecke's analysis.

21. Russell Grigg, "Signifier, Object, and the Transference," in *Lacan and the Subject of Language*, ed. Ellie Ragland-Sullivan and Mark Bracher (New York: Routledge, 1991), 100–15. Grigg also notes that in *The Interpretation of Dreams*, this term is translated as "transcript."

22. No one who has read Heidegger's "The Essence of Truth" will fail to see the proximity of this claim of Freud, who "always kept his distance from philosophy," to Heidegger's remark's on the *lethe* that "is not *steresis* (privation)" and precedes all disclosure, is "older than letting-be itself," and is a "concealment of beings as a whole." It "does not first show up subsequently as a consequence of the fact that knowledge is always fragmentary," but rather marks a fundamental withdrawal that makes possible the "openness," the "place" or "opening" that Heidegger will call *lichtung* and that Lacan in *Seminar XI* associates with Medieval German reflections on *Ort*. See Martin Heidegger, "On the Essence of Truth," trans. John Sallis, in Heidegger, *Basic Writings*, ed. David Farrell Krell (New York: Harper and Row, 1977), 117–41.

23. It should come as no surprise, then, that the psychotic, for whom lack has not been given a place, for whom lack has been *foreclosed* (so that primary repression can be said not to have occurred), will be (1) not only unable to inhabit language in the manner of the "normal neurotic," but also (2) unable to *mark time*—unable (and we recall here the two forms of the "question of being" that are decisive for the neurotic) (a) to distinguish birth and death, and (b) unable, like Schreber, to find a place within sexual division, even at the level of a question. Without lack, the psychotic is outside sex and mortality. See Alphonse De Waelhens, *Schizophrenia*, trans. Wilfried Ver Eecke (Pittsburgh: Duquesne University Press, 1978), 140–62.

24. For "non-positive affirmation" (Freud's *Bejahung*), see "What is an Author?" in Michel Foucault, *Language, Counter-Memory, Practice*, ed. and trans. Donald F. Bouchard (Ithaca: Cornell University Press, 1977), 113–38.

25. See, among many texts, Jacques Derrida, "Nombre de oui," *Psyche: Inventions de l'autre* (Paris: Gallilée, 1987), 639–50: "That a *yes* is presupposed each time, not only by every statement of yes by the subject, but by every negation and every opposition, dialectical or not, between the *yes* and the *no*—

this is perhaps what gives affirmation from the outset its irreducible and essential infinity" (640). My translation.

26. Here again, Derrida's relation to Lacan calls for examination. When Derrida suggests, in *The Post Card*, that in "Beyond the Pleasure Principle," Freud promises to explore a "beyond" that never actually arrives, a death drive outside the order of pleasure, for which all the evidence actually remains within the pleasure principle, this is not because Freud "doesn't deliver" or because Freud's thesis is simply wrong, but because the death drive itself is not, strictly speaking, "outside" the pleasure principle. It is an "internal" beyond, a limit that *does not appear*, that does not have the mode of being of "manifestation," though it organizes what appears. What Freud sees in the jubilant accomplishment of the Fort-Da game is also, he insists, a moment "beyond the pleasure principle," an instance of primary masochism—which would therefore *never appear* except *within* the pleasure principle: an internal "beyond." See "To Speculate—On 'Freud,'" in *The Post Card*, trans. Alan Bass (Chicago: University of Chicago Press, 1987), 259–409.

27. See Jacques Derrida, "Freud and the Scene of Writing," *Writing and Difference*, 196–231.

28. The relation between genesis and structure (the "opening of historicity") has been discussed by Derrida, whose work, although it bears more directly on the phenomenological problem of constitution than on psychoanalysis, would have to be carefully considered in relation to Lacan here. The question of the "subject" in psychoanalysis is more closely tied to the problem of constitution than most commentators have suggested. Like Freud, though with less irony, the analytic community has "carefully avoided philosophy," though unlike Freud, whose ethics led him to philosophy in any case, the analytic community has preferred to remain within the confines of their "science." See Jacques Derrida, "'Genesis and Structure' and Phenomenology," in *Writing and Difference*, 154–68.

29. Jean Piaget, *Structuralism*, trans. Chaninah Maschler (New York: Harper and Row, 1970), 55–56.

30. One can also see the importance of Lacan's remark that the "mother" is to be understood, not as the "primordial object," but as the "signifier of the primordial object" (E, 197). This formulation should give pause to those who have been so quick to assume that the "mother," in Lacanian theory, is confined to the imaginary order, left out of the symbolic, which for its part would be entirely under the legislation of the "father." In fact, the father has an imaginary function, just as the mother has a symbolic one, and only a *psychological* reading of Lacan, in which the symbolic function is not given its role, could reproduce the familiar, tedious, and deplorable positions of maternity and paternity that tradition has for too long sustained.

31. See Joan Copjec, "Cutting Up," in *Between Feminism and Psychoanalysis*, ed. Teresa Brennan (New York: Routledge, 1989), 227–246, esp. 228–29.

32. Rainer Nägele has shown clearly the abyss between Freud and advocates of the Enlightenment in *Reading After Freud: Essays on Goethe, Hölderlin, Habermas, Nietzsche, Brecht, Celan, and Freud* (New York: Columbia University Press, 1987).

33. I have addressed this point further in "On Fate: Psychoanalysis and the Desire to Know," in *Dialectic and Narrative*, ed. Dalia Judowitz and Thomas Flynn (Albany: State University of New York Press, 1993), 271–302.

34. Jean Laplance and J.-B. Pontalis, *The Language of Psychoanalysis*, trans. Donald Nicholson-Smith (New York: Norton, 1973), 245.

35. Marie-Hélène Brousse, "La formule du fantasme?" in *Lacan*, ed. Gérard Miller (Paris: Bordas, 1987), pp. 107–22, cited from 112, translation mine.

36. See Slavoj Žižek, "The Truth Arises from Misrecognition," in *Lacan and the Subject of Language*, ed. Ellie Ragland-Sullivan and Mark Bracher (New York: Norton, 1991), 206.

37. The fact that this is not a contradiction, a mere reversal of position, may be seen in Lacan's remarks on the shift from signifier to sign (the one represents the subject, the other is intended *for someone*), as well as in the shift Freud's formulation makes from the symbolic labor that grasps or destroys "something," to the formulation regarding the transference, where Freud's statement speaks of destroying "any*one*"). See Grigg, "Signifier, Object, and the Transference," 110.

38. Hamlet, of course, poses the life or death question from the side of the obsessional, in the speech beginning "To be or not to be." But we should recognize that this question, in which Hamlet appears "partly outside life," has a clear origin, for it is in response to the demand of the Other, the mandate of the father's ghost, that Hamlet, bound by love, dedicates nothing less than himself:

> Remember thee!
> Yea, from the very table of my memory
> I'll wipe away all trivial and fond records,
> All saws of books, all forms, all pressures past
> That youth and observation copied there:
> And thy commandment all alone shall live
> Within the book and volume of my brain. (1.5. 97–103)

It is worth noting the lines on "woman" that result from this.

6. Human Diversity and the Sexual Relation

1. Sander J. Gilman, *The Case of Sigmund Freud: Medicine and Identity at the Fin de Siècle* (Princeton: Princeton University Press, 1993), 2.

2. See: Guenter B. Risse, "Epidemics and History: Ecological Perspectives and Social Responses," in *AIDS: The Burdens of History*, ed. Elizabeth Fee and Daniel M. Fox (Berkeley: University of California Press, 1990), 33–66; and Mary Catherine Bateson and Richard Goldsby, *Thinking AIDS: The Social Response to the Biological Threat* (New York: Addison-Wesley, 1988).

3. Thomas Laqueur, *Making Sex: Body and Gender from the Greeks to Freud* (Cambridge, MA: Harvard University Press, 1990).

4. Michel Foucault, *The History of Sexuality, Volume I: An Introduction*, trans. Robert Hurley (New York: Vintage, 1978), 149–50.

5. Lucius Outlaw, "Towards a Critical Theory of 'Race,'" in *Anatomy of Racism*, ed. David Theo Goldberg (Minneapolis: University of Minnesota Press, 1990), 58, my emphasis.

6. Carl N. Degler, *In Search of Human Nature: The Decline and Revival of Darwinism in American Social Thought* (Oxford: Oxford University Press, 1991), 264.

7. Marvin Harris, *Our Kind: Who We Are, Where We Came From, Where We Are Going* (New York: Harper and Row, 1989), 296–300.

8. Degler, *In Search of Human Nature*, 257.

9. Ibid.

10. Ibid., 264.

11. Ibid., 262.

12. Ibid., 265, 264.

13. Ibid., 266.

14. Peter J. Bowler, *Evolution: The History of an Idea*, rev. ed. (Berkeley: University of California Press, 1989), 305.

15. Ibid.

16. Degler, *In Search of Human Nature*, 261.

17. Ibid., 264–65.

18. Ibid., 257.

19. Ibid. 248.

20. Ibid., 246.

21. Michel Foucault, "Power and Sex," in *Michel Foucault: Politics, Philosophy, Culture: Interviews and Other Writings*, ed. Lawrence Kritzman, trans. David J. Parent (New York: Routledge, 1988), 120–21.

22. Jacques Derrida, "Cogito and the History of Madness," in Derrida, *Writing and Difference*, trans. Alan Bass (Chicago: University of Chicago Press, 1978), 42–43, 54, 57.

23. See: Jo Ann C. Gutin, "End of the Rainbow," *Discover: The World of Science*, special issue "The Science of Race" (November 1994), 73; Michael Banton and Jonathan Harwood, *The Race Concept* (New York: Praeger, 1975), 47–49.

24. Gutin, "End of the Rainbow," 73, my emphasis. It should be noted that this group is distinct from the Human Genome Project. As Gutin explains,

the effort to "map the human genome" aims to give an exhaustive account of the entire human chromosome complement, consisting of twenty-three pairs, each of which comprises numerous genes ("Every human carries about 6 billion base pairs—the chemical rungs of the DNA ladder—in the nuclei of his or her cells"; ibid., 72). The sample from which this DNA is drawn, however, is severely limited and represents "a mere handful of U.S. and European scientists." Thus, Gutin comments: "As one wag observed, when they're finally mapped, those chromosomes will tell researchers everything there is to know 'about one French farmer and a lady from Philadelphia'" (ibid.). The Human Genome Diversity Project, by contrast, is an effort to expand the range of material by gathering samples from a great variety of populations, many of which are quickly disappearing, either because of migration or assimilation, or because of extinction.

25. Ibid., 73.

26. See: Peter J. Bowler, *Theories of Human Evolution: A Century of Debate, 1844–1944* (Baltimore: The Johns Hopkins University Press, 1986), 106, 128; Outlaw, "Towards a Critical Theory of 'Race,'" 62–64.

27. Michel Foucault, "Nietzsche, Genealogy, History," in *The Foucault Reader*, ed. Paul Rabinow (New York: Pantheon, 1984), 76–100.

28. See: Richard A. Goldsby, *Race and Races* (New York: Macmillan, 1971), 31–49; William Coleman, *Biology in the Nineteenth Century: Problems of Form, Function, and Transformation* (Cambridge: Cambridge University Press, 1977), 92–117.

29. Stephen Jay Gould, "The Geometer of Race," *Discover* (1994): 65–69.

30. Michael Albert, Leslie Cagen, Noam Chomsky, et al., *Liberating Theory* (Boston: South End Press, 1986), 26.

31. Jared Diamond, "Race Without Color," *Discover* (1994): 83–89.

32. Goldsby, *Race and Races*, 56.

33. Gutin, "End of the Rainbow," 73.

34. Diamond, "Race Without Color," 88.

35. Matt Ridley, *The Red Queen: Sex and the Evolution of Human Nature* (New York: Macmillan, 1993), 26–40.

36. Ibid., 134.

37. Charles Darwin, *The Origin of Species by Means of Natural Selection; or, the Preservation of Favoured Races in the Struggle for Life* (New York: Collier Books, 1962), 97–98.

38. Ibid., 98, my emphasis.

39. Ridley, *The Red Queen*, 9.

40. See: Harris, *Our Kind*, 296–300; Frans B. M. de Waal, *Good Natured: The Origins of Right and Wrong in Humans and Other Animals* (Cambridge, MA: Harvard University Press, 1996), 29–34, 182–86.

41. Ridley, *The Red Queen*, 8.

42. Ibid.

43. Theodosius Dobzhansky, *Mankind Evolving: The Evolution of the Human Species* (New Haven: Yale University Press, 1962), 346–47, my emphasis.

44. Ibid., 347.

45. Michel Foucault, *The Order of Things: An Archaeology of the Human Sciences* (New York: Random House, 1970), 351.

46. Ibid., 352.

47. Ibid., 352–53.

48. Ibid., 357.

49. Dobzhansky, *Mankind Evolving*, 347.

50. Gutin, "End of the Rainbow," 73, my emphasis.

51. Outlaw, "Towards a Critical Theory of 'Race,'" 66.

52. Ridley, *The Red Queen*, 13.

53. Paul Hoffman, "The Science of Race," *Discover* (1994): 4.

54. Gutin, "End of the Rainbow," 72.

55. Ibid., my emphasis.